History and Society No.12 – Labor Et Fides

True Piety

**Various treatises by Jean Calvin and
The Confession of Faith by Guillaume Farel**

Texts presented by Irena Backus and Claire Chimelli

Translated by Felicity McNab

Published by New Generation Publishing in 2013

First Edition

www.newgeneration-publishing.com

New Generation Publishing

Table of Contents

JEAN CALVIN

SELECTIVE BIBLIOGRAPHY AND ABBREVIATIONS

J. CADIER Sadolet and Calvin in Revue d'Histoire et de Philosophie religieuses 45 (1965), 79-82.
Opera Calvini quae supersunt omnia, ed. G. BAUM, E. CUNITZ, E. REUSS, Braunschweig 1863-1900, 59 vols. (= Calv. Opp.)

Johannis Calvini Opera selecta, ed. P. BARTH, G. NIESEL, D. SCHEUNER, Munich 1926-52, 5 vols. (= O.S.)
Jean Calvin, Treatise on relics followed by the Excuse to the Nicodemites, Introduction and notes by Albert AUTIN, Paris 1921.

Three treatises by Jean Calvin: The Letter to Sadolet, the Treatise on Holy Communion, the Treatise on Scandals, ed. A,-M. SCHMIDT, preface by J. PANNIER, Paris/Geneva 1934.

[J. Calvin] Three French treatises: Treatise on relics, Treatise on Holy Communion, Excuse to the Nicodemites, critical ed. By F. HIGMAN, London 1970.

Jean Calvin, Letter to all lovers of Jesus Christ, with Introduction on an French edition of the Institution from 1537, by Jacques PANNIER, Paris 1929 (Publications of the Calvinist Society of France No. 2)

Bettye Thomas CHAMBERS, Bibliography of French Bibles, Geneva 1983 (Works on Humanism and Renaissance 192).

H. DENZINGER, Enchiridion symbolorum, Barcelona, Freiburg, i. Br. Etc. 1965.

R.M. DOUGLAS, Jacopo Sadoleto 1477-1547. Humanist and Reformer, Cambridge (Mass.) 1959.

Guillaume FAREL, The manner and method that one uses in the places that God by his grace has visited. 1533.

Guillaume FAREL, Summary and brief declaration of some places which are very necessary for every Christian in order to place his confidence in God and help his neighbour. 1534.

A.GANOCZY, The young Calvin, genesis and development of his reforming vocation. Wiesbaden 1966.

HERMINJARD A-L. (ed.) Correspondence of the Reformers in French-speaking countries, Geneva 1866-1897, 9 vols.

Olivier LABARTHE, The relationship between Calvin's first catechism and the first confession of faith of Geneva. Thesis Licence No. 525. Autonomous faculty of protestant theology, Geneva 1967 (typewritten).

Patrologiae Cursus completusJ-P MIGNE: Patrologia graeca, Paris 1857-96, 161 vols; Patrologia Latina, Paris 1844-1903, 221 vols. (=Migne PG/Migne PL).

Jurgen QUACK, Evangelische Bibelcorreden von der Reformation bis zur Aufklarung, Gutersloh 1975.

E. REUSS, Literary fragments relating to the history of the French Bible in the Review of Theology (3e series, Strasbourg), 3 (1865), 217-252; 4 (1866), 1-48, 281-322.

A. RILLIET, Notice on Calvin's first stay in Geneva, introd. to the publication of the Catechism of 1537, Geneva 1878.

Abraham RUCHAT, History of the Reformation in Switzerland, ed. L. Vuillemin, Nyon 1835.

Letter of Jacques Sadolet, Cardinal, sent to the Senate and People of Geneva...With Jean Calvin's Reply; translated from Latin into French. Printed in Geneva by Michel du Bois, 1540 (Reprinted Geneva under the care of G. Revilliod at J-G. Fick, 1860).

Hermann SIEBERT, Beitrage zur vorreformatorischen Heiligen-und Reliquiensverehrung, Freiburg i. Br. 1907 (Erlauterungen und Erganzungen zu Janssens Geschichte des deutschen Volkes (hgb. Ludwig Pastor) 6: 1).

F. WENDEL Calvin, sources and development of his religious thought, Paris 1950 (2nd ed. Reviewed and completed, Geneva 1985).

TRUE PIETY
Various treatises by Jean Calvin
And
Confession of Faith by Guillaume Farel
Translated by
Felicity McNab

"TRUE PIETY"

HISTORY AND SOCIETY

Collection managed by Jean BAUBEROT,
With the collaboration of Roland CAMPICHE
Philippe JOUTARD, Elisabeth LABROUSSE, Marc
LIENHARD
Jean-Paul WILLAIME.

HISTORY AND SOCIETY No. 12

"TRUE PIETY"

Various treatises by Jean Calvin
And Confession of Faith by Guillaume Farel

Texts presented by
Irena Backus and Claire Chimelli

From the same publisher:

The Christian Institution (3 vol.)
Commentary on Genesis.
Commentary on the Gospel of John.
Commentary on the Epistle to the Romans.
Commentary on the Epistles to the Galatians,
Ephesians,
Philippians and Colossians.
The true way to reform the Church.
Calvin, man of the Church (selected works).

Denise HOURTICQ, Calvin my friend.
Gabriel MUTZENBERG, the Calvinist obsession.
Jacques de SENARCLENS, On the true Church
according to Jean Calvin.
Gilbert VINCENT, Ethical exigency and interpretation
in Calvin's work.
Francois WENDEL, Calvin.

ISBN 2-8309-0072-3

If you wish to be kept informed of our publications,
It is sufficient to let us know at our address

C. 1986 by Editions Labor et Fides
1, rue Beauregard, CH – 1204 Geneva

"…they gain nothing because they do not worship the Eternal God but the dreams and reveries of their heart instead of God. Now true piety does not lie in fear…but rather it consists in and pure and true zeal which loves God also as the Father…"

(Catechism 1537)

PREFACE

In presenting this collection of texts upon the request of the Committee of the 450th Anniversary of the Reformation in Geneva, we are giving ourselves the aim of showing – would it not be only in a tendentious and incomplete manner – the theological background of this Reformation. In fact, it is difficult to talk about the *historical* coherence of our texts. Only one among the five texts (the *Confession* of 1537 written by Farel) can be considered as coming into a direct relationship with the events of 1536. The *Epistle to all enthusiasts*, composed by Calvin in 1535 as one of the prefaces to the Bible of Olivetan, on a date before the Reformation (of 1536), even if its survival is directly concerned with applying the doctrines and practices of the Reformation after Calvin's return to Geneva in 1541. As for the *Reply to Sadolet* (published here with the *Epistle* of the Cardinal to the Genevans, 1539/40) and the *Little Treatise on The Last Supper (1541)*, both were composed by the Reformer at the time of his "exile" in Strasbourg.[1] The *Treatise on Relics*, on the other hand, dates from the period (1543) when Calvin was multiplying his reforming activities after his return to Geneva.

In spite of this lack of historical coherence, the great lines of the *theology* expressed by the five treatises remain unchanged. Here we note some of them among the most striking. The idea of man as the author of evil in difference from God who is the author of good and salvation, is underlined by the five treatises. The role

---

[1] To judge from Calvin's letter to Veit Dietrich of 17 March 1546, the *Little Treatise* was already composed in 1537 and only appeared in 1541. *V. Calv. Opp.* XII, nr. 781, col. 315-317; O.S. I, 501.

of civil government in the accomplishment of divine justice is highlighted by the *Epistle* and by the *Confession.* These two treatises, as well as the *Reply to Sadolet*, place the emphasis on the Scripture as the sole foundation of the Christian doctrine and of the Church. The latter, Calvin replies to Sadolet, must be governed in conformity with Scripture. If it does not conform to it, it must be reconstituted. The same idea is taken up again in the *Little Treatise* and, implicitly, in the *Treatise on Relics*, where it is a question of purifying the Church from *all* human work which hides the glory of God, and mainly from relics.

In fact, none of our texts forms an erudite or systematic theological treatise. It is a question of works of piety or polemics addressed to the public at large. The modern reader would be wrong to be surprised at the bitterness of these polemics, especially in the *Confession* and in the *Little Treatise on The Last Supper.* He would also be wrong to conclude that there was then no chance of agreement between the Roman Catholic Church and the various reformed Churches. In fact, there were several attempts to find a common language. It suffices to mention here the interconfessional colloquiums in Worms (1540/41) and Ratisbon (1541). By studying the attempts at union between erudite theologians and, as it is said, "professionals", we are struck by the fact that the confessional situation was fairly modified. Among the official delegates at the Colloquium[2], some of them, e.g. Gaspard Cruciger (1504-48), represent the theology of Wittenberg. Others, such as Jean Eck (1486-1543), represent the doctrine of Rome just as clearly. Even others, such as Jean Gropper (1503-59) apparently on

---

[2] The best work on this subject is that of C. Augustijn, *De Godsdienstgesprekken tussen Rooms-Katholieken en Protestanten van 1538 tot 1541,* Haarlem 1967.

the Roman Catholic side or Martin Bucer (1491-1551), the Strasbourg reformer (who, also, had an important influence on the Eucharistic doctrine of Calvin), are more difficult to place clearly and we are obliged to say that the represent a unionist theology. Calvin himself, to judge by his letters written at Ratisbon where he represented Strasbourg at Bucer's side, was not radically opposed to the union with the Church of Rome[3], while remaining sceptical and considering as dangerous loose objects[4] the articles on transubstantiation which prevented the success of the Colloquium in the first place. (Besides, it was the failure of an agreement on the doctrine of substantiation that prevented the Colloquium from succeeding in the first place).

However, our five texts are addressed to the public at large, and the central preoccupation of Calvin and Farel is not to draw up a modified theology, but to convince their public of the fundamental usefulness of the Reformation which had not been achieved. This public, at least as regards France in the years 1530 and 1540, was qualified by Pierre Imbart de la Tour as follows:

"Villagers, monks, students, small regents, schoolmasters or general practitioners, companions, and with them the wives, sisters, daughters of those workers who follow them in secret meetings, in the court, or even at the stake, are the first supporters of the new faith. In this way it affirms its democratic nature and its free attractions, its radical denials, the fierce

---

[3] V. CALVIN, Ratisbon, to Farel, Neuchatel, 24 April (1541) in *Herminjard 7*, no. 967, p. 87.
[4] Ibid. no. 976, p. 115.

spirit of its proselytism…Religion of the little people the king its advisers will say"[5].

This global description finds a confirmation in Calvin himself. In writing to the Nuremberg theologian Veit Dietrich in 1546 about the *Latin* version (1545) of his *Little Treatise on The Last Supper*, the Reformer states: "My intention was to teach simple and unschooled people by [the French version of] this treatise. Normally I write more precisely when I address the public who know Latin"[6]. The *Little Treatise* having been translated into Latin unknown to Calvin, he finds it necessary to explain to his correspondent that it is not a question of a learned treatise and to suggest to him that he should read *The Institution* where "the same doctrine is exposed with more solidity and more clarity"[7].

Even if the *Little Treatise* is, theologically, more elaborate than the other treatises in the vernacular languages, the great lines remain unchanged. Each time it is a question of outlining the theology of the Reformation without going into the shades of it and putting the population on its guard against the Church of Rome. As we have seen, the basic argument changes very little between 1535 and 1543 and one cannot talk about an alteration in tone when Calvin and Farel are aiming at the Genevan public[8].

We are not aiming to deal here with Calvin's French style which moreover was the subject of a recent

[5] Pierre IMBART DE LA TOUR, *The Origins of the Reformation*, v. 1-4, Paris 1905-35, v. 4, 264.

[6] *Calv. Opp.* XII, no. 781, col. 315-317.

[7] *Ibid.* col. 316.

[8] Geneva and its population play a more important role in Calvin's *predication*. V.R. PETER, *Geneva in Calvin's predication in Calvinus Ecclesiae Genevensis Custos. Die Referate des Congres International des etudes calviniennes,* ed. W.H. Neuser, Frankfurt a. M., Bern, 1984, 23-47.

study.[9] However it is right to emphasise that among the five texts that we are presenting, only two (the *Little Treatise* and the *Treatise on Relics)* were written in French by Calvin. The *Confession* is Farel's work. The *Reply to Sadolet* was written by Calvin in Latin before being translated into French by an author whose name is not known to us. As for the *Epistle to all enthusiasts*, it has never been proven that Calvin is the author of the French version or that the latter preceded the Latin version. Edouard Reuss in 1865 put forward the hypothesis towards which Olivetan was the author of the French version done according to the original Latin of Calvin[10]. Failing a critical edition of the two versions, the question remains up in the air. For the same reason, any attempt to analyse the developments in the different editions of the *Epistle to Sadolet* with the *Reply* of Calvin remains up in the air.

The texts that we have taken as a base here are either those of the existing critical editions (Higman's editions of the *Little Treatise* and the *Treatise on Relics*), or those published in the *Calvini Opera*, or those of the original editions (*Sadolet's Epistle* and *Calvin's Reply.*) In our original introductions to each treatise, we shall draw the reader's attention to the various 16th century editions only if they have special complexities.

We have tried very hard to make the French of the time of the Reformation legible to today's reader by modernizing the spelling and punctuation. The changes in the order of the words are minimal and we have not modified the vocabulary. Sometimes we have introduced sub-titles so as to clarify the argument of the treatises. The *Glossary* which appears at the end was

---

[9] Francis HIGMAN, *The Style of John Calvin in his French Polemical Treatises*, Oxford 1967.
[10] E. REUSS, *Fragments in Review of Theology* 3 (1865), 232-233.

compiled as far as possible with the help of Huguet's *Dictionary.*[11]

---

[11] E. HUGUET, *Dictionary of the French language in the sixteenth century,* v. 1-7, Paris 1925-67.

We would like to thank Mr Francis Higman for having kindly provided us with information on 16th century editions of the *Treatise* on Relics and the *Little Treatise.* We would also like to thank Miss Carole Lehmann and Mr Robert Chimelli for their assistance in collating the text and placing them in the net by typing.

Irena BACKUS and Claire CHIMELLI
Geneva, November 1985

TO ALL LOVERS OF JESUS-CHRIST
AND HIS GOSPEL, GREETINGS

[1535]

THE BIBLE
Which is all the holy scripture,
In which are contained/the Old Testament
And the New/translated
Into French,
The Old/from the Hebrew;
The New, from the Greek.

God in everything.

Isaiah.I.

Listen, sky and earth lend your ear;
As the Eternal one speaks.

THE NEW TESTAMENT

**From our Lord and only Saviour
Jesus Christ.**

Translated from Greek into French.

In God everything.

J. Calvin Epistle – Introduction

The Bible of Olivetan 1535

It is not within our intentions here to complete the statement of Edouard Reuss[12] about the genesis of this Bible. We shall content ourselves only with reminding the reader of the dates and circumstances of its composition insofar as they through a light on the *Epistle* of Calvin. Pierre Robert Olivetan (m. 1538), parent and compatriot of Calvin, arrived in Geneva towards 1533 and helped in the first reforming movements of this town. Threatened with persecution, he then left for Neuchatel and it was at this time that he came into contact with the Vaudois in Piedmont. In fact, it was they who financed the first edition of the Bible of Olivetan, the first reformed Bible in the French language, which appeared in Neuchatel in 1535[13]. Its printer was Pierre de Vingle (Pirot Picard), another Frenchman who had been obliged to leave Lyon and Geneva successively on account of persecutions coming from the Roman Catholic authorities[14]. We do not have clear information on the relations between Calvin and Olivetan before the appearance of the Bible. However, it is appropriate to remember that Calvin would have been converted towards 1533 and that he

---

[12] *Fragments litteraires et critiques relatifs a l'histoire de la Bible francaise,* 3e series in *Revue de theologie* (3e series, Strasbourg), 3 (1865), 217-252; 4 (1866), 1-48, 281-322.

[13] For the detailed bibliographical description, see Bettye Thomas CHAMBERS, *Bibliography of French Bibles,* Geneva 1983 (Works of humanism and Renaissance, 192), 88ss.

[14] He was staying at Serrieres near Neuchatel, from which the name "Serrieres Bible" sometimes comes.

would have left France to come and settle in Basle at the beginning of the year 1535. The Bible of Olivetan having appeared at the beginning of the month of June 1535, one must presume that Calvin was in contact with his cousin throughout the first half of the year 1535 and it was at that time that he made his contribution to the work on the Bible. It is generally presumed that Calvin did not touch the translation itself.[15] However, he wrote two prefaces. The first one, in Latin, was addressed "to all emperors, kings, princes and peoples, subjects of the empire of Christ"[16]. In this, Calvin attacks the Roman Catholic theologians, defending first of all the absence of privilege that the printers used to give themselves for their publications. According to the reformer, the Holy Scripture is itself a diploma coming from the King of Kings and needs no human recommendation. Calvin then defends the need to make the Bible accessible to the people by translating it into vernacular languages. He quotes the examples of Augustine, of Jerome and Chrysostom who made great efforts to spread biblical knowledge among simple people. This is followed by praise of "our Robert", the translator.

Epistle to all enthusiasts

It is the second preface, which is called *Epistle to all lovers of Jesus Christ and his Gospel*. Placed at the head of the New Testament, it is written in French and is addressed, as its title indicates, to a broader public. It is normally presumed that it was written in May 1535. We should note that this text also existed in a

---

[15] V. CHAMBERS, p. 91.
[16] "Ioannes Calvinus, Caesaribus, Regibus, Principibus, Gentibusque omnibus Christi Imperio subditis, salutem", gol. * 1v. of the Bible of Olivetan, V, also *Calv. Opp.* IX, 787-790.

Latin version and that it is this latter version that was published in 1576 by Theodore de Beze in his *Lettres et avis de Calvin*. Given the important differences that exist between the two texts, it would perhaps be rash to presume that it was Beze who quite simply translated Calvin's preface. Reuss[17] raised the question of Calvin as author of the two versions, but it is not here in our plan to develop this problem.

As J. Pannier pointed out already in his edition of the *Epistle* dated 1929[18], Calvin's preface consists of a plan of his *Institution* and some passages appear again almost literally in the French edition of the *Institution* of 1541. As for the sources and possible models of the *Epistle*, the latter have not been studied so far. Alexandre Ganoczy, in his *Jeune Calvin*[19], goes so far as to suggest an absence of sources by stating: "One has the impression that, in order to write it, Calvin has used no sources other than the Bible itself and – we shall willingly add – the resonances that his scriptural readings have stirred up in his own heart. Lutheran theological reminiscences only appear there in some statements on Adam's seed 'vicious, perverse, corrupt, empty and deprived of any good' on the Law which 'could lead no-one to perfection' and on the 'constitutions of men' which 'supplant those of God'. But the text taken as a whole is only an eloquent praise of Christ the only Mediator of the New Testament, in which is accomplished, as at his end, the entire ancient Law'. It is true that the biblical references bear witness to careful readings of the Bible. It is also true that its

---

[17] *Fragments in Revue de theologie 3* (1865), 232ss.
[18] Jean CALVIN, *Epistle to all lovers of Jesus-Christ, with introduction on a French edition of the Institution of 1537* by Jacques PANNIER, Paris 1929 (*Publication of the Societe Calviniste de France, No. 2*).
[19] P. 90ss.

tone is not especially marked by the Lutherian reform. However, the *Epistle* is not without a model, as regards its structure and its content. Before examining two possible models for it, we would like to give a brief resume of the main points of the doctrine of the *Epistle* itself:

Man, after having been created in the image of God, "slipped into ruin" only on account of his free will, and that is how God came to hate the human race. But God, in His goodness, did not want man to remain in this miserable state and he gave him, in creation itself, signs of the divine presence. These were aimed at the Gentiles in the first place. Then, "in order to show his goodness more fully", God made His voice heard by a certain race, that is to say Israel, whom he chose as his own. But this alliance was not enough to lead the Jews in the true way and they refused to obey the Law. As for the Gentiles, they did not honour their Creator in spite of the signs of His presence in nature, and they began to worship idols. In order to bring the Jews and the Gentiles near their Creator, a new alliance was therefore needed and a Mediator who places himself between the two parties (God and man) by conciliating them. This Mediator was Jesus-Christ.

The Mediator was a part of God's plan from the fall of Adam. It was even promised to Adam "incontinent after his ruin". This promise was then renewed to Abraham and in the whole Old Testament. By wishing to reassure the children of God in an even clearer manner, God gave them the Law whose ceremonies represented the "figures and shades of the great assets to come through Christ who was the only body and truth of them". He also sent them civil authorities, so that they should be well governed and well defended against their enemies. The Messiah came "in the fullness of time". The witnesses of the Old and New

Testament agree in order to say that Jesus-Christ was the Messiah. His "marvellous" works also show His divine virtue.

By His arrival he drew up the New Alliance which covers the Ancient and what is eternal, being confirmed by his death. The New Alliance is also called the Gospel because Christ, having become a man, made us children of Christ. As Christians we must not corrupt this new Alliance. That is what gives hope in front of the last Judgment. It belongs to princes, bishops and pastors to assure that it is achieved among all peoples.

And as regards the structure of the *Epistle*, a model is provided to us by the Latin preface to the Vulgate published by Robert Estienne (1503-59) in 1532[20]. Obviously shorter than Calvin's *Epistle*, d'Estienne's preface comprises the essential elements of the latter, even if it does not lean on the same biblical passages. According to the Parisian printer, God created man in His own image and the fall was solely due to Adam's disobedience. As a result of the fall, all men became sinners, but God promised Christ the Redeemer first of all to Adam himself and then to Abraham and the other fathers of the Old Testament. While awaiting Christ's arrival, God gave men the Law which enabled them to recognise their own sins. Christ came only on account of divine goodness and not on account of human merits. He came to unite us with the Father; it is thanks to Him that we could become sons of God; it is He also who will judge us at the time of the Last Judgment.

That is therefore a model of the *Epistle*, but is that the only one? In 1534, the Zurich reformer Henri

---

[20] *Biblia. Breves in eadem annotations ex doctissimis interpretationibus et Hebraeorum commentariis.* Paris, R. Estienne 1532. The second edition of the Bible was printed in Paris in 1534. It included the same preface.

Bullinger (1504-1575) published his treaty entitled *On the only and eternal alliance of God*[21]. Calvin certainly makes no mention of this treatise and it is impossible to *prove* that he knew about it. However, it is striking to note both the points of contact and the differences between the *Epistle* and Bullinger's work. According to the reformer of Zurich (who, we should note, does not base himself at all on the same biblical passages as Calvin), God makes an alliance with man only on account of His goodness and mercy. Immediately after Adam's fall, God gave us hope. The alliance with Abraham and his posterity applied to the Jews and the Gentiles who, however, neglected its conditions. God's promises in the Old Testament were about eternal heritage. In order to strengthen the Alliance drawn up with Abraham, God gave the Law which must be followed spiritually and that was always done by God's children, as the ceremonies of the Law make "living pictures" of the things to come. This same Alliance was at last confirmed by Christ and by His Incarnation. In becoming man, he made us all children of Christ. However, He himself has always remained the true God by witnessing the prophecies of the Old (and the New) Testament, as well as the miraculous works carried out by Christ himself. The difference between the Old and the New Testament, Bullinger concludes, is not an essential difference. It is always about the same Alliance promised to Adam, drawn up with Abraham, strengthened by the Law and finally confirmed by Christ.

Let us first of all note the points of contact between Bullinger's treatise and Calvin's *Epistle*. Like Estienne, they both think it is important to underline

---

[21] *De Testamento seu foedere Dei unico et aeterno Heinrychi Bullingeri brevis expositio*, Zurich, C. Froschouer 1534.

that God made his first promises to Adam already, and to underline the continuity of the divine promises which lead to Christ's coming by which we become "sons of God". Moreover, both of them (this time different from Estienne) underline that the Law was a prefiguration of things to come, that its conditions were neglected and that the Scriptures and miracles bear witness to Christ's divinity.

In his *difference* from Bullinger, Calvin agrees with Estienne by beginning with the description of the creation and the fall and by underlining divine goodness and the full responsibility of human freewill. However, he distances himself from his *two* sources by maintaining the distinction between Jews and Gentiles, and by noting that the civil government enjoyed by Israel was also a sign of choice. By this last comment, Calvin seems to reject the notion of Luther's "civil justice", as, according to the reformer of Wittenberg, "civil justice", otherwise human law and government, have no connection with divine justice.

As regards the differences between the *Epistle* and Bullinger's treatise, above all it is striking to discover that the man of Zurich makes a point of saying that there is only one Alliance which is drawn up between God and his people and that it is this Alliance which is confirmed in history until the coming of the Mediator. Calvin, as we have just seen, also underlines the continuity between the Old and the New Testament. However, different from Bullinger, he very clearly postulates two Alliances, one with the people of Israel which was considered inadequate, and the second (laid down by God from all time) which was drawn up with the Jews and the Gentiles through Christ. This second Alliance covers the first, while overtaking it.

We are led to conclude that Calvin, by writing the *Epistle*, used Estienne's preface and Bullinger's treatise. However, he did not hesitate to distance himself from his sources, in order to express his own theology. In the *Epistle* it is a question of rejecting the notion of "civil justice" peculiar to Luther and especially to reject the Zurich doctrine of the single Alliance. It will only be from 1539 that Calvin rallies to the doctrine of Bullinger's Alliance[22] that he expressed in the *Christian Institution*. (7,1).

As for the survival of the *Epistle*, it is revelatory. The text disappeared from the French *New Testament* published in Geneva in 1539 while Calvin was still "in exile" in Strasbourg. It is replaced there by a preface entitled *On the only and eternal Alliance* and written by Henri de la Mare and/or Jacques Bernard. The *Epistle* does not appear either in the first French Bible published in Geneva after Calvin's return, that is, in 1543. The *Epistle* is found, including the additions that we point out below, in the form of notes, as a preface to the Geneva Bible of 1544. From 1551, it appears under the title of the "Epistle to the faithful showing how Christ is the end of the Law" and has the same additions.

What happened? Without knowing if the New Testament of 1539 was printed before or after the conciliation between Calvin and the Genevan ministers which took place in March 1539, it is impossible to say whether the insertion of the preface on the *only and eternal Alliance* represents an anti-Calvinian measure or an echo of the change in the reformer's theology. The absence of the *Epistle* of the 1543 Bible would make one believe in this last hypothesis. But then why does the *Epistle* re-appear in 1544?

---

[22] On his adoption of the Zurich doctrine v. Jurgen QUACK, *Evangelische Bibelvorreden von der Reformation bis zur Aufklarung,* Gutersloh 1975, 104ss.

The answer to is look in the additions themelves. These appear for the first time in a separate edition of the *Epistle* which appeared in Geneva in 1543 in the following form (we will hereafter call it the *Treatise*):

TWO//EPISTLES, //ONE SHOWS HOW our Lord Jesus Christ //is the end of the Law, and the sum// of all that one must seek // in scripture. // Composed by M.I. CAluin.// The other in order to console the faithful who suffer // for the Name of Jesus: and to teach// them to govern themselves in times of adver//sity and prosperity and to// confirm them against the temp//tations and assaults // of death. Composed by M.P. Viret, // 1543[23].

As can be seen[24], the two most important additions do not concern the question of the two Alliances, but Jesus-Christ as being the sum of all of Scripture on the one hand and, on the other hand, the direct link which exists between divine justice and human justice. The accent of the *Epistle* undergoes a radical change. The main question is no longer that of the number of Alliances. In future it is a question of showing that Jesus-Christ is in *all* holy Scripture and to underline the manner in which civil government constitutes an instrument of God's justice. It is therefore on these two counts that the *Epistle* is re-incorporated into the Calvinian Bibles of the sixteenth century.

The text of the Epistle that we reproduce here represents the modernized version of the text published in the *Calvini Opera* IX on pp. 787-822. It should be noted that the latter is faulty, especially as regards the variants (relatively minor on the whole) in the

---

[23] *V. Calv. Opp. IV, LXIIss.*
[24] V. nn.8 and 11 of the text of the *Epistle*.

additions. A critical edition of the Latin and French versions remains to be made. The text presented here is however adequate for any reader who does not take on highly specialized works on this subject.

Irena Backus, Claire Chimelli

J. Calvin Epistle – Text

God, the very perfect creator and excellent worker of all things, even above his other creatures in whom He had already shown himself more than marvellous, had made man as a masterpiece to which one could attribute a singular excellence.[25] For He had formed him in his image and likeness [Gn 1,26 s.], such that the light of his glory shone clearly in him. Now, what could make him consist in this state where he had been created, it was that in humility he should always lower himself before the majesty of God, magnifying this with thanksgiving, and that in himself he should not seek his glory, but seeing that everything had come from above, he should also look upwards in order to glorify only one God, to whom the praise belonged.

But the wretched one, wishing to be something in himself, immediately began to forget and fail to recognise from where the goodness was coming to him and, by outrageous ingratitude, he undertook to raise himself and become proud against his maker and author of all his graces. For this reason, he stumbled into ruin, he lost all the dignity and excellence of his first creation, he was skinned and denuded of all his glory, he was alienated from the gifts which had been placed in him, in order to confound him in his pride and to teach him[26] what he had not wished to hear from goodwill: that is to say, that it was only vanity and had never been anything else, other than that the Lord of virtue had helped him.

---

[25] The editions of the Bible and the New Testament (printed in Geneva or elsewhere) which reproduce this preface entitle it, from 1551: "Epistle to the faithful showing how Christ is the end of the Law."

[26] Later editions, from 1543, add here: "by force".

Therefore, God also began to have him in hate and, as he well deserved it, to disown him for his work, in view of the fact that His image and likeness were erased from him and the graces of his goodness were not within him. And as He had placed him and ordained him to delight and take pleasure in him as a father in his very dear child, on the contrary He held him in scorn and abomination, so much that everything that pleased Him beforehand displeased him, what He wanted to take pleasure in him irritated him, what He wanted to look upon with a benign fatherly look, He started to hate him and look upon with regret. In short, man as a whole, with his affiliations, his deeds, his thoughts, his words, his life, have completely displeased God, as if he had been his special enemy and adversary, so far as to say that He was sorry He had made him. Having been dejected in such confusion, he was fertile in his cursed seed to create a generation in his likeness, that is to say vicious, perverse, corrupt, empty and without any goodness, rich and abundant in evil.

However the Lord of mercy, who not only loves, but is himself love and charity, wishing even by His infinite goodness to love what is not worthy of being loved, did not at all waste, lose and damage men as their iniquity required it, but upheld and supported them with sweetness and patience, giving them a medium and leisure to return towards Him and to pick themselves up again in the obedience from which they had turned away. And even though He hid himself and kept quiet, as if He wanted to hide from them, leaving them to follow the desires and wishes of their lawless wickedness, without a regime, without any correction from his word, nevertheless, He gave them plenty of warnings which had to encourage them to look for

Him, taste and find in order to know and honour Him as was his due.

For He raised up, in all places and in all things, his signs and arms, even under coats of arms of such clear intelligence that there was no-one who could claim ignorance of knowing such a sovereign Lord, who had so fully exalted his magnificence. It is when in all parts of the world, in heaven and on earth, that He wrote and almost engraved the glory of his power, goodness, wisdom and eternity. Saint Paul therefore has spoken the truth, that the Lord has never left himself without a witness, even towards those to whom He has sent no knowledge of his word, considering that all creatures, from the heavens to the centre of the earth, could be witnesses and messengers of His glory to all men, in order to draw them to seek Him and, after having found him, so powerful, so wise and eternal, and even helped each one in his own place in this search [Rm 1,19 ss]. As the little singing birds sang for God, the animals cried for Him, the elements feared Him, the mountains resounded for Him, the rivers and fountains winked at Him, the herbs and flowers laughed at Him, how true it is that it was not necessary to look for Him far away, considering that everyone could find Him in himself, insofar as we are all sustained and preserved by his virtue dwelling within us.

However, in order to more fully show His goodness and infinite mercy between men, He was not content to teach them all by such lessons as we have stated, but He especially made His voice heard by a certain people, who, by His goodwill and liberal grave, He elected and chose among all the nations on the earth. It is the children of Israel to whom, by His word, He clearly showed what He was; and by His marvellous works, He declared what he knew how to do. So He took them away from the subjection of Pharaoh, king of

Egypt, under which they were detained and oppressed, in order to liberate them and place them in freedom. He travelled with them night and day in their flight, being like a fugitive in their midst. He fed them in the desert. He made them owners of the promised land, He gave them victories and triumphs into their hands. And as if He had been nothing to other nations, He wanted to be expressly called the God of Israel, and they were called His people, under such a convention that they would never acknowledge another lord and would not accept another God. And such an alliance was confirmed and passed under true instruments, by the testament and witness that He opened up to them.

Nevertheless men, all of them feeling their cursed fate and showing themselves true heirs of the iniquity of their father Adam, in spite of such types of reprimands, were not at all moved and did not listen to the doctrine by which God was warning them. The creatures in whom the glory and magnificence of God resided did not give any advantage to the Gentiles to make them glorify Him to whom they bore witness. The Law and the prophets did not have the authority towards the Jews in order to lead them onto the straight path. They were all blind to the light, deaf to the warnings, hardened to the commandments.

It is true that the Gentiles, amazed and convinced by so many advantages and blessings that they saw with their eyes, were restrained from seeing the secret benefactor from whom so much goodness was coming. But instead of giving glory to the true God, which was due to Him, they wrought for themselves a God for their pleasure and according to what their crazy fantasy in its vanity and untruthfulness had imagined Him to be. And not only one, but as much as their rash presumptuousness could pretend and cast, so that there was no nation or region which did not create new gods, as it seemed right to them. That is how idolatry, the pandering traitor, made men turn away from God and amuse themselves with a pile of illusions to which they themselves had given a shape, name and being.

On the subject of the Jews, as much as they had received and accepted the messages and directions that the Lord sent them through his servants, however being unchaste distorted their faith in Him, thoughtlessly turned away from Him, broke and scorned His law, which they held in hate and followed that path to their regret, they estranged themselves from His house and ran immediately after other gods, practising idolatry in the manner of the Gentiles against His will.

That is why in order to come close to the men of God, both Jews and Gentiles, it was essential that a new alliance was made, certain, confident and inviolable. And so that this could be established and confirmed, it was essential to have a mediator who would intercede and intervene between the two parties in order to make them agree, without which man would always remain under God's anger and indignation and would have no means of recovering from the curse, misery and confusion into which he had slipped. It was our Lord and Saviour Jesus-Christ, the true and only eternal Son of God, who had to be sent and given to men through the Father in order to be the founder of the world which was otherwise dissipated, destroyed and desolate, to which from the beginning of the world was always the hope of recovering the loss made in Adam. For even to Adam, straight away after his ruin, in order to console and comfort him, the promise was given that by the seed of the woman the head of the serpent [Gn 3,15], would be broken, which was to say that through Jesus-Christ born of a virgin the power of Satan would be knocked down and broken.

Since then, this promise was fully renewed to Abraham when God told him that by his seed all the nations of the earth would be blessed [Gn 12,3]: it was that from his seed Jesus-Christ would come according to the flesh, by the blessing from which all men, from any region whatsoever, would be sanctified. And once more it was continued to Isaac in the same form and same words [Gn 26,24], and after being denounced often, repeated and confirmed by the witness of various prophets, until it showed completely for much greater faith from whom He would be born, at what time, in what place, what afflictions and death He would suffer, the glory in which He would rise, what His reign would be, into what salvation He would lead his people.

First of all, it was foretold to us in Isaiah how He would be born of a virgin, saying: "Here you are, the virgin shall be pregnant and shall give birth to a son and shall call His name Emmanuel" [Es 7,14]. In Moses[27] the time is described when the good Jacob said: "The sceptre will never be taken from the line of Judah nor the driver of his army until the one who must be sent shall come, and He will be the hope of people " [Gn 49,10], which was proven at the time that Jesus-Christ came into the world. For the Romans, having taken away from the Jews all government and leadership, had about thirty-three years before they appointed Herod as king over them, as a foreigner, for his father was Antipater Idumeen and his mother an Arabian[28]. It sometimes happened that the kings failed the Jews, but had never been seen without counsellors, governors and legislators as at that time. And another description of it is made in Daniel by the calculation of the seventy weeks [Dn 9,24].

---

[27] Genesis, of which Moses is taken to be the author.
[28] Herod the Great, whose biography is known mainly by the 1st century history Flavius Joseph.

The place of birth was clearly shown to us by Micah, saying: "And thou, Bethlehem in Judea, thou art the smallest among the thousands of the cities of Judah, from thee will come for me the one who shall be the ruler in Israel, and His issue is from the beginning of the days of eternity" [Mi 5,1].   As for the afflictions that He had to bear for our deliverance and the death that he had to suffer for our redemption, Isaiah and Zachariah have fully and strongly spoken. The glory of His resurrection, the quality of His reign and grace of salvation that He would bring to His people have been richly treated by Isaiah, Jeremiah and Zachariah.

Such promises, announced and testified by these holy people full of the Spirit of God, have calmed and comforted the children and chosen ones of God. They have nourished them, upheld and maintained their hope, while waiting for the Lord's will to be to exhibit what He promised them; between whom several kings and prophets have greatly wished to see their fulfilment, however much in the meantime they did not cease to understand in their hearts and minds by faith what they could not see with their eyes. And again to confirm to them even more in every way during the long wait for this great Messiah, God opened up to them His written Law to them, in which were included several ceremonies, purifications and sacrifices, which things were only numbers and signs of the great blessings to come through Christ, for he alone was the body and truth of them.   For the Law could lead no-one to perfection, but only showed and like a teacher addressed and led to Christ, who was, as saint Paul said, its end and achievement [Ga 3,24; Rm 10,4].

Noticeably, several times and in various seasons, He sent them kings, princes and captains to deliver them from the powers of their enemies, to govern them in true peace, recover their losses, make their reign flourish and in great exploits make them famous among all the other peoples in order to give them some taste of the great wonders that they would receive from this great Messiah, to whom all the virtue and power of the kingdom of God would be unfurled.

But when the fullness of time came and the time pre-ordained by God was due, this great Messiah who was so much promised and so much awaited came and perfected and achieved everything which was required for our redemption and salvation [*cf* Ga 4,4]. And it was given not only to the Israelites, but to all men of all peoples and regions, so that human nature should be reconciled to God, so that it is fully contained and only shown in the following book, which we have translated as faithfully as possible to us, according to the truth and aptness of the Greek language, so that all Christian men and women who understand the French language can understand and acknowledge the law [29]that they must keep and the faith that they must follow. And the said book is called New Testament in relation to the Old which, inasmuch as it must reduce itself and relate to the latter, was in itself infirm and imperfect, and yet it

---

[29] Instead of the passage:"as it is fully contained…the faith that they must follow", one reads in the *Treaty* of 1543 as well as in the editions of the Bible which reproduce it:

"To clarify such a matter, Lord Jesus, who was its foundation and substance, commanded his apostles to whom he gave charge and commandment to publish his grace throughout the world. Now the apostles, in order to fully and correctly carry out their work, have not only taken trouble and diligence to carry out their ambassadorship by preaching by word of mouth, but in the example of Moses and his prophets, in order to leave the eternal memory of their doctrine, have reduced it to writing, where they have first of all recited the history that our Lord acted and suffered for our salvation; then after they have shown that all that was worthwhile and what gain we receive and in what way we must take it. All this collection is called the New Testament. And is so called in the light of the Old…"

was abolished and repealed. But this one is the New and eternal, which will not grow old and it will never be necessary, since Jesus-Christ was its Mediator who ratified and confirmed it by his death, in which he achieved total and complete remission of all prevarications which remained under the first Testament [Hb 9].

Scripture also calls it the Gospel, that is to say Good and Joyful News, because it is in this that it is stated that Christ, the only natural and eternal son of the living God, was made man in order to make us children of God his Father, by adoption [Rm 8,15; Ga 4,5]. And thus He is for us the only Saviour in whom there lies our completely our salvation, peace, justice, sanctification, grace and life, who has died for our sins, rose again for our justification, who went up to heaven in order to bring us there, take possession for us in our name, and forever be present before his Father as our advocate and perpetual sacrificer, who sits at His right hand as a king, having been made Lord and Master over all, in order to compensate for everything in heaven and earth; what all the angels, patriarchs, prophets, apostles could never have done nor known how to do. [Hb 7 and 8]. For they were not ordained by God for that purpose.

And as the Messiah had so many times been promised in the Old Testament, by several witnesses of the prophets, also Jesus-Christ through some undoubted witnesses stated himself to be none other than the one who was to come and who was expected. As the Lord God, by His voice and His Spirit, through his angels, prophets and apostles, even through all His creatures, gave us so completely surely that nobody could contradict this without resisting and rebelling against His power.

First of all, God eternal, by His own voice and without any doubt irrevocable truth, testified about this saying: "Here is my beloved Son in whom I am well pleased, listen to Him!" [Mt 3,17; 17,5]. The Holy Spirit is the great witness of this in our hearts, as Saint John said [I Jn 5,6.]. the Angel Gabriel sent to the Virgin Mary said to her: "Behold, you shall conceive in your womb and shall give birth to a son, and you shall call His name Jesus. As He shall be great and shall be called the Son of the Most High. And the Lord God shall give Him the throne of David his father, and He shall reign in the house of Jacob eternally and there shall be no end to His kingdom". [Lk 1,31 ss]. This same message in substance was given to Joseph [Mt 1,20]. Also later to the shepherds to whom it was said that the Saviour, who was Christ, the Lord, had been born. And not only was this message brought by an angel, but approved by a great company of angels, who, all together, gave glory to the Lord and announced peace on earth [Lk 2,11 ss]. Simeon the wise, in a prophetic spirit, confessed Him in a high degree. For holding the little child in his arms, he said: "Now, Lord, you are leaving your servant in peace according to thy word. For mine eyes have seen thy salvation, which thou hast prepared before the face of all peoples" [Lk 2,25 ss.] John the Baptist spoke about it also as was his duty, when seeing Him come to the river Jordan said to Him: "Behold the Lamb of God, behold the one who takes away the sins of the world" [Jn 1,29]. Peter and all the apostles confessed, witnessed and preached everything relating to salvation and foretold by the prophets to be done in Christ, the true Son of God. And those that the Lord had ordained to be witnesses up to our time have, by their writings, fully shown, as readers can easily see.

All these witnesses accept so well in unity and agree so well together that by such agreement, it is easy to know that it is a very certain truth; for there could not be such agreement in a lie. However, not only the Father, the Son, the Holy Spirit, the angels, prophets and apostles give witness of Jesus Christ, but moreover these wonderful works show his most excellent virtue. The sick, the lame, the blind, the deaf, the dumb, the paralysed, those possessed of the devil, even the dead revived by Him, have brought the signs of it. In His virtue He is created, in His name He forgave sins. And however He did not say without reason that the works that his Father had given Him to do were fairly good witnesses [Jn 5, 36]. Besides, even the wicked and enemies of His glory were compelled by the force of truth to confess it and acknowledge something, like Caiaphus [Jn 11,49], Pilate and his wife [Mt 27, 19 s]. I do not want to bring in the witnesses of the devils and revolting spirits, considering that Jesus-Christ drove them out [Mc 1,25 et al].

To sum up, all the elements and all creatures gave glory to Jesus Christ. At His command, the winds ceased, the rough sea was calmed [Mt 8,26 par], the fish in His stomach brought pebbles [Mt 17,24]; the stones, in order to give witness to Him, were broken, the veil of the Temple is torn in half, the sun went dark, the monuments opened up and several bodies were brought back to life [Mt 27,45 ss, par.] And there was nothing, in heaven or on earth, which had not testified Jesus Christ to be its God, Lord and Master, and the great Ambassador of the Father sent down below in order to give salvation to humans. All these things are announced, shown, witnessed and signed in this Testament by which Jesus Christ made us heirs in the kingdom of God His Father and declares His will, as a testator to his heirs, in order to be brought to fulfilment.

Now we are all called to this heritage without exception of people, male or female, small or large, servant or lord, master or disciple, clerk or laymen, Hebrew or Greek, French or Latin, no-one is rejected; whosoever by certain faith will receive what is sent to him will embrace what is presented to him, in short, who will acknowledge Jesus Christ inasmuch as it is given by the Father.

And yet, all of us men and women who bear the name of Christian men and women, shall we allow ourselves to steal, hide and corrupt this Testament, which so rightly belongs to us, without which we cannot claim to any right in the kingdom of God, without which we do not know the great blessings and promises that Jesus Christ has given us, the glory and the blessing that he has prepared for us?

We do not know what God has ordered us or forbidden to us, we cannot discern the good with the bad, the clarity of shadows, God's commandments of the constitutions of men, without the Gospel, all were useless and vain to us, without the Gospel, we are not Christians, without the Gospel, all wealth and poverty, wisdom and folly before God, strength is weakness, all human justice is damned by God. But through knowing the Gospel, we have been made children of God [Ga 4,6], brothers of Jesus Christ, fellow-citizens of the saints [Ep 2,19], citizens of the kingdom of heaven [Ph 4,201], heirs of God with Jesus-Christ [Rm 8,17], through whom the poor are made rich, the weak powerful and fools wise men; the broken-hearted comforted, the doubtful sure, and slaves freed. The Gospel is the word of life and truth. It is the power of God for salvation of all believers and the key of God's science which opens the door of the kingdom of heaven to the faithful, the slaves freed. The Gospel is the word of life and truth. It is the power of God for the salvation of all believers and the key of God's science which opens the door of the kingdom of heaven to the faithful, freeing them from sin, and closes it to the unfaithful, tying them up in their sins [cf Mt 18, 18]. Happy are those who hear it and keep it [Lk 11,28]. For through that, they show that they are children of God. Unhappy are those who do not want it, nor hear it nor follow it, as they are the devil's children.

Oh Christian men and women, hear now and learn, for surely the ignorant man with his ignorance will perish and the blind man following the other blind man will fall with him into the ditch [Lk 6,39]. There is only one way to life and salvation, that is faith and certainty in God's promises, which cannot be found without the Gospel, through hearing and understanding from which living faith is given, with certain hope and perfect charity in God and burning love for one's fellowman. Therefore where is your hope if you despise and disdain to listen, see, read and take in this holy Gospel? Those who have their affections fixed in this world obtain by any means what they think belongs to their happiness, without sparing either labour, or body, or life, or fame. And all these things are done in order to serve this wretched body, whose life is so healthy, wretched and unsure. When it is a question of immortal and incorruptible life, of eternal and inestimable blessing, of all the treasures of heaven, shall we not make every effort to follow them?

Those who devote themselves to mechanical arts, however low or vile they are, take such great trouble and work to learn them and understand them, and those who wish to be known as virtuous and torment the spirit night and day in order to understand something in human sciences, which are only wind and smoke. How much, at a price, must we use and endeavour in the study of that celestial wisdom which surpasses everyone and penetrates into the mysteries of God, which it has pleased him to reveal through his holy word [Ep 1,7 *ss*].

What then will it be that can estrange and take us away from this holy Gospel? Will it be insults, curses, shame, deprivation of earthly honours? But we know well that Jesus Christ has travelled the same road, which we must follow if we wish to be his disciples, and it is not to refuse to be condemned, mocked, lowered, rejected before men in order to be honoured, prized, glorified and exalted in God's judgment. Will it be banishments, proscriptions, deprivation of wealth and richness? But we know well that when we shall be banished from a country, the earth belongs to the Lord, and when we shall be through out from the whole world, we will not however be outside His own kingdom; that we will shall be stripped and poor, that we have a Father who is rich enough to feed us, and even that Jesus-Christ has been made poor so that we could follow him in poverty. Will it be afflictions, prisons, tortures, torments? But we know that through the example of Jesus Christ it is the path to reach glory. Will that finally be death? But it does not take away the life that is to be desired[30].

In short, we have Jesus Christ with us, we will not find anything so cursed that is not blessed by Him, anything so dreadful that cannot be sanctified, anything so bad that does not turn us to the good. Let us not be made uncomfortable when we see all the worldly powers and forces, on the other hand. For the promise cannot let us down that the Lord on high will mock all assemblies and effort of men who will want to create against him [Ps 2,4]. Let us not be distressed as if all hope were lost, when we shall see the true servants of

---

[30] All this passage is inspired in the drift of Rm 8,35*ss*.

45

god die and perish before our eyes, as it has truly said by Tertullien, and was always been proved and will be until the centuries have been consumed, for the blood of martyrs us the seed of the church.[31]

And yet we have a better and stronger consolation: it is to turn our eyes away from all this world and abandon everything that we can see in front of us, while patiently awaiting the great judgment of God through whom in a moment everything that man have every devised against him will be knocked down, wiped out and turned over. That will be when God's reign, that we see now in hope, will be manifest and when Jesus Christ will appear in majesty with the angels. Then the good and the bad will have to appear before the judgment throne of this great King. Those who remain strong in this Testament and will have followed and kept the will of this good Father, will be on His right hand like true children and will be blessed, the goal of their faith, which will be eternal salvation. And insofar as they will not have been ashamed to acknowledge and confess Jesus Christ, in the time that he was scorned and condemned before men, they will also take part in his glory, eternally crowned with him. But the wicked, rebels and the condemned, who will have condemned and rejected this holy Gospel, and equally those who, in order to maintain their honours, wealth and high estates, will not have wished to be humble and lowly with Jesus Christ and for the fear of men will have

---

[31] This famous sentence is not found as such in TERTULLIEN; in the *Apologeticum* (50,13) one reads: "Every time that you harvest us, we become more numerous: it is a seed that is the blood of Christians " (ed. Waltzing, Les Belles Lettres, Paris 1961, p. 108). St-AUGUSTINE will take up the image then others after him. *Cf* for example *In Psalm 39, I pr.:* "Innocent blood has been spilt, and from this blood, as sown by everyone, the harvest of the Church has grown."

abandoned the fear of God, like bastards and rebels to this Father, will be on his left hand side. They will be thrown into a cursed state and for the wages of their unfaithfulness will receive eternal death [*cf* Mt 25,31 *ss*].

Now, since you have heard that the Gospel gives you Jesus Christ, in whom all the promises and graces of God are fulfilled, and tells you that He was sent from the Father, came down to earth, talked with men, perfected everything which was for our salvation, as it was foretold in the Law and the prophets, it must be very certain and manifest that the treasures of heaven are open to you, God's wealth is spread out and eternal life is revealed. For such is eternal life: to know only one true God and the one that He sent, Jesus Christ, in whom he set up the beginning, the means and the end of our salvation. It is Isaac, the beloved son of his father, who was offered in sacrifice but however did not succumb to the power of death [Gn 22]. It is the watchful shepherd Jacob, taking such care of the flock that he keeps [Gn 30]. It is the good and pitiful brother Joseph who, in his glory, was not ashamed to acknowledge his brothers, however humble and miserable they were [Gn 45]. It is the great sacrificer and bishop Melschisedek having made an eternal sacrifice once for everyone [Hb 7,27]. It is the sovereign legislator Moses writing his law on the tables of our hearts by his Spirit. It is the faithful captain and guide Joshua for leading us into the promised land. It is the noble and victorious king David making any rebel power subject to his hand. It is the magnificent and triumphant king Solomon, governing his kingdom in peace and prosperity. It is the strong and virtuous Sampson who by his death crushed his enemies [Jg 16].

And even everything which could be thought or wished good is found in this one and only Jesus Christ.

For he humbled himself in order to raise us up, and became a servant in order to free us, He became poor in order to make us rich [2 Cor 8,9], He was sold in order to buy us back, captive in order to liberate us, condemned in order to absolve us, He was cursed in order that we should be blessed [cf Ga 3,13], an offering of sin for our justice, He was disfigured in order to represent us, He died that we might live, so much so that through Him, harshness was softened, wrath was calmed, shadows turned into light, injustice justified, weakness became virtuous, discomfort was comforted, sin prevented, scorn was scorned, fear became confidence, debt was paid, toil lightened, sadness turned to joy, ignominy ennobled, rebellion subdued, threats threatened, traps trapped, fighting is fought, war waged against, vengeance avenged, torment tormented, damnation damned, damage damaged, hell is made into hell, death is killed, mortality became immortal. In short, pity swallowed up all wretchedness and goodness all unhappiness.

For all those things which used to be the devil's weapons for fighting us and a sting of death for wounding us, have turned us towards exercises from which we can gain something. If we can glorify ourselves with the Apostle saying: "Oh hell, where is thy victory? Oh death, where is thy sting?" [I Co 15,55]. From which it comes that, by such a spirit of Christ promised to His elected people, we do not live any more, but Christ in us [Ga 2,20] and we are by spirit sitting among the heavenly spirits, while the world is no longer the world to us, although we converse in it, but being content in everything, whether it is our country, homes, conditions, clothing, food and such other things. And we are comforted in tribulation, joyful in sadness, glorious in rage, wealthy in poverty, warm in nudity, patient in trials, living in death [2 Co

6,8 ss]³². There³³ is included all the wisdom that men can understand and must learn in this life, to which neither angel, nor man, nor death, nor living being can add or take away. However, it is the aim where we must stop and limit our understanding, without mixing anything of ourselves in there or receive any doctrine whatsoever which may be added to it. For the one who dares to undertake to teach a syllable beyond or above

---

³² In the *Treatise* of 1543 and in the Genevan editions of the New Testament which followed it, the following passage appears at this place:

"That is what we must all in all look for in all Scripture: it is to know Jesus Christ and the infinite richnesses which are found in him and through him are offered by God His Father. For when one thoroughly examines the Law and the Prophets, one will not find a single word which does not turn us and leads there. And on this account, since all the treasures of wisdom and intelligence are hidden in Him, there is no question of having another aim nor place if we do not want, as a deliberate plan, to turn away from the light of truth in order to make the mistake of going into the shadows of lies. However Saint Paul rightly states, in another passage, that he never considered himself to know anything, except Jesus-Christ, and Him crucified [1 Co 2,2].

For how much it seems to the opinion of the flesh that it is vulgar and contemptible that this knowledge, however it is enough for us to take in .for all our lives. We will not have wasted our time when we have used all our studies and applied all our understanding to gain from it. What would we want to ask more for our souls' spiritual doctrine than to know God to be transformed in Him and have His glorious image imprinted in us, in order to take part in His justice, in order to be heirs of His Kingdom, in order at the end to own it completely? Now is it so that from the beginning,

He gave himself and even now more clearly gives himself to be looked at in the face of his Christ. Therefore it is not lawful to turn away or divert here or there, however little it may be. But our understanding must be stopped at this point to learn in Scripture to know Jesus Christ only, in order to be directly led by Him to the Father, who in Himself holds all perfection."

³³ The *Treatise* adds here, in order to make the union with the preceding: "I told you once more".

what is taught to us must be in a curse before God and his Church[34].

And you, kings, princes and Christian lords, who are ordained by God to punish iniquities and keep good people in peace according to the word of God, it is up to you to have this holy doctrine which is so useful and needed, published, taught and understood by all countries, regions and lordships, so that through you God may be magnified and his Gospel exalted, as by right it is fitting that all kings and kingdoms, in all humility, should obey and serve his glory[35].

---

[34] Several Genevan editions of the New Testament place the last point of the preface here, as the publisher of the *Calvini Opera,* t.IX points out.

[35] The following piece, missing from the 1535 and in the Latin version, was added in the 1535 edition, was added in the *Treatise* of 1543: it is taken up in the later editions of the New Testament.:

"May you remember that the sovereign empire, above all kingdoms, principalities and lordships, was given from the Father to the Lord Jesus, so that he should be feared, held in awe, honoured and obeyed everywhere, both by adults and children. May you remember what was foretold by the prophets, that all the kings of the earth will pay him homage as to their leader and will adore him as their Saviour and their God [cf So 2,11], must be verified in you. And that it will do you no harm to be the subjects of such a great Lord, as if through that your majesty and eminence were in any way diminished. For it is the greatest honour that it is desirable to wish to be recognised and accepted as officers and lieutenants of god, which cannot be, at least that Jesus-Christ, in which he wishes to be glorified and exalted, does not dominate above you. And in fact, it is the reason why this pre-eminence may be given by you, in view of the fact that your power is not based, other than in him alone. Otherwise, what ingratitude would it be to wish to shut out the one who has set you up in the power in which you are placed and who holds and keeps you there?

What is even more important is, you must know that, as there is no better or stronger foundation, to keep your lordships in true prosperity than to have him for Leader and Master and govern your peoples under his hand, and that without him not only they cannot

Oh all of you that you call bishops and pastors of the poor people, see that the flock of Jesus-Christ is not deprived of its proper pasture and that it may not be prohibited or banned for any Christian to be able freely, in his own language, to read, discuss and hear this holy Gospel, seeing that God wishes it, Jesus-Christ orders it. And in order to do this, he has sent his apostles and servants through the whole world, giving them the grace to speak all languages, so that in all languages they should preach to all people. And He has made

---

be permanent or long-lasting, but are cursed by God and, as a result, they will fall into confusion and ruin.

Since it is therefore, that God has given you the sword in your hand to govern your subjects in his Name and his authority, since he gives you this honour to grant you his name and his title, since he has sanctified your state above others in order partly to have his glory and majesty illuminated, that each of you is used, in his place, to magnify and exalt what is his true glorious Image in which he is shown in full to ourselves. Now, in order to do this, it is not enough to confess Jesus-Christ only and to profess to be his people to have that title without the truth and possession; but one must give room to his holy Gospel and to receive him in perfect obedience and humility, which is the duty of everyone. But it is especially your duty to ensure that it is heard and that it should be published by your countries in order to be heard by all those who are placed in charge, so that they acknowledge you as servants and ministers of this great king, in order to serve him and honour him by obeying you under his hand and guidance.

It is what the Lord wants of you when, by his prophet, he calls you guardians of his Church [cf Es 32,3]. As this guardianship or protection does not exist to increase wealth, privileges and honours to the clergy with which it may become proud afterwards and raises up, lives pompously and in all dissolution against the order of its state; much less it lives to maintain it in its pride and in its untidy pomp. But it is ensuring that the doctrine and purity of the Gospel remains whole, that the holy Scripture should be faithfully preached and read, that God may be honoured according to his rule and that the Church may be well policed, that everything which goes against either the honour of God or the good policy of the Church should corrected and destroyed, so much so that the reign of Jesus-Christ should flourish in the virtue of his Word.

them feeders to the Greeks and barbarians, wise men and simple men, so that nobody should be excluded from their doctrine. Certainly, if you are truly vicars, successors and imitators of them, your duty is to do like them, watching over the flock, looking for all the ways that is possible for everyone to be taught in the faith of Jesus-Christ, by the pure word of God. Or otherwise, the sentence is already pronounced and registered that God will ask for their souls from your hands.

The Lord of light, by his Holy Spirit, wants this holy and wholesome Gospel to teach the ignorant, strengthen the weak, give sight to the blind and make his truth reign in all people and nations, so that the whole world may know only one God and only one Saviour, Jesus-Christ, one faith and one Gospel. So be it.

CONFESSION OF FAITH

Which all citizens and inhabitants of Geneva
And subjects of the country must
Swear to keep and hold,
Taken from the instruction that
Is used in the Church
Of the said city.

1. Peter.
2. Like newborn children, wish for pure milk which has no impurities.
3. Be clothed to reply to everyone, who asks you the reason why you have the hope that is within you.
4. If anyone speaks, may it be with the words of God.

G. Farel – Introduction

In the month of May 1536, won by the preaching of Farel, the Councils and people of Geneva solemnly proclaimed their decision to "live according to the Gospel."

This is not the place to re-tell this story, neither that of the re-organization of the educational system or the structure of the life of the church and its discipline. However, it should be noted that a great deal of work was required to have the resolution of May 1536 passed in the reality of the institutions, so as to guarantee to this life "according to the Gospel" a period and stability that the turmoil of the time threatened to compromise.

From the beginning, strong resistances appeared, and the Reformers, in a memoir presented to the Small council at the end of 1536, stated that a resolution was not sufficient to transform the city and they proposed the adoption of a confession of faith which would enable one to know who was a member of the Church:

"Now, as there is no greater division that that of faith, we pray you to command that all the inhabitants of your city should make confession and state the reason for their belief, so that one may now those who hold to the Gospel and those who prefer to be in the kingdom of the Pope rather than that of Jesus-Christ. You will achieve, Sir, a deed of Christian magistrates if each of you, in this Council, made a confession of faith which showed to all the world that the doctrine that you profess is in fact that through which the union of the faithful reigns in the Church. After having given this example, you will charge some of the members of your Council to go, with one of the ministers, to require each inhabitant of the city to do so; which would only take place for this time, because up to now, the doctrine of

each person has not been recorded, which is however the true beginning of a Church."[36]

In fact, the very title of our *Confession of Faith* does not reveal anything more of the unique founding character of the project. On the contrary, intended to be the subject of an oath of "all citizens and inhabitants of Geneva", the *Confession* was going to be considered as compulsory, which gave rise to long-lasting resistance. The text was printed and widely distributed so that everyone could become familiar with it, in the various "tenths" or circumscriptions of the city, after which the *dizeniers* were obliged to visit each house and to advise everyone to take the oath. That was done by districts, all through 1538, but unanimity could not be obtained. This enterprise was not without incident, the resistances not causing the fight to be abandoned. In February 1538, changes in the government of the city were going to give the enemies of the Reformers increased power. The outcome of this conflict is known, of which one of the issues was admission to communion: Calvin and Farel had to leave Geneva, at least for a while, at least as regards the former.

The *Confession of Faith* has come down to us without the name of the author or date of its appearance. The first edition, of which there remains only one known copy[37] came out of the presses of the German publisher Wigand Koeln, who was settled in Geneva from 1521. Dated 10 November 1536, the Register of the Council of Geneva describes articles about the government of the Church that Farel gave to the Council of the Two Hundreds. Did the text of the

---

[36] A. RILLIET, Notice on Calvin's first stay in Geneva, introd. To the publication of the Catechism of 1537, Geneva, Georg. 1878, p.XXVI s.
[37] Ibid., p. IX.

Confession go with these articles of reformation? Some people think they can prove this.[38] However up to now, the date of this first edition remains uncertain: November 1536 or even before that? Or the beginning, even Easter 1537?

On the other hand there is the question of the author of this text. Nicolas Colladon and Theodore de Beze, biographers of Calvin, have attributed its composition to the Reformer, while another tradition brings back the Confession to Farel.[39] This second hypothesis can be considered as accepted, from the degree thesis of Olivier Labarthe, upheld in 1967[40]: a minute analysis of the biblical texts traditionally contained in the catechism (Decalogue, Our Father), as they appear in Calvin's[41] *Instruction and confession of faith* and in our *Confession* has made it possible to establish the following: the formulation which appears in the *Instruction* is very close to that which is found in the *Institution* of 1536, which is not surprising, Calvin's paternity moreover not being in question as regards the *Instruction*. On the other hand, in the *Confession of Faith*, the form of these same texts is so close to that which appears in the two previous works of Farel, the *Summary*[42] and *The manner and method...*[43]

---

[38] Abraham RUCHAT, *History of the Reformation in Switzerland*, ed. L. VUILLEMIN, Nyon, 1835, t. IV, p. 111, and the publishers of the *Opera Calvini* (E. REUSS, BAUM, CUNITZ), t. V, p. XLI ss. Et t. IX, authors quoted by O. Labarthe.

[39] RUCHAT, loc. Cit.

[40] O. LABARTHE, *The relation between the first catechism of Calvin and the first confession of faith in Geneva*, Degree thesis No. 525, Independent faculty of Protestant theology, Geneva, 1967 (typewritten).

[41] CALVIN, *Instruction and Confession of Faith which are used in the Church of Geneva (Opera Calvini* t, XXII).

[42] FAREL, *Summary and short declaration of several places which are really necessary for each Christian to put his trust in God and help his coming. 1534.*

The title of the *Confession of Faith* presents it as an extract from the catechism (*The Instruction)* in use in Geneva. If the design of the two works is compared, several differences are noticed in the arrangement, and the *Confession* is much shorter and does not contain the theological developments of the *Instruction.* However, the main great themes of the Reform have their place there, as will be seen in briefly reviewing its 21 sections. It opens with the affirmation of the Word of God, the Scripture (sect. 1) as the sole foundation of the Christian doctrine (sola scriptura).

After having insisted on the uniqueness of God (sect. 2) before any idolatry and against the abusive place given to the saints, the *Confession* presents the Decalogue (*Exodus* 20, 2-17), as the only law and only rule of behaviour; to the difference of catechisms, it gives no commentary on the various commandments (sect.3). Sections 4 and 5 have as their subject the corrupt and perverse nature of man left to himself and delivered into God's anger. Under the heading "Salvation in Jesus" (sect. 6) there appears, also without a commentary, the text of the Symbol of the apostles. The blessings that God gives us in Jesus-Christ are justification and forgiveness of sins (sect. 7) and regeneration by the Holy Spirit (sect. 8). While we live here below, this regeneration is not however definitively obtained, but we must constantly turn to Jesus-Christ (sect.9). All these blessings are the effects of the sole grace of God (*sola gratia*), without any merit intervening on our behalf (sect. 10), and we can only reach that by faith alone (*sola fide*, sect. 111). In order to live by this divine grace, prayer is required, in the name of Jesus-Christ alone: the *Confession* formally

---

[43] FAREL, *The manner and method that one uses in the places that God with his grace has visited,* 1533. It deals with the first liturgy intended for the French-speaking reformed communities.

rejects mediation (intercession) of the saints (sect. 12). Prayer must be sincere, and intelligible, on the model of the Dominican Prayer (sect.13), the text of which appears without a final doxology, and without a commentary on the different requests. The only two sacraments whose Scripture is guaranteed by the Lord (sect. 14) are baptism (Sect. 15) and Holy Communion (sect. 16). The polemical note against the Roman septenarian is explicit, as is also the affirmation of the legitimacy of the baptism of children, based on the covenant which is open to all. Perhaps it is in the passages dedicated to Holy Communion and, later, to the Church that the tone is hardest and the attack against the "Pope's mass" the most violent, a sign that the struggle is far from being finished. All the rules intended to keep the Church in good order are considered as coming from God (sect. 17), while those that enslave consciences are only "human traditions" and "perverse doctrines of Satan": still there, the tone is bitter against all sorts of Roman practices.

The Church is recognised by its "brands": faithful preaching, but also listening and accepting the Gospel, "right-wing" administration of the sacraments (sect. 18). A stumbling-block and subject of profound disagreement between the Reformers and the Genevan authorities, excommunication (sect. 19) appears here like a measure which is never definitive, but which at the same time acts to guide sinners towards repentance and to protect the faithful against the contagion of sin.

It is the ministers of the Word (sect. 20) who are the true shepherds of the flock, responsible for the life of the faithful and for the purity of the doctrine which is taught; their authority has its roots only in the Word, of which they are the servants.

At last, the magistrates (sect. 21) have their place in the world governed by God: they have a vocation to exercise power on his behalf and to make goodness reign. Also must Christian people be subject to these and pray for them. The case of the impious sovereign, an author of unjust laws, is not called up here. It is a question which appears later in the works of the reformers.

One may notice that this text, by its conciseness, the clarity of the writing, the simplicity of the vocabulary and the concrete nature of the images used, responded well to the aim which was followed: to be accessible to all so that everyone can swear to adhere to it.

Finally, let us note that the bitterness of the polemical language does not constitute an isolated fact at the time. Most of the controversies of the time were full of verbal violences which, perhaps, only astonish today's reader because the subjects of current polemics have become different.

Claire Chimelli

G. Farel – Text

1   THE WORD OF GOD

First of all, we protest that for the rule of our faith and religion, we wish to follow Scripture alone without mixing it with anything which was fabricated from the sense of men without the Word of God, and let us not claim, for our spiritual government, to receive any doctrine other than that which is taught to us by this Word, without adding to it or taking away from it, as our Lord commands it [Dt 4,2; 12,32].

2   ONLY ONE GOD

Therefore following the institution which is contained in the Holy Scriptures, we acknowledge that there is only one God, whom we must adore and whom we must serve [Dt 6,13; Mt 4,10], in whom we must place all our trust and hope, having this assurance that only in Him is all knowledge, power, justice, kindness and mercy contained, and as He is a Spirit, that we must serve Him in spirit and in truth [Jn 4,24]. And however we claim it is an abomination to place our trust and hope in any creature, to worship anyone other than Him, either angels or any other creatures, and to acknowledge another Lord of our souls than Him alone, either holy men or holy women or men living on the earth; equally, to constitute the service which must be given to Him in external ceremonies and bodily observations, as if He delighted in such things, to make an image to represent his divinity, neither any other image to be adored [cf Ex 20,4: Dt 4,16].

3   LAW OF GOD, THE ONLY ONE FOR ALL LAWS

While He is the only Lord and master who has domination over our consciences and also that his will is the only law for all justice, we confess that our whole life must be governed by the commandments of His holy law, in which is contained all perfection of justice [Rm 7,12], and that we must not have any other law for good and righteous living, nor invent any good works in order to take pleasure in Him, other than those who are found therein, as follows:-

Exodus 20

I am the Lord thy God, who has brought thee out of the land of Egypt, from the house of slavery. Thou shalt have no other gods but me. Thou shalt not make unto thyself any image or likeness of the things which are in heaven above, nor in the earth beneath, nor in the waters under the earth. Thou shalt not bow down to them nor serve them, for I am the Lord, thy God, strong, jealous, visiting the iniquity of the fathers upon the children in the third and fourth generation of those who hate me, and showing mercy in a thousand generations to those who love me and keep my commandments. Thou shalt not take the name of the Lord, thy God, in vain, for God will not hold innocent the one who shall take his name in vain. Remember the day of rest to sanctify thyself: six days shalt thou labour and do all thy work; on the seventh, it is the day of rest of the Lord thy God. Thou shalt not do any work, neither thou nor thy son, nor thy daughter, nor thy servant, nor thy maidservant, nor thy beasts, nor the stranger who is within thy gates, for in six days, God has made heaven and earth, the sea and all that in them is, and rested on the seventh day. However He has blessed the day of rest and sanctified it. Honour thy father and mother that thy days may be long in the land which the Lord thy God shall give thee. Thou shalt not kill. Thou shalt not swear. Thou shalt not steal. Thou shalt not bear false witness against thy neighbour. Thou shalt not covet thy neighbour's house nor desire his wife, nor his servant, nor his maidservant, nor his cattle, nor his ass, nor any other thing belonging to him.

4   MAN IN HIS NATURE

We understand man in his nature to be blind to everything, in shadows of understanding, and full of corruption and perversity of heart, such that of himself he has no power to be able to understand the true knowledge of God as it is his, nor to devote himself to good works. But on the contrary, if he is released by God into his true nature, he cannot otherwise live in ignorance and be abandoned to all iniquity. [Rm 1,28]. By which he needs to be illuminated by God to come to the true knowledge of his salvation and also to be in his affection turned around and reformed to the obedience of the justice of God.

5   MAN DAMNED IN HIMSELF

Since man is naturally, as it was said [cf Rm 7,18 ss], deprived and destitute in himself from all the light of God and from all justice, we acknowledge that in himself, he can only expect the anger and curse of God, and yet he must look elsewhere than in himself for the means of his salvation.

6 SALVATION IN JESUS

We confess therefore that Jesus-Christ is the one who was given by the Father so that in Him, we would recover everything that has made us lacking in ourselves. Now everything that Jesus-Christ has done and suffered for our redemption, we hold it to be true, without any doubt, as it is contained in the Creed which is recited in Church, that is to say:

I believe in God, the Father almighty, creator of heaven and earth, and in Jesus-Christ, his only Son, our Lord, who was conceived by the Holy-Spirit, born of the Virgin Mary, suffered under Pontius Pilate, was crucified, died and buried, and descended into hell; on the third day He rose from the dead, and went up to heaven, is seated at the right hand of God, the Father almighty, from whence He shall come to judge the living and the dead. I believe in the Holy-Spirit, the holy catholic Church, the communion of saints, the remission of sins, the resurrection of the body, and life everlasting. Amen.

7 JUSTICE IN JESUS

However, we acknowledge the things that follow to be given to us by God in Jesus-Christ:

First of all, that being by our nature enemies of God [Rm 5,10], subject to His anger and judgment, we are reconciled with Him and placed again in his grace through the intercession of Jesus-Christ [Rm 8,34], so much that in His justice and innocence, we have the remission of our sins and that, through pouring out His blood, we are purged and cleansed of all our stains [Hb 9,11 ss.I Jn 1,7 *et al*].

8   REGENERATION IN JESUS

Secondly, that by His spirit, we are regenerated in a new spiritual nature, that is to say that the bad lusts of our flesh are mortified through his grace, in order not to reign in us [Rm 6,14] and, on the contrary, our will is made true to that of God in order to follow his way and to look for what is agreeable to Him [Rm 12,2] and, however, that through Him we are delivered from the servitude of sin under the power by which we are held captive by ourselves, that that through this deliverance, we are made capable and apt to do good works, and not otherwise [Rm 6,17 ss; Hb 13,21].

9   REMISSION OF SINS ALWAYS NECESSARY FOR THE FAITHFUL

Finally, that this regeneration is so made in us that until we have cast off this mortal body [Rm 8,11], a great many faults and infirmities always remain in us, so that we are always poor and miserable sinners before the face of God.   And how much we had day after day to grow and benefit in God's justice, while there is never fullness nor perfection while we converse here. We always need God's pity in order to obtain remission from our faults and offences.   And so we must always look for our justice in Jesus-Christ and not in ourselves, and in Him we rest and are secure, attributing nothing to our own works [Ph 3,9].

10   ALL OUR WELFARE IN THE GRACE OF GOD

And in order that all glory and praise should be given to God, as it is due, and that we can have true peace and rest in our consciences, we hear and confess that we receive all blessings from God above recited by his sole clemency and pity, without any consideration of our dignity and merit of our works, to which no retribution is due other than eternal confusion [Ep 2,9 s]. Nevertheless our Lord, through his kindness, having received us in the communion of his Son Jesus, has the works that we do in the faith which are pleasing and agreeable, not that they deserve it, but however, not imputing to us the imperfection that is in us, he acknowledges nothing in these other than that which proceeds from his Spirit.

11   FAITH

We confess that the entry that we have into such great treasures and such great richnesses of the kindness of God which is spread out over us, is by faith, when in certain confidence and certainty of heart we believe in the promises of the Gospel and receive Jesus-Christ as he is presented to us from the Father and that he is described to us by the Word of God.

12   INVOCATION OF GOD ALONE AND INTERCESSION OF CHRIST

As we have stated that we have no confidence and hope of our salvation and all blessing in none other that in God through Jesus-Christ, also we confess that we must invoke Him in all our needs in the name of Jesus-Christ [Ph 4,6. 19], who is our mediator [Hb 9,15; 12, 24] and judge [1 Jn 2,11], through whom we have access to Him [Ep 2,18]. Likewise, we must acknowledge that all blessings come only from Him and we must give

Him thanks. On the contrary, we reject intercession by saints as a superstition invented by men against Scripture, even considering that this only comes from defiance that the intercession of Jesus-Christ may not be sufficient.

13   INTELLIGIBLE PRAYER

Moreover, since prayer is only hypocrisy and trickery if it does not come from the inner affection of the heart, we understand that all prayers must be made in sure intelligence. And for this reason, we learn the prayer of our Lord in order to understand properly what we must ask Him for. Our Father who art in heaven, hallowed be Thy name. Thy kingdom come. Thy will be done on earth as in heaven. Give us this day our daily bread and forgive us our sins, as we forgive those who sin against us; and lead us not into temptation, but deliver us from Evil. Amen.

14   SACRAMENTS

We understand that the sacraments that our Lord has ordained in His Church must be to us like exercises in faith, as much in order to strengthen it and to confirm to God's promises as for witness to men. And there are only two of them in the Christian Church that are constituted by God's authority: baptism and the Holy Communion of our Lord; however, what is held in the kingdom of the Pope of seven sacraments, we condemn it as a legend and a lie.

15 BAPTISM

Baptism is an outward sign by which our Lord testifies that He wishes to receive us as His children, as members of His Son Jesus. And however, in this the purgation of our sins that we have through the blood of Jesus-Christ is shown, the mortification of our flesh that we have through his death in order to live in Him through his Spirit [Rm 6,4 ss]. Now, since our children belong to such an alliance of our Lord, we are sure that by right the outward sign is passed to them.[44]

16 HOLY COMMUNION

Our Lord's Last Supper is a sign through which, under bread and wine, it represents to us the true spiritual communication that we have in his body and his blood. And we acknowledge that, according to his command, it must be distributed to us in the company of the faithful so that all those who want to have Jesus for their life may be participants in it [Mt 26, 26-28 *par*]. Now, more especially as the Pope's mass has been a cursed and diabolic order in order to overturn the mystery of this Holy Communion, we declare that to us it is an execration like an idolatry condemned by God, beyond the other execrable blasphemies and superstitions that are contained in it and the abuse of the Word of God which therein is taken in vain, without any fruit or edification.

---

[44] This remark insists on the legitimacy of baptising infants in the light of the Anabaptist doctrine which cast doubts on it.

17 HUMAN TRADITIONS

The circumstances which are necessary for the external policies of the Church and belong only to maintain peace, honesty and good order in the company of Christians, we do not hold onto them for human traditions, more especially as they are included under this general commandment of Saint Paul where he wants everything between us to be done decently and in good order [I Co 14,40]. But all laws and constitutions made to bind consciences, in order to oblige the faithful to things that are not ordained by God, in order to establish another of God's services that He requires, and tending to break Christian liberty, we condemn as perverse doctrines of Satan, considering that our Lord states that he is honoured in vain by doctrines which are from the commandment of men [Mt 16,9 *par*]. And in such opinion we have pilgrimages, monasteries, differences in food, defences of marriages, confessions and other similar things.[45]

18 CHURCH

As much as there is only one Church of Jesus-Christ, however we acknowledge that necessity requires companies of the faithful to be spread in various places, from which assemblies each one is called a Church. But more especially while all companies do not meet in the name of the Lord, but rather to blaspheme and pollute Him by their sacrileges, we understand that the clear mark to discern the Church of Jesus-Christ is when His holy Gospel is purely and faithfully preached,

---

[45] Differences in foods: an allusion to the lean days prescribed in the Catholic Church and during which certain foods were forbidden. It is not a question of fasting, practised in the Churches of the Reformation.

announced, listened to and kept there, when His sacraments are strictly administered, even when there may be some imperfections and faults as there will always be among men. On the other hand, where the Gospel is not declared, heard and received, we do not recognise the form of Church at all, and however the Churches governed by the commandments of the Pope are rather synagogues of the Devil than Christian churches.

19 EXCOMMUNICATION

However, because there are always those who hold God and His sacred Word in contempt, who do not take admonishment, exhortation or reprehension into account, but on the contrary have a career in a much greater punishment, we hold the discipline of excommunication to be a holy and salutary thing among the faithful, as truly it was instituted by our Lord for a good reason [Mt 18,15 ss]. This is so that the wicked ones, by their damnable conversation, do not corrupt good people and do not dishonour our Lord and also that, being ashamed, they return to penitence. And however we understand that it is expedient, according to God's commandment, that all manifest idol-worshippers, blasphemers, burglars, thieves, bawdy people, liars, rebels, quarrelsome people, detractors, batterers, drunks, wastrels, having been duly admonished, if they do not come to reform, should be separated from the communion of the faithful until they are known to have repented.

20 MINISTERS OF THE WORD

We do not consider any other pastors of the Church than faithful ministers of the Word of God, and feeding the flocks of Jesus-Christ [Jn 21,15 *ss*] through Him in instructions, admonitions, consolations, exhortations, reprehensions, on the other hand resisting all false doctrines and mythical deceits, without mixing among the pure doctrine of the Scriptures their dreams or foolish imaginations. And we do not grant them any other power or authority, except to conduct, rule and govern the people of God to those committed by this Word, in which they have the power to command, defend, promise and threaten, and without which they cannot and must not achieve anything. Now as we receive the true ministers of the Word of God as messengers and ambassadors of God, who must be heard as himself, and we consider their ministry to be a commission from God which is needed in the Church; also, on the other hand, we hold that all tempters, false prophets who, abandoning the purity of the Gospel, stoop to their own inventions, must not in any way be tolerated or upheld, whatever title of pastor they claim, but rather as ravishing wolves [Mt 7,15] must be chased and dismissed from the people of God.

21   MAGISTRATES

We hold the super-eminence and domination as much of kings and princes and other magistrates as other magistrates and superiors for a holy thing and good ordinance of God. And like them, in carrying out their duties, they serve God and follow a Christian vocation, either in defending afflicted and innocent people, either by correcting and punishing the evil of the depraved; also, on our behalf, we must bring honour and reverence to them, give obedience and subjection, carry out their orders, bear the duties which are imposed by them upon us as far as possible without offending God; to sum up, we must consider them as vicars and lieutenants of God, to which one can in no way resist except by resisting God himself, and their authority is like a holy commission from God, which he has given them so as to govern us and reign over us [I P 2,13 s]. Through which we understand that all Christians are obliged to pray to God for the prosperity of superiors and lords of the country where they live [I Tim 2,2 s], to obey statutes and ordinances which do not infringe God's commandments, to achieve goodness, peace and public service, striving to uphold the honour of superiors and the peace of the people, without contriving anything or acquiring anything at all in order to stir up trouble or discord. And on the contrary, we state that all those who behave unfaithfully towards their superiors and do not have honest affection for the public good of the country where they converse, therein show their infidelity towards God [Rm 13,2].

EPISTLE FROM JACQUES SADO-/LET CARDINAL

SENT to the Senate & People of Geneva:
By which he tries to reduce
Them under the power of the Bishop of Rome.
With the Reply of Jean Calvin:
Translated from Latin into French:
Printed in Geneva by Michel du Bois.
M.D. XL.
INTRODUCTION

Letter from Cardinal Sadolet to the Genevans

Jacques Sadolet (1477-1547) was born in Modena. He received an education in classical letters in Ferrara before coming to settle in Rome in 1502. In 1513, he became apostolic secretary of Pope Leon X and four years later he was nominated Bishop of Carpentras. Obliged to leave Rome upon the accession of Adrian VI, he stayed in his diocese until 1523, the date upon which he was recalled to Rome by the new Pope Clement VII. In 1536, he was appointed Cardinal by Paul III. A year later, he took part in the Commission called by the Pope to examine the question of the reform of the Roman Catholic Church and to prepare the general Council of which there had been a question for a long time. A Latinist, theologian and philosopher, Sadolet is counted among the most influential Roman cardinals of the first half of the 16th century. As the Papal Legate in 1542, he tried unsuccessfully to bring about a reconcilement between King Francis 1st and the Emperor Charles V. The last years of his life were almost entirely devoted to attempts to reform his own Church. Without being present himself at the first session of the Council of Trent (1545-47), he

72

particularly contested its decrees on Biblical translations, considering the maintenance of the Vulgate as a retrograde step. An author of writings on the education of children (De pueris recte instituendis, 1533) on theological treatises on the church (De exstructione catholicae ecclesiae, 1538) and on original sin (De peccato originali, 1543), he was often considered as theologically suspect by his colleagues. His *Commentary on the Romans,* dating from 1535, was censured by the Vatican as placing too strong an emphasis on human freewill.

As for his *Epistle to the Genevans* dated 18 March 1539, in fact it represents the third attempt on behalf of the Cardinal to bring back to Rome a Church which had adopted the Reformation. His first attempt dating from 1537 was a letter sent in 1538 and addressed to Philippe Melanchthon, to whom the Wittenberg theologian never replied. The second was a letter to Jean Sturm of Strasbourg which sparked off a considerable polemic. It was on 26 March 1539 that the Small-council of Geneva received the original Latin manuscript of the Church from the Cardinal, by the hand of the messenger "Jean Durand, citizen of Carpentras." The circumstances which would have led Sadolet to take this initiative remain mysterious. Even if one accepts that his letters to Melanchthon and to Sturm set a precedent and truly showed his "unionist" tendencies, nothing, nothing, in Sadolet's career, indicates that he was interested in Calvinist theology or, more generally, in the fate of Catholicism in Switzerland before 1539. The letter itself contains no precise information about this. Rather it leaves an innuendo that it is a question of a spontaneous step, motivated only by "the care and solicitude that I am taking on your account".[46]   However, some historians have supposed, without a good reason, that Sadolet had been at the colloquium organised in Lyon in December 1538 by Paul III and whose aim was to re-introduce the Roman-Catholic religion to Geneva.[47]   One of the instigators of this colloquium being Pierre de la Baume, a bishop expelled from Geneva after the Reformation of 1536, it is completely probable that it was he who *later* asked Sadolet to take the first step towards the Genevans.

Whatever the background of the *Epistle*, the Little-Council of Geneva only took one day to decide that "having seen the missive from the said Cardinal, together with his book, that an amiable reply should be sent to him concerning his missive and that, concerning the reply to the book, that in time and place a reply will be sent to him".[48] The reply to Sadolet's letter which accompanied the *Epistle* was given to the messenger Jean Durand the next day. As to the reply to the *Epistle* itself, the situation was more complicated.

Sadolet's Epistle and Calvin's Reply: Latin and French versions

Jean Calvin and Guillaume Farel had been expelled from Geneva in April 1538. From September of this same year, Calvin had been settled in Strasbourg as the pastor of the French church, without however losing contact with his faithful Genevan flock to whom he wrote "pastoral letters". The situation in Geneva was difficult more and more often there were requests for Calvin and Farel to return.   Discipline was going

---

[46] V. below, p. 65.

[47] V. on this subject HERMINJARD V, p. 261ss; DOUGLAS, p.147, 280.

[48] V. HERMINJARD V, p. 262 n.3.

downhill. Berne, for its part, was doing very little to protect the Genevans against the attacks of the Savoyards. Nevertheless, in principal was under the protection of the "gentlemen of Berne" and it is to the Council of that town that the Genevan authorities applied, by sending them a copy of Sadolet's *Epistle*. Here is the reply of the Council of Berne dated 23 May 1539: "We have received the book by the Cardinal of Carpentras and understood your rescription about that…On the former we have counselled to send a lengthy reply to the said Cardinal and on this matter we have instructed to some of our preachers to do so."[49] The "preachers" in question have either refused, or are considered incapable of carrying out this task. On 24 July 1539, one of them, Pierre Kunz (1480-1544), suggested that Calvin should be asked to reply to Sadolet. His suggestion was accepted on condition that no reference should be made to the Bernese in the reply. It seems that at that time, Simon Sulzer (1508-1585) was charged with taking a new copy of the *Epistle* to Strasbourg. In a letter to Farel, written towards the middle of August 1539[50], Calvin states that Sulzer had truly and properly brought the manuscript to him. He adds that he did not wish to answer it, but that he had yielded to the pressure of "our people" (that is to say, Strasbourg preachers M. Bucer, W. caption and J. Sturm, the latter himself being always engaged in debate with Sadolet). Once accepted, Calvin continues, the work takes up all his time. However he hopes to be able to finish it in six days. Whatever amount of time was taken by Calvin to write his Latin reply, the latter was published in Strasbourg by Wendelin Rihel in

---

[49] V. HERMINJARD V, nr. 792, p.321-323.
[50] V. HERMINJARD V, nr. 811, p. 372-373.

September 1539 with Sadolet's text[51]. Meanwhile, the Cardinal himself had had his *Epistle* slightly altered[52] in Lyon. The small volume containing it only includes the year 1539 as the date, without indicating the month. However, it is clear that it must have appeared some months before Rihel's volume. It should be noted that the "Strasbourgian" version of the *Epistle* was printed according to a Bernese copy sent to Calvin by Sulzer.

As for the French translation of the Epistle and Calvin's Reply, its author remains unknown. Some notes about his identity appear in the correspondence from Calvin and Farel in 1539, but they are too vague to allow us more than an attempt at conclusion. On 4 October 1539, Antoine Pignet (an old student friend of Calvin in Orleans), who was then pastor of Ville-la-Grand near Geneva, wrote to Calvin saying that he has just read his *Reply* to Sadolet, in Rihel's edition, it must be supposed. Struck by the elegance and importance of the treatise, he offers to translate it, so that "this treasure" becomes accessible to less cultivated people[53]. To our knowledge, there is no other exchange on this matter between Pignet and Calvin. On 21 October 1539, Farel wrote to Calvin from Neuchatel stating that he had given the French translation of the *Reply* to "a Genevan" and that he had asked that person to bring it to Calvin for verification. The messenger,

---

[51] IACOBI/ SADOLETI ROMA-/ ni Cardinalis Epistola ad Sena-/*tum populumque Geneuensem, qua in obe-dientiam Romani Pontificis eos /reducere conatur./ Ioannis Caluini Responsio. /Argentorati per Vuendelinum/Rihelium./*Mense Septembri./ANNO M.D. XXXIX. Cf. Calv. Opp. V, XLV.

[52]IACOBI SA-/DOLETI ROMA-/NI CARDINA-LIS/Epistola ad Senatum Populumque Geneuen-/sem, qua in obediendiam Romani Pontifi-/cis eos reducere conatur./LVGDVNI APVD SEB./GRYPHIVM, /1539, Cf. Calv. Opp. V, XLVI. Sur les retouches au texte v. HERMINJARD V, 262-263.

[53] V. HERMINJARD VI, nr. 821, p. 37.

continues Farel, claims that he had done so. Also, he would have lodged the translation reviewed by Calvin[54], at Basle. The idea of the latter was on all evidence to have the *translation* printed in Basle. But who was the translator? Calvin's letter to Farel dated 27 October 1539 very clearly suggests the existence of two concurrent versions. The author of the *Reply to Sadolet* explains that it had been impossible for him to collate the whole text of the French translation, "since such work would have taken him a whole day". However he examined some selected passages, which he found satisfactory, but not free from mistakes. These mistakes had to be corrected before the manuscript was sent to press. But, Calvin continues, if the translator does not hurry up in getting it printed, he will be pre-empted by Antoine Pignet who has nearly finished his translation, having, it seems, begun it on 4 October[55].

Calvin does not mention the *Epistle to Sadolet* but, as we know, the French translation of the *Epistle* and the *Reply* was not published in Basle, but in Geneva, by Michel du Bois who had obtained the authority from the Council on 30 January 1540:

EPISTLE / OF JACQUES SADO/LET CARDINAL, Sent to the Senate and People of Geneva: / By which he tries to reduce them/ under the power of the Bishop of Rome./ With the Reply of Jean Calvin:/ translated from

---

[54] V. HERMINJARD VI, nr. 830, p. 103.

[55] V. HERMINJARD VI, nr. 832, p. 116-117 and *Calv. Opp.* V, XLVI. The editors of *Calv. Opp* re-punctuate this Latin letter by inserting a comma between *Antonius* and *Pignaeus*, which gives the following meaning: "if Antoine does not hurry up he will be pre-empted by Pignet". The anonymous translator would therefore according to them be called *Antoine* but, as HERMINJARD VI, p. 116-117, comments, this first name does not correspond with any convincing candidate in Calvin's circle.

Latin into French./ Printed in Geneva by Michel du Bois./ M.D.XI.

The translation made from the Latin text printed in Strasbourg in 1539 by Ribel was not published again in the 16th century after 1540[56]. Are we referring here to the version of the anonymous translator who, finally, gave Michel du Bois and not a Basle printer the printing work? Or is it a question of Antoine Pignet's translation which had, as Calvin suspected, pre-empted its competitor without perhaps his even being aware of its existence? The question is open. Neither do we know if the corrections required by Calvin were incorporated. However, the French text, especially that of the *Epistle*, contains some important differences in relation to the original Latin[57].

As for the Latin version, altogether it was known in three editions in the 16th century. Apart from the Lyonnais edition of the *Epistle* alone in 1539 and the Strasbourg edition of the two treatises which appeared in the same year, Michel du Bois published, at the same time as the French translation:

IACOBI/SADOLETI ROMA-/Cardinalis Epistola ad Se/natum Populumque/Geneuensem:/ Qua in obedientiam romani Pon/tificis eos reducere conatur:/ ad exemplar ipsum Sa-/doleti recognita. /Ioannis Caluini Responsio./ GENEVAE /Apud Michaelem Syluium./M.D. XL[58].

The text of this edition of the *Epistle* would be revised according to the "Sadolet copy", otherwise according to

---

[56] V. *Calv. Opp.* V, XLVI.
[57] The Latin texts are printed in *Calv. Opp.* V, 369-416 and in *O.S.*I, 441-480.
[58] Cf. *Calv. Opp.* V, XLVI.

the manuscript sent by Sadolet to the Little-Council of Geneva in March 1539[59]. The text of Calvin's *Reply* is included in Rihel's Strasbourg edition.

Content of Sadolet's Epistle

This is a brief synopsis of this content. The French version occupies pp. 3-48 of the volume published by du Bois. The Cardinal begins by stating the affection that he holds for the Genevans and by regretting the fact that they have fallen victims "of the enemies of Christian union and peace" and thus are "separated from our mother Church". They have yielded, says Sadolet, to human wisdom, to "vain philosophy", instead of listening to the word of God as it is communicated by the Church. This word teaches us to have faith in Jesus Christ and to carry out charitable works for the eternal salvation of our souls. Faith, contrary to what "inventors of new things", includes several virtues, in particular charity which expresses itself in good works carried out within the Church. As for the latter, its authority is unchanging since it is the Holy Spirit himself which has established it and which through the centuries has inspired its doctors to prescribe the standards that all Christians must follow. The Cardinal continues that "the great diversity of opinions touching true or false religion "can lead 'simple people" astray. In order to avoid this trap, one must submit "to the judgment of the wisest people", in other words to the consensus of the Church.

Having this rejected the doctrine of justification by faith, he attacks the reformed doctrine of the Eucharist,

---

[59] Unfortunately there is no critical edition of Sadolet's *Epistle* which would enable us to estimate the importance of the variants in the Genevan and Bernese manuscripts as well as in the versions printed in 1539 (Lyon and Strasbourg) and in 1540 (Geneva).

by stating that: "They think they can enclose the Lord of heaven and earth and insert his spiritual power which is free and infinite "in which there is shown humility, which is free and infinite in the joints of a human body". Then he defends private confession "in which there is demonstrated humility, the main foundation of our salvation" and the prayers of saints as showing the immortality of our souls. Then, Sadolet builds the image of God's court before which the true and the false Christian will answer. The true Christian is the one who has always persisted in the way of the Church, even if he has found out that a certain number of priests were corrupt. The false Christian is motivated by cupidity and by the wish for the respect enjoyed by the priests among the people.

It is striking to note that the Cardinal's attack is based on two main arguments: 1) the Roman Catholic Church established the standards of Christian life, and that was because of the whole of its traditions go back to the Holy Spirit. 2) In order to achieve his salvation, the Christian must act on his own behalf inside this Church. Sadolet does not mention the divine aid from which man will benefit while carrying out good works. He is happy only to mention Christ as an example. It seems therefore that Sadolet has not abandoned the "semi-pelagic" theology of his Commentary on the Romans.

Calvin's Reply

This is much longer than that of his adversary and occupies pp. 49-160 of du Bois' edition. Therein Calvin quotes or paraphrases the greatest part of the Epistle, without however following the exact order of Sadolet's argument. He begins by refuting the accusations of greed and personal ambition by stating that, contrary to what Sadolet says, the aim of the Genevan reformers was "to multiply and grow the Kingdom of God". Then he contests his adversary's definition of the Church. For Calvin, the Church is the same as the propagation of the word of God; therefore it rests on Scripture above all. Human traditions play a completely secondary role in it. The Church as it is is not unchanging; on the contrary, it is a question of putting it back into "first place" (that is to say, apostolic). It is the Roman Catholics who are to blame for having seduced the people by their "vain philosophy", far away from the word of God.

As for works, they are of no value for justification, man being justified by the death of Christ. The reformed doctrine of the Eucharist affirms the universal presence of the Lord; it is the Catholic doctrine which tries to "bury" the Lord in descriptions. Private confession is only a human innovation and the theology of intercession of saints has blocked out the importance of the redemptive work of Christ from human memory. The Roman church no longer holds any authority after abuses committed by its priests, by its bishops and by the Pope himself. Calvin then takes up the accusation of personal ambition against which he defends himself against "God's court". In spite of the personal tone of this defence, in fact it only constitutes – moreover, like the rest of the treatise – a general apology of Luther's Reform, from which Calvin knew the Latin works well. He explains (echoing Luther in his *Commentary on Galatians* of 1538 and elsewhere) that he had been brought up in the faith of the Roman Catholic Church, where the understanding of "divine philosophy" had been recognised solely by the dignitaries of that Church. The people had only to submit passively to their decisions. He points out, however, that the Church had provided him with the essential teaching on

81

the one and only God and Redemption by the Son. What the Church could not give him, was hope of salvation. He continues that the priests said that God was only merciful towards those who made themselves worthy and that had to be done through works. Besides, they claimed that man, a sinner by his nature, constantly fell into sin. It was therefore necessary to confess and give satisfaction. However, the priests pointed out, according to Calvin, that God's look was so terrible, one had to apply in the first place to the saints. Thus, the reformer continues, the doctrine of the Church inspired in him such a fear of God that he began to despair of his salvation.

At that time, he became aware of another doctrine that moreover he found repugnant first of all. However, little by little he began to share the point of view of preachers who stated that the Church itself had fallen into error. While listening to them condemning papal infallibility and other abuses, Calvin would have realised his own errors which, with the fear of being perpetually damned, would have enabled him to apply in the first instance to God himself.

One must wonder whether Calvin, by debating against the universalist idea of the Church on which Sadolet insists, does not himself fall back into a certain separatism. This does not seem to be the case. He states clearly that the Church, even in its corrupted state, knew how to provide him with the essential teaching to enable him to have faith in God and in the event of Redemption. As for errors and abuses, it is a case of the visible Church which should not be abolished, but reconstituted on the apostolic model. Thus, Calvin does not call into question the validity of the sacraments which had been administered to him by the Roman Catholic Church. He restricts his criticisms to institutions and structures inside that Church, which he considers to be purely human!

Differing from Sadolet's *Epistle*, Calvin's Reply puts the accent mainly on the power of God: everything depends on him. The justification of the Christian is free. In order to obtain the salvation of one's soul, one does not have to act on one's own behalf, but to have every confidence in God while listening to his word.[60]

The present edition

The text of Sadolet's *Epistle* and the *Reply* that we reproduce here under a modernised form is that of the edition of Michel du Bois of 1540.[61] The text of the *Reply* as it was published by A.-M. Schmidt unfortunately contained too many errors and omissions to be able to be republished without any reference to the original.

Irena Backus

---

[60] V. also GANOCZY, 321-327, to analyse the pastoral vocation expressed by Calvin in the *Reply*.

[61] According to the copy in the Bibliotheque Nationale, Paris: shelf Res. z, 2206. There is also a reprint of this edition published in 1860.

Sadolet Text

Jacques Sadolet, Bishop of Carpentras, priest, Cardinal of the Holy Roman Church named after Saint Calixte: To his beloved brothers the managers, Council and citizens of Geneva.

Very dear brothers in Jesus-Christ, peace be unto you and with us: that is to say love and concord be with the Catholic Church our mother and yours, by God the Father and his only son Jesus-Christ our Our Lord with the Holy Spirit, who is one perfect unity in three, to whom praise and Lordship belong from centuries to centuries. Amen.

I truly think, very dear brothers, that none of you are without knowledge that as, for the moment, I am living in Carpentras, where I have retired from Nice, after having accompanied the sovereign bishop, who had come from Rome to pacify the princes. For I love this Church and city, which God has wished to be my country and spiritual consort, and brings to this my people a love and truly paternal charity, separating me from a wish to be with them. For if this honour of cardinalship (which was conferred on me and given in my absence and without my knowledge) obliges me to return to Rome (as is certainly necessary, so that in the vocation in which I am called, I serve God), however if it will not take away my affection and love for the people that I must have always printed in the deepest innards of my heart.

As therefore I am in Carpentras, hearing a great many reports of you, which were partly causing me sadness and partly were giving me hope not to dare that ourselves and you (who in the past have been with courage in God's true and straight religion and union of spirit, he seemed good for the Holy Spirit and to me (for Scripture speaks thus, and also all things done with zeal and full courage towards God come from the Holy Spirit [cf.Ac 15,28; Rm 9,1] – it seemed right, I said, to write something to you and to state to you in writing the care and concern that I have on your account.

And to tell the truth, my dear friends, it is not just from now that I have such goodwill and good affection towards you. But so it is at this time that, by God's will, I was elected Bishop of Carpentras (about twenty-three years ago) for the familiar contacts that you had with my people, in my absence should have heard of your activities; from that time, I began to hold in esteem and love the nobility of your town, the order and form of your republic, the excellence of the citizens and especially your exquisite and praiseworthy humanity towards all people and foreign nations. And thus as neighbourly presence and closeness of houses in a town give rise to love between men, so the surrounding countries act so that the people are swept along and encourage this. In view of the foregoing, it did not happen that you felt either the fruits of this my affection towards you (which is certainly yours), or to see some sign or appearance of it. As the opportunity has not yet been given. But now, it is not only offered to me, but necessity requires me to state to you in what affection and courage I hold you, if at least I wish to hold faith in God and practise Christian charity towards my neighbour.

For having heard that some cunning men, enemies of Christian union and peace, had placed and sown in your city the seeds and beginnings of discord and dissent (as they had already done in certain towns and villages which are subject to the virtuous and powerful nation of the Swiss), turning the faithful people of Christ from the path of its ancient fathers, turning them from the Catholic church and filling everything with discords and divisions (which certainly those who, while opposing the Church's authority, have always done, and seek unaccustomed honours and new powers for themselves) I call upon as my witness Almighty God, who now sees and knows my innermost thoughts, that I was greatly grieved and felt my affection touched with double pity and compassion. For on the one hand I heard the tears, sighs and groans of our mother the Holy Church, lamenting that in one blow it was deprived of such a great number of her beloved children. On the other hand, my dear friends, I was moved on account of the dangers and discomforts which could happen to you.

For I knew a fair number of people who were innovators of things which were set up well a long time ago, such troubles and dissensions, to not only bring the plague (which is however the most contagious illness) to souls, but also hugely pernicious to public and private affairs. What by experience of things you have obviously been able to know. What therefore? Certainly, the affection that I have to you and the fear of God oblige me to write to you as brother to brother from my heart, asking you affectionately not to deny your usual facility and humanity, which I ask you now to use towards me, by receiving my letters and reading them.

For I hope, if you are carefully and patiently reading what I am writing to you, while you do not esteem and approve my advice, at least you will know my heart to be straight and whole, above all wishing for your health and well-being, and will see that I do not look at all for what is my own, but your gain, goodness and usefulness. However I shall not begin by subtle, difficult and prickly disputations (which Saint Paul calls vain philosophy [Col 2,8], exhorting the faithful not to give a place easily to them)   by which these people have seduced you, bringing I know not which obscure interpretation of Scripture among ignorant people, covering their malice and deceit with a false assumption of the name of doctrine and wisdom. I would only suggest what is clear and obvious, without any hiding-place for error, palliation of fraud or deceit, as truth has always been. For it shines even in the midst of shadows [cf. 1 Jn 2,8], being seen by all and known both by the ignorant and by the wise. And singularly, in the Christian doctrine it does not lean and is not based on syllogisms or deceptive words, but in humility, piety and obedience of the Lord. For the word of God is alive and efficient and more penetrating than all double-edged swords and reaches up to the division of the soul and the spirit, also joints and marrow, and if it does not intertwine spirits by difficult arguments, but bringing a certain holy affection of heart, it clearly and manifestly represents to our spirits, so that in order to hear it, God by his vocation works hard in us [cf. Ph 2,13] more abundantly than our human reason.

Which God, father of all right intelligence, I humbly pray to wish to help me to say and make you so disposed to hear, that once we might both consent to the Lord with one heard and one thought. Now, so that my beginning may be taken from the most suitable place, I really think, my very dear brothers, that I, you and all others who have placed their faith and hope in Christ, have not done such things and do not do them in this mortal transitory life, so to try salvation for our souls and to seek eternal and permanent life, which can be obtained only in heaven and not on this earth and dwelling. To which our service is so equally divided and arranged that, after having sat in the foundation of faith, we work down here in order to have rest up there, that we sow on earth in order to reap the harvest in heaven [*cf.* Rm 6,22]. And how much the way of Christ and the reason for living according to his statutes and prescriptions seems very difficult to us, since it orders us to draw our hearts away from the sensuous mire of this world and to place them in God alone, to scorn the present wealth that we have in our hands in order to hope for wealth which is invisible to us; nevertheless, the salvation of ourselves and of our souls is so well recommended, that nothing is harsh or laborious, so that once we have the hope of life which is offered to us, the kindness and mercy of God always going in front of us in our affairs, we could through many tribulations and cares, at last obtain this eternal salvation and perpetual happiness.

In this hope, Christ, who has announced true goodness, was already received in great affection and assent of the universal world. For this he is served and worshipped by us and acknowledged as God and the Son of the true God. Because he alone in all time has brought to life Almighty God, to whom alone is life, the hearts of all men, asleep and half-buried in the obsolete and deceivable vanities of this world, which were universally given over to eternal death, reviving them from death, in other words from that which is the most damnable type of death. And he at first wishing to be our salvation, deliverance and instruction by suffering the death of the flesh, then after taking on an immortal life, by his example taught us and taught us to follow another path that we had not done and to die to this flesh and the world, in other words to sin, so that we could live in God [cf. Rm 6,10] putting all our hope of goodness in him and happily live forever. Which is the true resurrection of all of us, and suitable for the glory and majesty of Almighty God by which neither one nor two, but all humanity was recalled from a horrible and miserable spiritual death, in order to live a heavenly and abiding life. Paul the apostle, considering in his own mind and thinking about this resurrection, finding in that a great argument and approval of Christ's divinity, said: I am separated in order to preach the Gospel of God, which he had previously promised by his prophets in Holy Scripture about his Son who was created from the seed of David according to the flesh, and was declared the Son of God in spiritual power, which is the true virtue of God [Rm 1, 1-4], inasmuch as he does not perform his miracles physically but spiritually.

For controlling the winds, giving light to the blind by his word and reviving the dead was not at all done by physical power, but in spiritual and divine virtue. Christ is therefore declared the Son of God by this spiritual power belonging only to God. And what the Apostle places after the resurrection of the dead [Rm 1,4] is not understood at all by this revival by which the body of Lazarus [Jn 11,43] the widow's son [Lk 7,14] or the daughter of the prince of the synagogue [Mt 9,25] were restored to life (how much also these are works of God), but rather he speaks of this revival by which he delivered Mary Magdalene from seven devils [Lk 8,2] and called Matthew from the Revenue Office [Mt 9,9] and called several others from this earthly and obsolete life, and generally all humanity from sin, from the death of sin and the power of these earthly shadows to a hope of heavenly affinity and company. Of which also he set right and lifted up to heaven the minds of men who were plunged into this mire and earthly corruption. Which is the great gift of Jesus-Christ towards us and the main argument of his divinity.

And for this purpose, he was in himself ordained by God in the mission of his Son who took this responsibility upon himself, which in his time he achieved and gave it to us, helped and rescued in one

Christ of all counsel, divine and human comfort and virtue, could present our cured souls before God. The nobility of the soul is so eminent, its price is so excellent and its worth was such that, in order to save it and reach God and ourselves, all natural laws were reversed and the order of things was totally changed. God came down to earth in order to be made man and man went up to heaven in order to be made equal to God. We all therefore believe in Christ in order that (as I have already said) we should find health for our souls, that is to say, life in ourselves, which is the most desirable thing beyond which no more precious, familiar or more fitting good can come to man. For the more each man loves himself, the more his salvation must be dear to him. Which, if he is scorned and rejected by him, what other home can find which would be like that? What will man give in reward for his soul, said the Lord, or what will it profit a man to gain the whole world if it is harmful to his soul [Mt 16,26]. Therefore this rule which is so broad, so dear and precious, in which the salvation of our souls is contained, must be to us in such price and value that we should watch over it with all our strength, power and understanding. All other possessions that we want and desire in this world are external and foreign. But this one asset, to keep our souls, is not only ours, but we ourselves are part of this asset. From which if anyone withdraws from this by neglect, cannot recover the fruitfulness of another asset, given that he has alienated himself from the asset from which he should enjoy. Moreover, this asset of eternal life comes only by faith in God and in Jesus-Christ [cf Rm 5,1-2].

When I say: by faith alone, I do not understand, as do fabricators of new things, that in neglecting the charity and duty of a Christian, I have only a persuasion or trust in God by which I believe that all my sins will be forgiven in the death and blood of Jesus-Christ. Certainly that is really opens up our first entry towards the Lord, but it is not enough. For thus we must bring to God all our thoughts and furnished with the fear of Him, wishing to carry out His will, in which the virtue and power of the Holy Spirit lies and consists. Which thoughts, while they never come to work outwardly, if it is however within us, ready by themselves to do good, wishing promptly and willingly to obey God in all things, which is the true property of divine justice living in us. For otherwise, what meaning could give us, or what intelligence and knowledge could bring us this name of *justice,* if one did not have some regard for good works? For Scripture says that God has sent his Son so that he should have an agreeable people for him, followers of good works [Tt 2,14]. And in another passage: in order, says the Scripture, that we should be built in Christ for good works [cf. 2 Co 9.8].If therefore Christ was sent so that, doing good works, through him we should be agreeable to God and if we are built in him for good works, surely, the faith (that we have in our God through Jesus-Christ) does not only lay down confidence in him, but wishes that in doing good, with the intention of always doing good, we should have this faith in Christ. For this word *faith* is broadly and fully taken and usurped. Which does not only include a belief or persuasion, but also it includes hope, obedience and reverence in God, and mainly that which was so broadly declared in Jesus-Christ, the princess and highest of all Christian virtues, that is: love. In which the Holy Spirit is naively manifested, and to speak properly, is love himself. For, as the Scripture says: God is love [1 Jn 4,8]. When therefore we declare that only faith and God and Jesus-Christ can save us, in that same faith we mainly understand love which is the first and main cause of our salvation.

But in order that we may leave this dispute in order to return to our first subject: we have stated to you, my very dear brothers, or to say it better, we have made great efforts to show you (for our prayer is not equal to the size of the matter) how important and how necessary it is for us to care for our soul and its health, since by such concern we stop completely at our mind which is our true, our own and unique asset; and all other assets are distinguished and separated from us, from which same assets we could have no benefit if we are frustrated from this sole and sovereign asset. For which asset of the same to defend and keep to itself, so many glorious martyrs of God have formerly given up their life, so many doctor saints have worked day and night in vigils and sweating, in order to make us, command and prescribe the straight way in order to come to salvation, so many persecutions, injuries, calamities and serious oppressions have in old times been done by tyrants and marshals of pagans to the universal Church, which for this cause bore them patiently. All of which things were allowed by Almighty God and also received, suffered and fought by this virtuous people, true worshippers of Christ, in order that the Church, being forged as by several hammers by all sorts of experiments and trials, made worldly in great heat and also melted, soldered and put into shape by so many trials and torments of the saints, obtained enormous grace of his fidelity towards God and sovereign authority towards men.

This Church has regenerated to us God in Christ, he who fed, confirmed and taught us, teaching us how we must feel and believe, in whom our hope must lie and who is the true way to reach eternal life. We travel in this common faith of the Church and in observing its laws and commandments. If, by weakness or incontinence, we fall once into sin (at my own wish that

that does not happen so often), it is by this same faith of the Church that we are set right. And according to what she teaches, we use atonements, penances and satisfactions through which (and always presuming God's mercy) we are restored into our first innocence, and our sin is erased from us. In so doing, we hope to find grace and pity towards God. For we do nothing beyond the sentence and authority of the Church, which we consider to be prudence and know and hear sobriety. We do not carry a pride to condemn the Church's decrees, being puffed up in our minds. We do not at all show our understanding among the people, and we do not boast of a new knowledge and uncommon science; but (I speak of new and true Christians) travel in humility and obedience. And everything which was laid down to us and left by the authority of the holy fathers and wise men, we receive these with faith, as things that were dictated and truly ordained by the Holy Spirit.

For we know and recognise well how humility is of great price and respect towards God. Which is a virtue between all Christians and which Jesus-Christ, our Lord, has always shown in all his deeds, sayings, reprimands and commandments, saying that the kingdom of heaven is only offered to little ones, in other words to the humble [Mt 19,14]. For the greatness or smallness of our body is not very useful in this matter; but the main thing is to know if our mind is humble and low, or haughty and uplifted by pride. The same arrogance which threw the angels out of heaven prevents men on the path to heaven. And from there where the angel, a heavenly being, was chased out by arrogance, man, an earthly being, is lifted up, by his humility, so that thereby we may know that our whole being consists in humility, which is a perpetual help to our salvation and an assurance and foundation of that

93

happy hope, through which we aim for the sky. Which things being so, my very dear brothers, considering also that in the first place and on all things, our salvation, the true life and eternal happiness, must be very dear to us, and that finally towards ourselves (all other things postponed) we must have a singular respect and hold ourselves precious and in perfect recommendation; considering in the same way that, if we lose ourselves, there will be nothing of ours or belonging to us that we could find for our help; considering also that there is no more serious loss, nor dangerous evil, or more harmful calamity than the ruin and perdition of our soul, in which diligence, I ask you, in what therapy and care must we provide so that our salvation and life do not fall into such peril and danger?

Certainly, you will not deny me, therefore for me you will consider the loss of the soul to be the most miserable and pernicious thing that could happen to a man. You will grant me too, as I think, that our greatest work must be to beware that that does not happen to us. For we must be wonderfully afraid of the dangers of an evil, from which, if it happens to us, the end and fate surpass all other evils. And insofar as the evil is great and heavy, so much greater the fear must be. Thus those who were frightened and feared falling into the sea not only dare to go near those who have a horror of the dreadful judgment and condemnatory sentence of the Lord, withdraw first of all and go far away from the things that they know to be near and half-attached to this half-eternal misery. I do not say this in this place in order to make sure that we should be free from sin or that, during this life, we may be exempt and free from all dangers. For surely we are there, and we make mistakes, sin, commit offences, fall, all of them once, some more often rather than others, according to the virtue that God gave to each person to beware of.

However, all sins that one has committed and perpetrated deliberately or by fragility have their easy recourse to the mercy of God. But this so horrible and terrible sin of only serving God as he asks clearly and sincerely, or to feel falsely and mistakenly from him who alone is the real truth, this same sin, I say, not only places us in danger of eternal death, but it takes away all hope and almost any effort to avoid and run away from this great danger, misery and calamity. For in relation to these other sins, as in the middle of the waves and floods of our life, that anchor of the vessel is good and safe which keeps us from crashing into rocks and losing the ship in that, once throwing our thoughts over to God, being spurred by the compunction of our sins, in sighs and groans, in confessing them, we invoke, demand and need his mercy. Who, as he is full of all goodness and kindness, is moved beyond limit and inclined to pardon and, like a good-natured father, he peacefully receives the prayers of his children. But this miserable and dreadful sin of false and perverse religion deprives us both of God and of all hope of him. Why, very dear brothers, if we wish to be saved, we in all diligence carefully avoid and run away from this danger and withdraw from this risk. One could say here: there is such a great diversity of opinions today on true or false religion, the sentences are so variable, one exposes in this way, the other in another; it therefore seems to us to be enough if in good affection we believe that will be said to us, always submitting to the judgment of people who are wiser and more experienced in these things. I know enough, very dear brothers, that such words are spoken commonly by simple people who naturally have a heavy and dazed mind (however the sin is greater on those who take them away from the straight path) for such words do not fall on a crafty man who has experience of these things. I know enough, although because of the time, I confess that these things are uncertain both to the scholars and to the uneducated (which is not so, for the Catholic church has some rules for discerning the truth or a lie). But still, let us make the case that it is in doubt. However, so that our salvation may depend on this matter and that we have our souls, that is, very is, ourselves, in high esteem and that now it is not a question of wealth or bodily health, nor even of this mortal life (what constant and magnanimous servers of God have not feared to lose for their souls), but that this consultation and deliberation is made on ourselves, in order to live either in eternal blessing or in perpetual misery, we must diligently consider, look and assess (I speak as if the thing was uncertain, which however it is not) to place ourselves in such a place and withdraw where there will be less fear and danger, and where greater hope and certainty will be offered to us. There is no-one, I think, who in a doubtful matter, mainly where it is a question of our life and salvation, who does not rather follow advice based on good reason than a stupid and adventurous boldness.

Therefore let us look at what side and in what sect there is more danger either of being withdrawn from God, or to go near to more eternal perdition. Which thing I shall propose and follow, as if you were still thinking it over, and not decided, from which you must rather either run away from freewill, or believe in the advice. It is a question of knowing which is more necessary for your salvation or that you think it is more pleasing to God: if you believe and follow what the Catholic Church through the universal world already through more than one thousand five hundred years, or – if we look for the most certain and fresh memory of things – more than thirteen hundred years, has approved with one consent, agreement and freewill, or what some sly men, and as it seems to them, subtle people, have only in twenty-five years since then innovated, against all seniority and perpetual authority of the Catholic Church, those who certainly are not the Catholic church. For the Catholic church (to define it briefly) is that which, in all time, in every country on earth, is always one and accepting in Christ, being ruled and governed in everything and everywhere by the Spirit of Christ alone, in which there can be no disagreement, inasmuch as it is bound and united in a Spirit. For if such discord or division occurs, that body certainly remains whole, even if it makes some apostasy, by which the corrupt flesh is divided and separated from the Spirit invigorating the whole body, and is no longer the substance of the body of the Church.

The Eucharist

Here I will not come to scrutinize each dispute on things and I shall not annoy your ears in a surplus of words or arguments. I shall say nothing of the eucharist in which we adore the true body of Christ. Certainly those, not hearing at all who the arguments should applied and use reasons in one science only, think by some unsuitable insane reasons, princes of dialectic and vain philosophy [Col. 2,8], that they enclose the Lord of heaven and earth and imprison his spiritual power, which is free and infinite, in the corners of a human body which is surrounded with his aims and has certain proportions.

Confession of sins

I shall keep quiet on the confession of sins made to a priest, in which the main foundation of our salvation, that is humility, is shown by Scripture, ordained and ordered by the Church. From which humility these people by slander have been mocked and by their arrogance have tried to reject it and ruin it.

Prayer and the immortality of the soul

I shall say nothing about prayers, both of saints towards God for ourselves and our own prayers for the dead. But what do they mean, because they laugh at them and scorn them, saying they are useless and worth nothing? Similarly in that they take away all ecclesiastical rules and their subjection, giving themselves a freedom and licence for all greed. For if the soul is mortal, let us drink and eat, says the Apostle, for we shall die tomorrow [Co 15, 32]. What if it is immortal (as certainly it is), where does this sudden dissent and division of the body by death come from, that the souls of the living and the dead have nothing in common as a whole, do not communicate with us at all and that they may have lost all affinity and common society with us? In view of the fact that charity (which is the main gift of the Holy Spirit between Christians) always benign, profitable, never being idle [cf. 1 Co 13, 4-6] always remains in full efficient force in the one and in the other life.

God's court

But in order that I may leave such difficulties, reserving them to another time, let us consider and return to our first plan to know and understand what is most necessary and useful to do, and more suitable to obtain the grace of God the sovereign, or to feel with the universal Church and to obey in faith, comply with his laws, decrees and sacraments, or to agree with contentious people, always seeking divisions and new things. The point is here, my very dear brothers, and here is the forked way which leads in two contrary directions, from which one pulls to life and the other to eternal death.   In this difference however and choice, everyone has to deal with the salvation of his soul and the deposit for future life, that is to say if we shall be destined to eternal happiness or to infinite misery? What therefore shall we say?

Let us take the case that for each person, that is to say the path of each person, he may be a constituent and assign before the judicial seat of the sovereign Judge so that he may know and scrutinize their cause, in order to absolve them or finally condemn them. They will be interrogated on whether they were Christians. Each of them will reply yes. *Item*: if they have faithfully believed in Christ. They will reply: yes. Now they will be examined on what they believed. For knowledge of the faith will be examined first before that of the works and habits of the man. When therefore they will be asked precisely the reason for their faith, the one who has been fed and taught in the bosom of the Church and according to its discipline will answer in this way:

Reply of the Christian who has always followed the doctrine of the Church

As I was taught by my parents, who also had received from their fathers and ancestors this same doctrine of obeying our holy mother Church in everything and reverently to observe its laws, statutes, prescriptions and decrees as coming from thee, Oh Lord God, and as I can see nearly all of those who were known as Christians and who in our time and in front of us, had marched us all under thy banner, to be and to have formerly been of this same opinion of acknowledging and honouring the Church as the mother of their faith and to consider it a sacrilege to leave and withdraw from its commandments and institutions, in this same faith that the Catholic Church keeps and teachers, I have tried to please them, Oh Lord God. And how some strange men have risen up, stirring up new things in scorn of the old ones, blaming the church and wanting us to withdraw completely from the obedience which we give to him, however I have preferred to persist constantly in that which already for a long time has been observed and almost hand in hand decreed by the consent of the old Church and the saints in person. And however much the customs and conditions of several prelates and ecclesiastical persons were such that they could cause me wrath and disappointment in my heart, however I have not been swayed from my opinion.

For I have resolved (as you my God has ordered it in the Gospel) to obey their holy commandments, leaving you Judge of all their life and actions. Waiting the same as I, horrible and stained with such great and enormous sins (which are manifest and obvious to you as on my face) I could not worthily and reasonably judge others. For which my sins I now stand on the floor before your judgment seat, asking and imploring not your severity, Oh kind God, but rather your leniency and pity.

The Reply of "the other"

Reply of "the other" deduced his case in such a way, the other will be called. He will compare. He, having obtained permission to speak, will begin thus – and let us set the scene that he should be one of the promoter of these divisions, for he will know better how to defend his case, he who publicly exhorted the people to leave the communion of the Church – therefore he will say thus: when I shall consider, oh sovereign God, the customs and actions of ecclesiastical people to be almost everywhere corrupt and that, notwithstanding this, the priests in favour of the religion were held in great esteem among the people, having their wealth in regret, I have been rightly (as I think) been moved in wrath upon meeting them, standing as their adversary and enemy. When I also considered in myself that I had spent so long as a student of both theology and in human science, having not however such a position in the Church that my labours could have deserved, also seeing a great many others, lesser than I, to be raised up in honours and in profit, I began, I confess to follow those whom I considered displeasing even to you. And in spite of being unable to take away their power, that first of all I shatter the laws ordained by the Church, I have let most of the people to scorn the decrees which were observed for a long time as impregnable. Which, if they were drawn up in general councils, I would have considered them as ignorant and without any knowledge of good intelligence. If by change they were bishops of Rome, I have constantly maintained that they had wickedly occupied this tyranny and falsely usurped the title of vicar of Christ. Finally, I have attempted in any event for this unbearable yoke [cf. Ac 15,10] of the church, forbidding meat, observing days, making us confess our sins to priests and keep our vows, oppressing and expecting servitude from men who are free and honest, Oh Jesus-Christ, to be rejected by us who serve you, having confidence that faith alone would justify us and not the works which are so highly recommended and preached in the Church. Given also that you had suffered for us and by your precious blood had erased everyone's sins and iniquities, so that, placing our faith and assurance in

101

thee alone, more completely we could do what seemed good to us. I have also studied the Scriptures more subtly than those old people, especially when I was looking for some passage which could be used against them. By which opinion and noise of doctrine and spirit, having achieved fame and great esteem among some people, I have been able to subvert and annihilate the Church's authority. But I have indeed been the author and cause of several rebellions in it.

After he has spoken and stated the truth (for there is no question at all of lying before this heavenly Judge, while he keeps quiet on a great many things about his ambition, his avarice, his desire for popular fame, his deceits and internal mischiefs that he himself knows to have inside him, and which will seem to him to be written on his face) what will be the end of it, oh my brothers in Geneva, whom I wish to be united with me in Christ and in his Church? And what judgment do you think will be made, not only of those, but also of all their followers? Definitely one who has followed the Catholic Church in that will bring nothing of his misdeeds into the open. First of all, in order for the Church having the Holy Spirit for its leader and governor of all its decrees, never makes a mistake and cannot make a mistake. Moreover, if it lost its way or the Church was wrong (which one cannot believe or think), even the mistake would not be charged to someone who with all his whole and humble heart would have followed the faith of his predecessors and his fathers' authority for the honour of God. On the other hand, the other one basing himself on his brain, scorning both the holy fathers and the general assemblies of bishops, attributing no faith to them, thus, attributing everything to himself, being readier to slander and malign than to learn or teach, when therefore he leaves the communication of the Church, what can he hope for the end? What defence can be use? What lawyers can he have before God, unless he must greatly fear to have been thrown out through the outer shadows, where there will be tears and gnashing of teeth [Mt 8,12], in other words where he must cry for his wretchedness forever, gnashing his teeth even against himself for being able, if he had wished, to have avoided this serious and miserable disaster, nevertheless he was not aware of it.

Now everyone can think in himself as if their whole life will be accompanied by unhappy despair and wretched anger, particularly as their unhappiness, wretchedness and disaster has no end. There is no end of it: rage, tears and groans continue in it. But again, if all their other wickedness could in some way be suffered and borne, however, how could they be excused considering that, as it seems to me, at that point they have no refuge to the goodness and pity of God, insofar as they have tried to dismember this one and only bride of Christ [cf Ep 5,25] and have not dared at all to divide, but to tear this garment of the Lord that the unfaithful soldiers themselves did not dare to tear up [cf. Jn 19, 23-24]?

For, from their beginning, how many sects have there been in the Church who did not agree either with those, or among themselves? Which is an obvious argument, according to any doctrine, to convict something of being a lie. For the truth is always one thing and a lie is variable and divided. The right thing is simple, but the tortoise breaks up into several parts. But is it the man knowing Christ and confessing him, in the mind and courage with which the Holy Spirit has sometimes enlightened him, who does not very well know this division and tearing asunder of the holy Church to be the sole work of God, but of Satan? What does the Lord say to us? What does Christ order us to do?

103

Certainly that we should all be one in him [cf.Jn 17,21]. For what purpose would this excellent and rare gift of charity be given to us from heaven, which is divinely inspired and sent to Christians only and not to other men? Is it not so that we should all with one heart and one mouth confess the Lord? Do these people think that the Christian religion is something other than a peace with God and charity towards his fellow-man? Let us look at the same thing that the Lord said, praying for his disciples: Holy Father, keep those by your Name which you have given me, so that they may be like us. Now I am not praying only for them, but also for those who shall believe in me by their word, that also they may be one in us, so that the word may believe that you has sent me. I have given them the glory, which you have given me so that they may be one, as we are one [Jn 17, 11. 20-22].

You see, very dear brothers, and by the evangelical light you can judge what it is to be truly Christian, since our faith in God and the glory of almighty God (which is from him towards us, and from us towards him) consists in this single union; since Christ does not require or ask for anything else from us to his Father, and that he thinks that by this means his work, his perfections, afflictions and works, the fragility of the human body that he took on for us, his cross and his death will bear fruit for him in this, as much to the glory of the Father (which he would wish absolutely) as for our salvation, for which he had to suffer death, if certainly between ourselves and we are one in him [cf. Jn 17,21]. And also the catholic Church works and always tries to create peace and union of spirit between us, and that the same men who are separated by the distance of regions or time intervals, even if they cannot all gather in one body [cf. Rm 12,5], the same Spirit however, which is similar everywhere, holds

104

them together and governs them. To that catholic Church and to the Holy Spirit the latter show that they have a great deal of contrary righteousness, which tries to break up the union, leads to diversity of spirit, undoes harmony and takes away any agreement in the Christian religion and with such greed, with such fervour, by so many machinations and inventions, so that there is no prayer that can properly express their concern and anxiety. Certainly against whom I do not pray at all that the Lord should destroy all their frauds and all high talk [Ps 11,4], nor also that he should add iniquity to their iniquity [cf Es 30,1]; but I shall humbly beseech my Lord, my God (as I always have), that he should wish for them to convert and come down in good spirit.

And you also, my brothers in Geneva, I would ask and urge you, after you have shaken off the fogs of error of your understanding and to have come into the light, raising your eyes to the heavens that God offered to you for land and perpetual heritage, if you live in the union of the Church – I urge you, I say, to return in harmony with us and give the loyal service to our holy mother Church, and that you should wish to worship God with us in one Spirit. And however may your courage not be changed at all, nor pulled into a diverse contrary opinion, if by chance our customs displease you or if, through the fault of some people, the splendour of the Church (which should be perpetual and uncontaminated) was sometimes knocked down and obscured. You may well, perhaps, hate our persons (if that is allowed in the Gospel), but you must not hate the doctrine and the faith. For it is written: everything that they shall say to you, do them [Mt 23,3]. And we do not say anything else, except that we show you the great wish that we have for your salvation. For if, dear friends in Geneva, you take it in good part and if you heed the words from me, who wishes you health, gain and usefulness, certainly you will not be sorry for having recovered the favour and grace that you had in God in former times, and praise to men. For myself, as much for my duty, as for the great friendship that I hold you in, I shall continually pray God for you, certainly being unworthy on account of my sins, but by chance charity will make me worthy and acceptable. Moreover, all my power, help, favour and the little piece of understanding that is within me, counsel, authority and diligence, is so much yours and for your commandment that I shall consider a great blessing to me, if you could receive some benefit and convenience from my trouble and work, as much in things of God as in things of the world. The end will be to ask you to deal with and receive this messenger, whom I have sent you with these letters, in such courtesy and kindness, so that your humanity and common righteousness, particularly, Christian modesty, demands, a thing which will be honourable to you and extremely pleasant to me. Dear brothers, may God speak to you and keep you by his goodness.

From Carpentras 18 March.
M.D. XXXIX.

Calvin Text

JEAN   CALVIN   TO   JACQUES   SADOLET
CARDINAL, GREETINGS

As it may be that by your excellent doctrine and
wonderful grace in speaking about it, you may have
(and rightly) deserved that between learned people of
our time you may be held in great admiration and
esteem, mainly from the true followers of fine writing, I
am wonderfully displeased that it should be necessary
for my expostulation and complaint (that you can now
hear) to be publicly obliged to touch and in no way
wound your good reputation and opinion.   Which
action I would truly never have undertaken, and would
not have been obliged and drawn into this battle by a
great need. For I am not unaware of what great malice
it would be to provoke that one unfairly by ambition or
simple envy, that one I say, who in his time has carried
out so well his duty towards fine writing and
disciplines.   And how much more odious it would be
between learned people if they heard that for one single
annoyance or trouble, without another fair reason, I
would have taken up my pen against the one who,
among them (and not by mistake) for his grace and
virtues is considered worthy of love, praise and esteem.
However, after I have said and set out the cause and
reason for my enterprise, I hope that I shall not only be
absolved and exempt from any crime, but also there
will be no-one, as I think, who judges the cause
undertaken by you to be unable to be abandoned by me
without the greatest shame and scorn of my ministry.

For a short time in this, you again wrote letters to
the Council and people of Geneva through which you
tried to test their hearts, to find out if they wished to

reduce themselves under the power and tyranny of the pope, from which they were once delivered and freed. And because it was not expedient to use harshness against them, for the favour that you needed in order to win your case, for them you used the office of a good orator. For from the beginning you tried by sweet words to flatter and deceive them, pretending to draw them into your opinion, rejecting all the malice and bitterness against them by means of which they were taken away from that tyranny. You come in there impetuously, and like a horse with a free rein, poured out against those who, according to you, under the shadow and pretext of the Gospel, by quibbling and deceit, have placed this poor city in such confusion of the Church (which you complain about) and in such trouble with the religion; as regards me, Sadolet, I want you to know that I am one of those against whom you speak in such great anger and fury. And how much the true religion was truly set up and established and the form of their Church corrected before it was called, nevertheless, for which I have not only approved by my voice and opinion, but also I have forced myself as far as I could, to preserve and confirm the things that were formerly instituted by Farel and Viret, I cannot be simply shut out or separated from them in this cause. If you in particular had accused me, doubtless I would easily have put everything straight for you, owing to your knowledge and for the honour of the written word. But I see with my ministry, which I know to be founded and strengthened by the Lord's calling, wounded and upset by the scourge that you are inflicting upon me, to me that will be disloyalty and not patience if, by keeping quiet, I hide in this place.

First of all and in my first duty, I have in this Church held the position of reader and then, afterwards, that of minister and pastor. In as much as I have undertaken the second charge, I keep as my right that I have done it legitimately and as a true vocation. Now in whatever documents and religion I have administered, there is no need to express it in long words. I shall not attribute to myself any subtle intelligence, erudition, caution, or dexterity, or even diligence. But however I know surely before Christ, my judge, and all his angels that I have travelled in that Church in such purity and sincerity that it belonged in the work of the Lord, in which also all faithful people give me good and plentiful witness of it. Therefore after my ministry shall be recognised as being from God – as surely, it is understood that the deduction of this matter will appear clearly - who will be the one, while I keep quiet, I suffer from being proscribed and slandered, does not judge my silence to be false and does not accuse me of prevarication? Therefore there is one who does not know that by great need I am not only cramped, but also I cannot escape, if I do not like a traitor leave the action that the Lord has put into my hands, that I do not confront and contradict your reproaches and accusations.

And however for the moment I may be discharged from administering the Church in Geneva, nevertheless that cannot and must not make me withdraw from bringing him paternal love and charity. On that account, I say, on which God ordaining me once, has forced me to be always faithful and loyal to him. Now therefore, seeing the traps being set against that, which the Lord wants me to care for and be concerned for, knowing also the great and eminent dangers, which, if by good means and diligence one does not provide for, it could fall swiftly, who would be the one who would wish to advise me to, in safety and patience, wait for the end and outcome of such dangers? How stupid would it be, I ask you, staying stupid and surprised, not to take into account the ruin of the one for whose protection one must be on watch day and night? Now I see that it would be superfluous for me, to use a long prayer in such a place when you yourself are delivering me from this problem. For if this neighbourhood that you describe (which however is not too close) was so strong against you, that, wishing to show the friendship that you bring to those in Geneva, you have not been afraid to set upon by such a great atrocity and fury and I and my good reputation, am allowed by a human right, wish to provide and understand the public good of the city, which I know is recommended, for a much greater reason than proximity: to prevent your enterprises and efforts, which doubtless have a tendency to its total ruin and destruction. And moreover, even though I may have no respect for the Church of Geneva (from which surely I cannot distract my mind, nor love less and hold more dear than my own soul), but even, given that I may not bring any affection to it, where I see my ministry being falsely proscribed and slandered – which, as I have known to be from Christ, also if it is required, I have to defend by my own blood – how is it possible that a hypocrite can endure such things? Because not only kindly readers may easily judge, but you also, Sadolet, can consider and think within yourself that for several fair reasons I am forced to go into this battle, if however the simple and moderate defence of my innocence must be called a battle! However much I cannot hold my right without understanding and joining with my fellow ministers with whom the reason for my administration has been so united, that I will gladly take on myself everything that one would wish to say in relation to them. However I shall apply myself totally to showing the same affection by putting myself to some trouble and dealing with this cause in relation to you, that I have taken on. For I shall make sure that everyone will hear that I surpass you in many ways in a good and just cause, in straight conscience, in purity of heart, frankness of words, and in good faith, but also that I am a little more constant in keeping a certain modesty, mildness and leniency. By chance, there may also be things that will dawn on you, and may also break your heart. However I shall take care that no bitter or bad word will come from me, except due to the iniquity of your accusation, by which I am first of all attacked, or the need of the cause to which I am constrained. Moreover I shall try to ensure that such bitterness and asperity will not come to an unbearable intemperance, so that kind minds, seeing such trouble, should not be offended in any way.

Now is it sure that in the first place, if you were involved with some person other than myself, he would not also begin his defence in the argument, all of which I have planned to omit and neglect. For he would have no problem in so dissecting his intent to write, that one would obviously know that you, as a writer, would have rather sought some other end than that which you conclude and claim. And for sure, if in the first place you do not have faith in your integrity, you make yourself wonderfully suspect, considering that you, who is a foreigner who has not up to now had any knowledge or familiarity with the people of Geneva, and now all of a sudden you are telling yourself that you have a singular love and benevolence towards them, from which nevertheless no fruit or evidence has ever come out. And you, such a man, that has served your apprenticeship almost from childhood in Roman institutions, which are learnt now in the court of Rome, in that shop of all delicacies and tricks, and even you who have been fed as if in the arms of Pope Clement and made cardinal in support, surely you have a great many stains which make you suspect, and almost to everyone, in this place. As for those subtle means and insinuations, by which you thought you could warm and surprise the simplest minds, they could easily be refuted by a man who is not at all stupid. However, the matter, which by chance could credible among some people, because it does not belong and does not fall readily to a man who is decorated with good writing and liberal sciences, I do not wish to attribute to you.

Therefore I shall proceed with you as if with great zeal, as is fitting for a man filled with such doctrine, prudence and gravity, you should have written again to the people of Geneva, leading them to listen in good faith to the things that seemed to you to be suitable for their health and prosperity. But however, inasmuch as I do not wish to annoy you in this place, whatever your intention may have been, nevertheless, insofar as you break up and make an effort to defile and slander to the end by outrages and hurts the things which were taught to them about the Lord by our own hands, I am constrained, whether you like it or not, to openly contradict you. For surely the structure of the pastors in the church is not only to lead the docile souls of the faithfully straight to Christ, but also to be armed to repel the machinations of those who struggle to prevent the work of the Lord. Now however much your Epistle may be full of ambiguous comments and circumlocutions of words, however the core and the main point tends to be that you are passing them on in the power of the Pope. What you call: turn around in the faith and obedience of the Church. But because in an unfavourable matter, one needs to weaken the bravery of the listeners by a long preface and prayer, you invoke the incomparable blessing of eternal life. Then approaching the matter more closely, you show that there is no more dangerous disease for the soul

112

than false religion. And in addition, that the true rule for serving God is that which is set up in your Church. By this conclusion to be made by them, and that all those who have broken the unity with that Church are completely lost, if they do not come to repentance and amendment. And later you claim that it is a manifest abandonment of the Church to those who have removed themselves and separated from your company. Moreover, in that they have received the Gospel from us, you state that it is only a pile and mixture of wicked institutions and false doctrines. From which finally you recall what judgment of God awaits them, if they did not comply with your warnings.

Now however much it would be of great service to your cause that all credibility should be taken away from our words, your real intention was to create suspicion of the diligence which they have found in us, for their salvation. And thus you come to accuse us mistakenly (even while you know very well that the opposite is true), if only to fulfil our ambition and greed. Considering therefore that by such causes and malicious interpretations, you wanted to smudge us with this wretched stain, bothering the minds of the readers to cause hatred towards us so that they may not have faith in our words, I shall come first of all to other points, briefly, and I shall reply to this objection. It is true that I do not willingly speak about myself. Nevertheless considering that I cannot keep completely quiet, as modestly as possible I shall speak about it.

Therefore, as for me, if I had been interested in making a profit, I would never have separated from your faction. And if I will not glorify myself at all in that I had the means to receive honours therein, that I have never wanted, nor was my heart ever able to live for (how I have seen several of my fellow creatures arrive in some dignity, which I could partly achieve and partly exceed!) It shall be sufficient to say only that for me it was permitted to obtain what I wanted on everything, in other words, to stop studying with some honest and free condition. Why, I shall never fear, that any man might reproach me, unless he was completely shameless, for claiming or asking for something outside the Pope's reign, which was not completely cast off from him. If he had been obliged to live from his industry and knowledge, the profit that he had already had from writing would not have left him in need of this, in spite of the fact that he came from such a grand house that he did not need anyone else. From both of us, because you marked me as if with your finger, I have wanted you to reply specifically. But because, it seems to me, you slander and, without any pretence, you bite all those who today uphold one cause with us, I would like you to understand that you do not know anyone for whom I do not reply better than for Farel and myself. There no people among us, whom you know by hearsay, from those for whom I call to your conscience. Do you think that hunger forced them to go away with you and that through despair for wealth they became separated and reduced to this change and new conversion as though they were bankrupt, or as they were in general abolition of old debts? But in order to avoid verbosity, without reciting a long catalogue of it, I would dare you to properly make sure that of all those who were leaders and chiefs in this matter, there is no-one who was so well and honourably received among your people, who did not need for that any new way of life. Now that there is judgment and renown between you and me, what honours and what powers have we obtained? Surely all those who have heard us will be witnesses that we have not wanted or tried to have any other riches or dignities than those which have fallen to us.

Considering therefore that in all our sayings and actions, not only have they not been suspected of any ambition of which you accuse us, but also they have seen, by obvious signs, as we had in horror and hatred, do you think that by a simple word, you enchant their understandings in such a way that they would rather believe in a vain sin of yours than so many sure teachings that they have received from us? And in order that we should work in deeds rather than in words, the power of the sword and other civil affiliations, which a pile of masked priests and bishops, under the pretext of immunity and franchise, had fraudulently taken away from magistrates, have we done nothing for them to be returned into their hands? Have we not detested and have we not been forced to abolish all the means of condemnation and ambition that they had usurped for themselves? If we had hope of amending these, that we may not hide this cleverly, so that such things should be returned to us with the administration and government of the Church? But why have we undertaken by such efforts to overturn this kingdom and power or, in other words, this extortion that they carried out on souls against the word of God? How did we not think that we were lost to such an extent for ourselves? As for matters relating to ecclesiastical wealth, most of that is still devoured by these chasms. If therefore we hoped that this would be taken away from them once – as surely it will be finally necessary – why did we not look for a means to make this come to us? But, considering that publicly we have pronounced and stated at the top of our voice that the supervisor or bishop was a thief, who converted the wealth of the Church for his own use more than is necessary to live soberly and reasonably, considering also that we have witnessed the Church to have been poisoned at that time with a pernicious poison, when

115

the pastors were burdened with wealth by which in the end they were blinded, given that we taught that it was not expedient that they should have so much wealth and that, finally, we have advised that funds should be given to ministers that were reasonable according to their condition, not to abound in surpluses and that the rest should be dispersed to the poor, as was done in the primitive Church, when also we have shown that serious and authoritative people should be elected who would bear the responsibility and administration, on condition that every year they were accountable to the Church and the magistrate, was that to purchase and continue to gather wealth or rather to reject this from us voluntarily?

Surely all these things show adequately not what we are, but we have wanted to be. If therefore everything that I have said above is so apparent and obvious to each one that nobody would deny the smallest point, from what audacity now could you reproach us for having coveted unaccustomed wealth and power, in the same way towards those who are not ignorant of these things? As for the large enormous lies that people of your kind sow every day in their own country, we are not at all impressed. For there is nobody who either notices them or even dares to contradict them. But, from swishing to persuade the opposite to those who have seen and heard the things that I have recited above, it is not at all the act of a wise man and is a thing which is a very ill-advised for Sadolet, a man of such esteem and doctrine, prudence and solemnity. And if it seems to you to be our complaint to have to be measured by the effect of the matter, it will be found that we have had no other consideration, other than by our small size and humility, to multiple and increase the kingdom of God. This is so necessary that, by a wish to dominate, we may have wanted to abuse your holy and sacred name. I am passing on and keep quiet about a great many other insults and disgraces that you pour out against us, as it is said, at the top of your voice. You call us cunning men, enemies of union and Christian peace, innovators of things that are well established in bygone days, seditious, plague-infested in our consciences, and even, both in public and in private, enemies to the common society of men. If you wanted to avoid reprehension, either you should not attribute haughtiness and deep language to us in order to make us odious to everyone, or you should completely give up this magniloquence. However I do not wish to stop at all your themes, but I would be very pleased if you could think in yourself how cunning – I am not saying nasty – it is to hunt by several long insults (which notwithstanding can be refuted in a single word) those who have not earned or deserved this from you. How is it that you say a few things, thus insulting men, at the cost of the indignity of such a great insult poured out by you on Jesus Christ and on his word, when you come to enter further in the matter.

In relation to the people of Geneva, taught by our preaching, who have withdrawn from the mire of error in which they had been submerged, almost drowned, and have been reduced to the pure doctrine of the Gospel, you call that: abandoning the truth of God. Because also they have withdrawn from subjection and papal tyranny so that between them, they could set up a better form of Church, you say that it is a real separation from the Church. Now therefore, let us go through all these matters in good order. As for your preface which contains almost a third part of your Epistle to preach the excellence of the blessing of eternal life, there is already no need for my reply to it should be made into a long file. For, while the recommendation of the future eternal life is something

117

worthy of being ceaselessly in our ears day and night, I do not know however you have described it in such long comments, unless it is to place you in the greatest esteem and recommendation, under the pretext and sign of religion. Or even, thinking of taking away any bad suspicion of you, you wished to make it appear that all your thought was of the blessed life which is towards God, or you thought that the minds of those to whom you were writing, by this long commendation, would be rather attracted and moved (I do not at all wish to guess what you intended). However that does not feel much like a true theologian to wish so much to bind man to himself than to order and teach him that the beginning of making his life a good one is to desire, increase and illustrate the glory of the Lord, considering that we are mainly born to God, and not to us. For while all things come from him and consist in him, also, as the Apostle says [Rm11.36], they must bring everything back to him. And thus he says that the Lord himself, in order to make the glory of his name more commendable to men, he has so much tempered and moderated the wish to exalt and amplify him, that he is constantly linked with our salvation. But considering that he has taught that such affection must overcome every care and desire for wealth and gain that he could bring to us, and that even natural right encourages us to respect him above all, if at least we wish to give him the honour which is due to him, certainly the duty of a Christian man is to go higher up than to look for and obtain only the salvation of his soul. Because there is nobody who is well taught and experienced in the true Christian religion, for whom this long and curious exhortation to study heavenly life (which only holds man therein, without lifting him with a single word to the sanctification of God's name) would not be considered to have no taste or flavour.

118

After this sanctification, I will gladly grant to you that in our whole life we must not strive for any other aim, nor have any other deliberation other than to reach this supreme vocation. For that is the main aim that is offered to us by God in all our deeds, sayings and thoughts. Truly, there is nothing which makes man superior to the animal in any case, but the spiritual communication with God in the hope of this eternal blessing. Even in all our sermons we almost tend to do nothing but to raise up and move the hearts of each person to meditating and studying this. Yet I willingly granted to you all the danger which could come to our salvation, in acting otherwise in the service of God in a corrupt and unseemly manner. And surely these are the first instructions and teachings which we habitually use to teach in true piety and religion, those that we wish to gain as disciples to Jesus Christ. That is to say, that they are careful not to stupidly discover and at their pleasure, some new way of honouring God, but know that only this service which from the beginning was pleasing to him, is legitimate. And moreover if we affirm what is approved by the holy oracle of God [1 S 15,22], that obedience is better than sacrifice. Finally we lead them and make them used, with all our power, to abandoning all services and manners of false and contrived superstitions, being happy with a single rule and commandment of God, to those stated by his holy word.

Why, Sadolet, is all the foundation of my defence by you put down and almost thrown out when willingly you have confessed and approved these things. For you grant that this is a horrible calamity for the soul, when by wicked opinions the truth of God is converted into lies, it remains to be discovered which of the two parties observes and keeps this honour and reverence to God, alone, true and legitimate. For your part, you say that this is the surest rule which is prescribed and ordered by the Church, however much you put this sentence into deliberation, as if we wanted to impugn it, as one does in dubious matters. But surely, Sadolet, seeing that you work in vain, I am forced to lift you up and relieve the great disagreement. For falsely and very mistakenly you persuade yourself that we others wish to withdraw the faithful people from true adoration, observed from all time by the catholic Church. Or you are mistaken in this word Church, or with a certain movement and in a trap, you want to deceive us; in which last thing I shall catch you in passing. It is also possible that you are wrong elsewhere. For first of all, in the definition of the Church, you are leaving what could be very useful to you in the true understanding of the word. When you say that you are the one who, in all past time as today, in the whole world, has always been one in Christ, consenting in one Spirit in Christ, from which in everything and everywhere it is ruled and governed, where is the word of God here, that clear mark, which was so often recommended by the Lord even in the description of the true Church? For, foreseeing how dangerous it would be to extol the Spirit without the word, he established that the Church was governed and administered by the Holy Spirit. But in order that such administration would be sure, stable and fixed, he united and allied it to his word. That is what the Lord proclaims, that God's people are those who hear the word of God [Jn 8,47], that they are his flock, who know his voice as they know their shepherd, rejecting any other voice as that of a stranger [Jn 10,27.5]. For this reason the Spirit speaks through the mouth of Saint Paul, that the Church is founded on the foundation of the apostles and prophets [Ep 2.20]. And this is even more clearly stated through the mouth of Saint Peter when he teaches us, the people will be born again to God by that incorruptible seed [1 P 1,23]. And, in brief, why is the preaching of the Gospel called the kingdom of God, unless because it is the sword with which the heavenly King rules and governs his people? What you will find not only in the writings of the apostles, but all and as many times that the prophets have foretold the restitution and establishment or even the propagation of the Church through the universal world, they have always assigned and given first place to the word.

For, they say, living water will pour out of Jerusalem which, divided into four rivers, shall water the whole earth [Za 14,8]. And some of them are those waters, which show and declare it, saying that the law shall come out of Sion, and the word of the Lord from Jerusalem [Es 2,3]. Therefore Chrysostom has truly advised that all those who, under the colour of the Spirit, want to take us away from the simple evangelical doctrine , should be rejected, considering that the Spirit is promised not in order to give rise to some new doctrine, but in order to write the truth of the Gospel in the hearts of men. And surely today we know through experience how badly needed this warning is. We are opposed by two sects which seem to be very different. For what do the Pope and the Anabaptists have in common? And however – so that you should know Satan never to be so secret, as he does not appear from some side – both of them use the same means, with which they try to oppress us. For, when they are boasting so arrogantly about the Spirit, they certainly do not deal with other things (the word of God oppressed and buried) except to make room for their lies. And you, Sadolet, stumbling at the first stop on the threshold of the door, have been punished for the insult that you have made to the Holy Spirit, separating

121

him and dividing the word. For, as if those who are seeking God's way were settled on a forked road or destitute of a certain aim, you are obliged to tell the doubtful ones to know, which is the most suitable: to follow the authority of the Church, or to listen to those whom you call inventors of new doctrines? If you had known (or that you had not at all wanted to pretend) that the Spirit lights the Church in order to open the intelligence of the word and that the word is like the touch when gold is tested in order to discern all the doctrines, would you have withdrawn from this very perplex and vexed difficulty?

You should therefore learn by your own fault that it is no less unbearable to boast of the Spirit without the word, than it is bleak to place the word in front without the Spirit. Now therefore, if you wish to endure and receive a truer definition of the Church than your own, tell me henceforth that it is the company of all the saints which, spread out all over the world, is dispersed in any time; however it being united together by a single doctrine of Christ and by his only Spirit, keeps and observes the union of the faith, a harmony and brotherly charity together. Now that we may have some argument with that, we deny it. But rather, so that we worship it as a mother, so we always wish to stay within her arms. But in this place you correct me, saying and striving to show that everything which was received and approved by the consent of the faithful for fifteen hundred years and more, is snatched away and repealed by our disorder. Here I shall find no need for you to walk with us in good and true faith – which however, not only a Christian, but a philosopher would gladly do – but I shall ask you not to come to this nasty licence to slander, which would greatly offend (while we keep quiet) your reputation and esteem among good and serious persons.

The old Church

You know very well, Sadolet – and if you deny it, I shall tell everyone from whom you have hidden it craftily and maliciously – that non only shall we agree better with antiquity that you others, but also that we shall ask for something else, unless that old face of the Church can be sometimes established and restored completely which, warped and polluted by unlearned people, later in a cowardly manner was torn apart and almost destroyed by the Pope and his faction. Now I do not wish to restrain you so much, nor to almost pester you, that I may wish to revoke that, reform and put it back into the state of the Church that was first of all established by the apostles, which we must comply with, if we do not make an enormous mistake and be in the wrong), but in order to spare you a little bit more, I ask you to consider and I am putting before your eyes the old state of the Church which was among the Greeks, at the time of Chrystostom and Basil, and among the Latins, in the time of Cyprian, Amboise and Augustine, as it is fully contained in their writings; afterwards look at the ruins which remain to you. Surely you will find so much difference there, as the prophets write about it, among which it has fallen into all types of superstitions, under Zedekiah and Joachim, the Church had completely corrupted the purity of the service of God, through zeal for sanctimony and old piety, not happy with the present corruption, the Church in all things would wish to try to improve and restore in their pristine splendour the things which are depraved and dissipated within it?

Therefore as it is thus that the health and firmness of the Church exists mainly and is adorned with three things: that is to say, from doctrine, discipline and sacraments, come the ceremonies in fourth place in order to rule the people in the duty of piety, in order to truly save your Church and keep its honour, by which of the four do you want us to judge it? First of all, the doctrine of the prophets and evangelical truth, in which the Church must be founded, is not only extinct among you, but by a great excess it is chased and followed by fire and blood. And you, will you really allege to me and would you dare state to me that this is a Church in which all the institutions of our faith, established by God's word, recorded in the writings of the holy fathers and even approved by the old councils, are furiously driven away and persecuted? Tell me, where are only the traces and marks of the order, so holy and true, that the old ministers and bishops observed in the Church? Have you not laughed at all their establishments? As for the sacraments, I cannot think, without being very horrified, how you have wickedly debased them. As regards ceremonies, you have done so more than enough. But considering that the more often their meaning is inane, silly and even corrupted by a thousand superstitions, what can they gain for the preservation of the Church? From everything that I say, there is nothing, as you see, that can in any way be attacked or increased in the manner of an accusation by me. All these things which are so notorious and obvious that one can even point one's finger at them, if one had eyes to make one careful. Now, if you please, ask yourself now in all diligence according to this rule and, without pointing out a mistake, if it would really be necessary for you to convict us of the crimes of which you accuse us. As for the sacraments, we have not touched on them, except in order that, when they have been put back into their simple purity of which they were stripped, they should receive their first honour and dignity. On ceremonies, mostly we have abolished them. But we have been forced to do this partly because, by their great number, they seemed to stay into Judaism and partially, so occupied the minds of the rank and file of the people and filled them with superstitions that they could not sustain at all, without harming the piety which they should increase. However we have kept some of them which seemed to us to be adequate for the place and time. We truly confess that we have not yet come to the discipline which was observed by the old church. But what right and reason is there in our being accused to have subverted it by those very people who alone have taken it away and abolished it, wishing to put it back into its original state, up to now you have prevented us from doing so?

To deal with doctrine, I am not at all afraid to draw attention to it and above all to bring it back to the old Church. And however, as by way of example, you have touched on some points through which you seem to have seen some occasion to slander us, I shall briefly show how you are mistakenly accusing us and falsely thought up these things, against the authority of the Church. However before I come to go into detail, I very much want to admonish you for thinking and consider twice for what reasons you criticise our people for having undertaken their studies to explain Scripture. For you know very well that, through their watching and literary writings, they have given such great clarity to the word of God that envy itself would be ashamed in that matter to deprive them of all praise. How much goodness and honesty is there in you to say that the people were charmed by us in difficult and subtle questions and almost tricked by this philosophy, of which Saint Paul [Col 2,8] orders Christians to beware. How? Do you not remember at all what was the time at which our people began to appear? What doctrine did those schools teach which tended to be administered by the Church? You know very well yourself that it was even not pure sophistication, so twisted, so mixed, so full of circumlocution and so intertwined that scholastic theology could be rightly called a certain type of secret magic. In which, the more each person obscured it with deeper shadows and hindered himself and the others in difficulties and obscure sentences, he was considered so much more ingenious and subtle in his doctrine. And also, when those who were trained in such a place wanted to show the people the fruit of their doctrine, with what dexterity, I ask you, did they edify the Church?

But in order that I do not decipher everything in great detail, what sermons were there at that time in the whole of Europe, which represented the simplicity, in which Saint Paul wanted the Christian people to live throughout their lives? Where even was the sermon in which the stupid old women did not learn more about dreams, that they could not have described a month later at their firesides? For their preaching was so arranged that one of the parts was in these obscure and difficult questions of the school in order to draw the poor and simple people in admiration; the other part was spent in happy tales and leisurely speculations in order to excite and move the hearts of those people to happiness. Some words of God were mixed in between so that, by their majesty, they might give some colour to their dreams and daydreams. But however our people took up their sign, in a moment all these shadows were lightened among us. Now, you preachers, partly having been students and having learnt from their books, and being partly constrained, by shame and murmuring of the people, to comply with the example of those described above, find it still impossible to feel deeply…this old stupidity and blunder. So that, if one compares our manner of preaching with theirs – even with that which is the most esteemed among them – one will easily find out that you have insulted us very badly. And if you had wanted to follow the words of Saint Paul a little further there is not such a small child who would not have know the crime of which you accuse us to be imputed to you, rather than to us the other ones. For the Apostle says that that philosophy is vain, which abducts the faithful consciences par the constitutions of men and elements of this word [Col 2,8], with which you have corrupted and ruined the Church.

Justification by faith

Now you relieve us of the charge of incontinence after your own testimony, when between so many of our teachings that you undertake to criticize, you do not allege that one of our teachings whose knowledge would not be hugely necessary to the enlightenment of the Church. In the first place you deal with justification by faith, which between you and ourselves is the cause of the main and most bitter conflict. Is that a vexed and useless question? But having taken away knowledge of that, the glory of Jesus Christ is dead, religion is abolished, the Church destroyed and hope of salvation completely destroyed. Why do we say that this article, which we hold to be supreme in our religion, was wickedly removed by you from the memory of men, which is fully and obviously proven and stated in all our books. And moreover, the great ignorance which still rules in all your Churches, bears witness to the fact that we are not complaining about it mistakenly. But also you are acting very maliciously here in saying that attributing everything to faith, we should not give it a place at all and that we should not take good works into consideration. Here I shall not set up an absolute dispute, which would surely require a whole book. But however, if you looked at the Catechism and Instruction which I have written to the people of Geneva being for the time being the minister in their town, at the first word, being overcome, you would keep quiet. Nevertheless, I shall here deal briefly with how we speak of this matter. First of all, we ordain that each person should begin by recognising himself, and not lightly, and not by way of payment, but as if to present his conscience before God's court, and that when he finds himself rather condemned by his sin, he considers over and over the severity of his judgment which is denounced against all sinners. And being thus confused and beaten in his own wretchedness, he prostrates himself and humbles himself before God, all confidence in himself having been taken away, as he groans pathetically as if he were condemned to eternal death.

Good works

Then later we show that the only haven of salvation is in God's mercy which is shown to us in Jesus Christ. For only in him, everything that belongs to our salvation is shown in Jesus Christ. Considering therefore that all human beings are condemned sinners before God, we say that Christ is the only justice; which, by his obedience, has wiped out our transgressions; by his sacrifice God's anger has been soothed; by his blood he has cleansed us of any stain; by his death he has fulfilled our needs for us. In this way we say that man was reconciled to God the Father, through Christ; not by the merit or dignity of his works, but by the goodness and free mercy of the Lord. Therefore when we by that embrace Christ and come as in his communion and participation, we call that, according to Scripture, justice by faith [Rm 4,13].What do you have here, Oh Sadolet, that you could have eaten into or taken back? Is it however that we attribute nothing to works? Certainly, for the justification of man, we deny that they are valuable, not even a hair of one's head. For Scripture says so clearly in so many passages that we are all lost, and there is nobody who is not driven by his conscience in this. That very Scripture does not give us another hope, except in the sole goodness of God through which our sins are forgiven to us and justice is imputed.to us. And it says that one and the other is a free gift so that it finally states that man is happy without the works [cf. Rm 4,6].

But, you say, what other thing do we understand by this word justice, if one does not consider good works? Truly if indeed you thought that it is what Scripture understands by this word justifier, you would not be in any doubt. For it does not refer to the proper justice of man, but to the mercy and goodness of God, which grants justice to the sinner, even if he had not given it to you, without imputing any injustice to him [cf Rm 4, 4-5]. That, I say, is our justice which is described by Saint Paul: to know that God reconciles us to himself in Christ [2 5,19]. The means is stated later: it is in not imputing our sins to us. Finally, it shows that we are participants in this asset by faith, when it says that the ministry of this reconciliation is found in the Gospel [cf 2 Co 5,18; 6,1 ss]. Yes but, you say, this word, faith, is a word which includes a great deal, the meaning of which is greatly broadened. But on the other hand, every time and often that Saint Paul the faculty of justifying to faith, he limits it and restricts it to the free promises of the benevolence of God, diverting it completely from the trust and respect for works. However he concludes so often: if it is by faith, it is therefore not by works. And once again: if it is by works, it is therefore not by faith. Indeed, but Christ is insulted if, under the pretext of his grace, good works are rejected, considering that he came to make a people pleasing to God, a follower of good works [Tt 2,14]. On which there are a great many similar testimonies through which it is shown that Christ came so that in doing good, we were through him acceptable to God. [cf 1 { 2,5]. Our enemies have hardly any other slander in their mouths, except that they say we have taken men away from the study of doing good by preaching justice freely ascribed, which slander is more frivolous than if from itself we could be put under a strain or hurried in any way.

For the justification of man, we deny that good works have no place, but we assign to them their reign in the life of good men. For if the one who is justified possesses Jesus Christ and Christ is never without his Spirit, it follows unavoidably that this free justice is always linked with regeneration. Because, if you want to understand properly how faith and works are inseparable things, look at Christ who, as the Apostle says, was given to us in justice and sanctification [1 Co 1,30]. Therefore some portion of justice by faith that we describe as free, Christ also is. And where Christ is, the Spirit of sanctification is present in order to regenerate the soul in newness of life. On the other hand, where there is no study of holiness, and innocence, or Christ, or his Spirit can be there. And where Christ is not present, there is no justice either, nor even faith which can comprehend Christ in justice without sanctification. Considering therefore that, as we say, Jesus Christ regenerates in a happy life those whom he justifies, after he has taken them away from the kingdom of sin in order to lead them to the kingdom of justice, transfiguring them into the image of God [cf 2 Co 3,18], and reforming them by his Spirit in obedience to his will, there is no appearance of wishing you to complain that by our doctrine we others give way to the desires of the flesh.

And if they do not mean something else, all the allegations that you put forward, which if you want to exploit in order to abolish free justification, see you are arguing ignorantly. Saint Paul says in another passage that we were all before the creation of the world chosen in Christ to be saints and blameless in the presence of God, through charity [Ep 1,4]. Who dare to conclude through that, that the election is not free, or that charity is not the cause of it? Rather thus, as free election tends to the aim that we live before God purely and without stain, such is also the end of free justification. Meanwhile however we remain firm and stable in that man not only is for once justified without any merit for his works, but also that his everlasting salvation lies only in this free justice. And that his works cannot be pleasing to God at all if they are not accepted and approved by this justice. Because I am greatly amazed, in reading your writings, that you say that charity is the first and main cause of our salvation, Oh Sadolet, who is it who would ever have thought of hearing such a word from you? Blind people, even in the midst of their shadows, are more sure of the mercy of God than to dare to ascribe most of their salvation to charity. But those who have one scintilla of the light of God, feel strongly that their salvation is not cut off by any other thing, unless they are adopted by God. For eternal salvation is the heritage of the holy Father, who is only preparing for his children [cf Rm 8,17]. Moreover,

131

would one wish to ascribe another cause to our adoption than that which is commonly placed in Scripture? One should know that the first love does not come from us, but that God with his own movement and goodwill has received us in grace and benevolence.

Penitence

Another mistake comes from your blindness, that you hold that sins are purged and wiped away by penitence and reparations. Therefore where will this single satisfactory host be from whom, if one withdraws from him, there is no other sacrifice for sins [cf Hb 10,12]? Have a good look in the whole of holy Scripture: that if the blood of Christ is offered to us for the price of our satisfaction and ablution, by what rashness do you dare to transfer this honour to your works? You do not have to ascribe this sacrilege to the Church of God. I confess truly that the ancient Church had its compensations. However, they were not such that through them sinners should think they should seek grace and have their sins atoned for. But it was in order to confirm their repentance that they showed outwardly that it was not at all false, and in order to wipe out the memory of the scandal which had come about from their misdeeds. And if they had not been united with each other, but so strongly to them, they would have fallen into some painful and large sin, with solemn observance.

Holy Communion

As for the sacrament of holy communion, you admonish us for what wanting to include and confine the Lord of heaven and earth, together with his divine and spiritual power (which is free and infinite) in the corners of a natural body, which has its certain measurements and proportions. Will the slandering never stop? We have always openly witnessed that not only the divine power of Christ, but also his essence is spread everywhere, and that it has no strict limits. And you, have you no shame in reproaching us for having confined him in the proportions of a natural body? Why is that? Because we have never wanted, like you, to subject his body to visible and earthly things. But if sincerely and truthfully you wanted to judge, surely you are not unaware of how much these two things are contradictory: to take way from the bread the local presence of Christ, or to restrain and imprison his spiritual power for the purposes of a natural body. And however, you should not slander me at all for our doctrine of innovation considering that this article was always sure in the Church. But because this dispute, due to its size, would be enough for a whole book, it would be better, in order to relieve our suffering, for you to read the Epistle from Augustine to Dardanus. In which you will find that the one and same Christ, through the size and magnitude of his divinity, is greater than heaven and earth, and however according to humanity is not spread everywhere. The true communication of his flesh and his blood which is shown to the faithful in holy communion, which we preach, in that he is in us, openly showing that flesh to be the true meat of life, and this blood to be the true drink, this is, not only by an imaginary idea, with which the soul is not at all happy, so truly it enjoys its virtue.? We do not at all reject the presence of Christ from holy communion , through which we are united with and grafted into him. And if we do not wipe him out, provided that this local district does not exist, and that the glorious body of Christ is not removed into these base elements, and that one does not pretend that the bread is transubstantiated into the body of Christ so that in the end it is adored like Christ. The dignity and usage of this high mystery, we magnify according to our power, stating how useful it can be to us. All of which things are despised and almost buried by you. For scorning God's blessing which is offered to us, and not considering the use of such a blessing (in which it had to come to rest), it is enough for us that the people, without any understanding of this spiritual mystery, should hold the visible and carnal sign in admiration. In that we have rejected your great and material transsubstantiation that you are instituting, in that we also have taught that this adoration which is so stupid (through which human minds, held by the elements of this world [cf Ga 4,3], were prevented from coming to Christ) is perverse and iniquitous, we have not done so without the actual consent of the primitive Church, of which you willingly (but in vain) would like to cover up the abominable superstitions which are still in force among you.

Confession

On heard confession, we have condemned this institution of Pope Innocent which orders everyone to tell all his sins every year to his own priest. How, and for what reasons we have abolished this, it would take a long time to tell. Nevertheless while it may be a wicked thing, it has an obvious place because the consciences of the faithful, freed from such torment, have only begun to rest and trust in the goodness and mercy of God, who in the past were in constant anxiety and disturbance. I shall not say a word about the great injuries that the Church has suffered through this confession, through which rightly we consider it dreadful. On what is being done now by you others, it is enough for you that there is nothing written about it, neither in Christ's commandments, nor in the institutions of the early Church. All the passages of holy Scripture which the scholars try to untwist in order to prove this confession, we have powerfully uprooted. And the ecclesiastical Histories that we have today in our hands hold that it was not a new thing, in that time when everything was purely observed; with which the testimonies of the fathers agree. It is therefore abuse and deceit that you say that there is humility in what is ordered and established by Christ and by the Church. For, however much there may be some appearance of humility, however it is very necessary for any lowliness, under the shadow of humility, is pleasing and agreeable to God. However Saint Paul teaches us that true humility is that which is true and ordained according to the pure word of God [Col 2,18].

Saints

In order to strengthen intercession by the saints, if your case is only that, by constant wishes, they ask for the fulfilment of the kingdom of Christ in which the salvation of all the faithful is contained, there is no-one among us who doubts any of that. Therefore you have gained nothing by dwelling so much on this point. But certainly, you did not wish to lose this gentle case, with which you are satirizing us, as if it were our opinion that the spirit would die with the body. For our part, we leave this philosophy to our bishop princes and to the College of Cardinals, by whom it was faithfully revered for many years and still is at the moment. And moreover, what you add later (that is, to live wantonly in pleasure, without any care for the future life and laughing at us other poor dwarves, who carefully work to advance the kingdom of God) is naturally suitable.

Moreover, as for intercession by the saints, we stop in such a place that it is no wonder if you do not do the same. For it was necessary to shatter countless superstitions, which had come to the point until then that the intercession of Christ was completely abolished from the memory of man. The saints were invoked as gods. The true qualities of God were attributed to them and there was no great difference between venerating them and that idolatry which you, rightly, hold in horror and detestation.

Purgatory

As regards purgatory, we know that some old Churches made some remembrance of the dead in their prayers, but this was rare, sober and consisting of a few words, which appeared to wish for nothing but to briefly bear witness to their charity towards the dead. But the master workers who had created your purgatory had still not been born, who then later expanded it so broadly and have placed it in such eminence and height that the greater part of your kingdom is supported and upheld by it. You know yourself what a huge mistake came out of it. You do not know how much witchcraft superstition has willingly created in order to deceive itself. You know how many deceits, bewitchments have been willingly created by superstition in order to deceive oneself. You can see really well what a loss true religion has suffered from it. For, in order that I should say nothing about the service of God, which has been beaten by it, the worst of it is surely that when men envying one another, without any commandment from God, wishing to help the dead, they have completely scorned the true works of charity which, however, are so much needed and prescribed.

I will not tolerate, Oh Sadolet, that in ascribing such sacrileges to the name of the Church, you bring it, against all right and reason to be slandered, and because this makes us obnoxious to stupid people, as if our plan was to make war against them. For, however much I confess that some foundations of superstitions were thrown out long ago, which in no way stained evangelical purity, you know well that these monsters of impiety (against whom we are mainly fighting) are not so old, or, at least, had not grown to such magnitude. And surely in order to fight, break, ruin and abolish your kingdom, we are not only armed with the virtue of the word of God, but we are also provided with the authority of the holy fathers. And in order that sometimes I can completely take out of your hands the authority of the Church – that you are always putting in front of us, like a shield of Ajax – I shall show you by some examples, how far different you are from this paternal and ancient sanctimony.

Abuses of the Roman Church

We accuse you of having subverted the ministry, the name of which you hold empty and without any effect on the matter. For, as for the need for spiritually feeding the poor people, the children themselves see clearly that your bishops and priests are nothing more than dead images, and test men in all conditions, that they are not brave, except in plundering and destroying. We cannot entertain the idea that instead of holy communion a sacrifice should be introduced which annihilates the virtue of the death of Jesus Christ. We shout against the abominable merchandising and fairground of the mass and we complain that the Christian people are almost deprived of the communion of the Lord. We rail against the wicked and sinful adoration of images. We can prove that the sacraments

137

were polluted and soiled by several profane and impure opinions. We are teaching that the pardons and indulgences were introduced, without being seen, to the great and horrible disgrace of the cross of Christ. And we complain that Christian liberty was submerged and oppressed by human traditions. And because we have given an order that the Churches that God has committed to us should purged and cleansed for such similar plagues. You may complain now, if you can, that we have harmed the Church, for having dared to violate its venerable establishments. Surely that is already so common that you will gain nothing by denying it, that in all these things the old Church agrees with us and that it is no less opposed than ourselves. Now I remember here that you said in I do not know which passage, as if you wished to belittle the matter, that it does not follow however, if your conditions are muddled, that we should separate from the holy Church. Certainly it could be with great difficulty – considering so much cruelty, greed, rapes, intemperance, insults, and so many examples of all licence and wickedness that are constantly being committed by people of your kind – that the bravery of the people should not be turned away from you and your side. But none of these things has led us to try what we have undertaken by a much greater need. What is sure has been, because the clarity of divine truth had been extinguished, the word of God buried, the virtue and effectiveness of Christ had been abolished by deep forgetfulness, and the position of the pastor completely subverted. However impiety was coming so much to the fore that there was hardly any Christian doctrine that was pure and without taint, no ceremony without a mistake, and no portion of the divine service free from superstition. Therefore those who drive away these sins, are they waging war on the church, or rather, are they not trying to help her, seeing her thus afflicted and oppressed on all sides? And still you come to us to allege your obedience and humility, that is to say, that the reverence of the Church prevents you from putting your hand to driving out such iniquities. What has a Christian man in common with this counterfeit obedience, despising the word of God, comes to serve and obey men? What is it to him with this contempt and rebellious humility, which in scorning the majesty of God, has only men in honour and reverence? Fi, fi to such false names of virtues, which are not put forward, except to cover up and hide vices. Let us come to the point without deceit. May there by humility between us which, at the beginning of the world, honoured everyone according to his degree, so that it ascribes to the Church the sovereign dignity and reverence, which however may in the end be attributed to Christ, its leader. May it be obedience which settles us to hear our superiors and those in charge of us, so much. However may it ascribe all our actions to the only rule of the word of God. Finally may the Church not try to do anything else, other than to look up the word of God in all religious humility and contain itself under his obedience.

But, you will say, what arrogance is it in you others, to boast that the Church is only with you, and however to wish to deprive the rest of the universal world? Surely, Sadolet, we do not deny at all that the Churches over which you preside are Churches of Christ, but we say that the Pope, together with the whole troop of its false bishops, who between you have taken the place of pastors, are cruel and dangerous wolves [cf Jn 10,12], which until now, have no desire, other than to consume and destroy the kingdom of Christ until, through ruin and desolation, it would be completely deformed and wiped out. And we are not the first people who have complained about it. With what vehemence did Saint Bernard blast against Pope Eugene and all the bishops of his time? But how much more tolerable was the state of that century than of the present? For today we have come to extreme and the highest degree of all wickedness, so that these spurious shadows of bishops (in whom you think the whole steadfastness or ruin of the Church consists) cannot already suffer either their own vices, or the remedies for them, through which we say that it was cruelly beaten and mutilated and that it was not at all necessary for it to be razed to the ground and sacked. Which is what without any mistake would have happened, if the singular goodness of God had not prevented it. So that in all the places occupied by the tyranny of the Pope, with difficulty there appeared some broken traces and remains, through which you might consider the Churches to lie there half-buried. And there is no need for that to appear strange, as you can hear by the mouth of Saint Paul: the siege of Antichrist must be nowhere but in the midst of God's sanctuary [2 Th 2,4]. Does this single and unique warning make us watchful in order to take care that illusions and deceptions are not brought into the church under that name and shadow?

Now, whoever they are, you say, nevertheless this is written: what they tell you, do it [Mt 23,3]. Yes, if they sit in Moses' chair [cf 23,2]. But considering that from the chair of vanity, they abuse the people for their daydreams, it is written: take care of their leaven [Mt 16,6]. It is not for us, Oh Sadolet, to take away from the Church its right which was not only granted by the goodness of God, but also was severely avenged and maintained by several threats and curses. For in the same way that the pastors are not sent by him to govern the Church with a licentious and irregular power, but are limited to a certain form of duties, which must not

140

be exceeded, so the Church is ordered to warn and to beware of how faithfully those who have taken over under that condition carry out their duty [1 Th 5,21; 1 Jn 4,1]. Because, either one will not largely stop at Christ's witness, or it will not be permissible to annul and diminish, however slightly, the authority of those that he has decorated with such pre-eminences and dignities. Surely you are very mistaken, if you think that the Lord may have put over his people tyrants who may govern everything according to their imagination, because he has given such great power to those that he sends in order to proclaim his Gospel. You delude yourself a great deal in that you do not see that their power is restricted before it is knocked down. Therefore we confess that the pastors of the Church must be listened to like Christ himself, not to say those who carry out the duties which they are called upon to perform. So it is, not in order that they should arrogantly come to introduce and put forward their decrees which are forged without thinking, but that religiously and in good faith, they proclaim the words that they have received from the word of the Lord. And Saint Peter does not ascribe anything else, nor allows others to do, but when they talk among the faithful, that it should be as if from the word of the Lord [1 P 4,11]. The Apostle Paul greatly increases this spiritual power that he had, but with such moderation that it can do nothing, other than enlightenment, that it should have no appearance of sovereignty, in the end, that it should not be given to extinguish and subjugate faith [2 Co 13,10]. For now your Pope glorifies himself so much that he would like the succession of Saint Peter. For, when he obtained that, if he will not achieve through it any obedience of the Christian people, unless he himself keeps his faith in Jesus Christ, without turning away from the purity of the Gospel. Surely the Church

141

of the faithful does not call you to an order other than that in which they Lord wanted you to remain, when it establishes you in the form and order in which all your power is restricted. And this is the order which is ordained by the Lord among the faithful; that the prophet, in his place as a teacher, should be judged by the group of listeners [1 Co 14,29]. Anyone who wants to exempt himself from this, must first of all wipe himself out from the number of the prophets.

Calvin's Reply to Sadolet's accusations and the justification for his ministry

Now at this time there is presented to me a very great matter for finding fault with your ignorance. For between the differences and controversies of religion, you do not leave any other means to the company of the faithful apart from, turning their eyes from the truth of the matter, they come to submit and fasten on to the judgment of men who are more learned and experienced. But considering that it is certain that the soul, depending moreover on God alone, is subject to Satan, how unhappy and wretched will be those who have such beginnings and foundations in their faith? Through that I see very well, Sadolet, that you have a theology that is much too stupid and lazy, almost like that of those who have never suffered the assaults on their consciences in good understanding. Otherwise you would not set the Christian man in a place which is so slippery and dangerous, in which he could not live for a moment if, as seldom as it may be, he stumbled. Show me, I am not saying a man of the average people, but the most foolish rough swineherd. If he is from God's flock, he must be ready for the fight which God has laid down to all the faithful. This poor wretch, he goes near, he fights, your enemy in the right way in

which no earthly power is impregnable. This poor
wretch, with what will he be protected? What weapons
can he have to protect himself so that at one blow he
will not be overpowered? There is only, says the
Apostle, one sword with which we must fight: that is
the word of God [Ep 6,17]. Therefore the soul, stripped
of the word of God, is delivered to the devil completely
unarmed so that he may kill it.

Now tell me, will the first act of the enemy be to
take the sword of Christ away from the opponent? But
the means of taking it off him, is that not to place it in
question, that is to say: if what he is attacking is the
word of God, or of men? What would you do here for
this poor wretch? Will you tell him that he is looking
here and there for scholars on whom, having depended
on them, he may find comfort and rest? But the
enemy will not let him only breathe in this subterfuge.
For if he has once forced him to place his confidence in
men, at all, he will force him and will subvert him more
and more, until he has confused him with everything.
Therefore he will either be crushed, or, in forsaking
men, he will look straight to the Lord. The sure thing is
thus that the Christian faith must not be founded at all
on the witness of men, nor upheld by dubious opinions,
nor even sustained by human authority, but engraved in
our hearts by the hand of the living God, so that no
enticement can wipe it out and destroy it. Therefore
this has nothing of Christ in it, which does not have
these rules and beginnings within it. That is to say,
that he is a God who is lighting up your minds in order
to learn his truth, which he signs and seals in our hearts
by his Spirit, affirming and assuring our consciences by
his sure witness. That is the firm and full certainty
(properly speaking) which is so much recommended to
us by Saint Paul. Which, in the same way that it
makes us confident without having any doubt or

defiance, also likewise it is not in uncertainty or wavering between men's altercations, to know to which side it would rather belong. But while everyone may upset it, nevertheless it remains firm and stable in its opinion.

Out of this, there comes and proceeds the power to judge what we ascribe to the Church, which we wish to be inviolably kept within it. For, however much the world is moved and blurred by the diversity of opinions, notwithstanding this, the faithful soul is never so neglected that it does not always follow the straight path to salvation. However, I do not here at all want to imagine a faith which is so perfect, which can never make a mistake or fail in the choice of good and bad, or pretend and dream of a reluctance and absence, which, as having pre-eminence and superiority, scorns and rejects all men, without stopping at judging anyone and without making a difference between the scholar and the ignoramus. But rather I confess that even those who have a purer and more devout conscience do not come to the knowledge of all the mysteries of God, but more often things are clearer and they do not see a speck. This is by the Lord's providence so that they should become used to all modesty and submission of the mind. Besides, I confess that they have all good people in such renown and esteem, and the Church even more, that they will only separate themselves from envy of a man that they know to have the true knowledge of Christ and of his word. So that they prefer sometimes to remain abandoned in their judgment, than to disagree lightly. I only maintain that, while they will dwell on the word of God, they will never be so surprised that they would be drawn to iniquity, and that the truth of the word is so sure and obvious that neither angels, nor men could draw them away from it. That is why, we should let go of this frivolous simplicity that you call seemly to rough and ignorant people, to look so much to these learned persons and dwell on their deliberations. For beyond that no persuasion of religion, as obstinate as one wants, which rests moreover that in God the name of faith is not deserved, who will be the one who will call any dubious opinion a faith, which not only is not easily extorted by a diabolic art, but also floats and wavers by itself according to the change in the weather, from which one can hardly expect another end, than that it is finally lost and disappears?

In that you falsely accuse us against what you know, that in rejecting this tyrannical yoke we have had no other consideration, other than to loosen our reins and place in irregular licence, which is above all abandoned by us (God knows) all reflection on future life, judgment on the comparison between your life and ours should be based. Certainly we are sinners, and there are sins abounding in us, and many of them. We fall more than too often and fail a great deal. However shame and scruple hold me back from daring to glorify myself (as much as truth allows) in how much better we are than you, and in every place. If by chance you did not want to exclude Rome, this very beautiful sanctuary of all holiness, which is placed outside the broken hinges and barriers of straight discipline, all honesty downtrodden, has so far boiled over into all sorts of wickedness, that such an example of abomination has hardly ever occurred. I think that we should submit our lives to so many risks and dangers, so that by their example we would not be forced into a more strict and narrow continency. For ourselves, we do not at all refuse to accept that the discipline ordained by the ancient Canons should be received today and that it should be maintained and preserved. But on the other hand, we have always declared that the miserable ruin of the Church did not come from elsewhere, but that, by over-licentious superfluities, it had lost all its power and strength and had remained as though it was completely weakened. For it is necessary for the body of the Church, in order to make it really united, to be held together with discipline as a body which is strengthened by nerves. But. I ask you, how is it held in reverence or desired between you others? Where are the ancient Canons through whom the bishops and priests were held, as though with a bit between the teeth, in their duty and position? How are those bishops elected among you? By what probationary period? By what examination? By what proceedings? By what precaution? How are they initiated in the duties of their position? By what means? By what religion? They are only made to swear as a form of receipt that they will carry out the role of pastor. But not (so it appears) except in order to make them, for another purpose, beyond the other unkind things, perjuries. Because therefore that in thus taking the responsibilities of the Church as if by force, it really seems to them to have a power which is not subject to any law and think that by such power everything is allowed to them. To such a degree that it is easy to believe that between pirates and sea-rovers, brigands and thieves, there may be a better administration, and that their laws are better kept than not between all those of your state.

And because in the end you have described us as criminals before God's court, leading somebody to defend our cause, for my part I am not afraid to call you there. As regards doctrine, our conscience on that is so sure that it is not afraid of that heavenly Judge from which it knows certainly that it comes. And it does not stop at these little jests where you have wanted to disport yourself, always rather unsuitably. For is there anything more troublesome than after having come before the face of God, to invent any kind of stupidities and therefore makes for us a rather inappropriate defence, which fails as incontinent? Every time and as many times as that day comes into the memory of Christian hearts, they fall into a greater reverence than may be praiseworthy to them and thus they disport themselves lazily. Therefore leaving out such delights, let us consider a little today the expectation with which the courage of men must always be engaged. And let us remember that it is not so desirable for the faithful that he must not, rightly, be held in fear formidably to the ignorant and wicked despisers of God. Let us prick up our ears to this trumpet sound that even the ashes of the dead will hear from their tombs [cf 1 Co 15,32], and by the only Spirit from his mouth he will confound all sins. For about our cause, inasmuch as it is based on God's truth, it will not be deprived of good and fair defence. I am saying nothing about our persons, of which salvation will not be built at all on quibbling and pleading, but in humble confession and imploring prayer. But as for the cause of the ministry, there will be no-one among us who cannot speak for himself as follows.

For my part, sir, I have experienced how difficult and distressing it is to hold towards men the envious accusation by which I was oppressed on earth. But with the same confidence with which I have always provoked and called before your court, from that very thing I compared now before you, knowing to find truth in your judgment. Under the confidence of which, forcing myself, I have first of all dared to undertake and been able to accomplish (being provided with its instruction) everything which has been done by me in your church. They have accused me of two very distressing crimes, that is to say, heresy and schism.

147

But they call heresy what I have dared to contradict to the institutions received between them. What should I have done? I have heard from your lips that there is no other light of truth, to lead our souls in the way of life, than that which was illuminated by the word. I heard that everything was vanity that the human mind invented by itself, and as for your majesty, veneration of your name and the mystery of religion. I knew that if the doctrines invented in the brain of man were sown in the Church instead of your word, that would be too arrogant a sacrilege. And surely, when I looked towards men, everything seemed to me to be contrary. Those who were received as superintendents of the faith, did not listen to your word, nor did they care very much. They deceived and abused the humble people with strange constitutions and were mocked by them with any kind of nonsense. For which people the greatest veneration of the word was worship it from afar, like something which one cannot reach and however one must refrain from any inquiry into it.

And it came about that through this lazy stupidity of the pastors, as well as through the stupidity of the people, that everything was full of injurious mistakes, lies and superstitions. They did call you a God, but transferring elsewhere the glory that you had taken for yourself, they became inventors and had as many gods as they wanted to worship for saints and patrons. Your Christ also was well worshipped as God and held the name of Saviour, but in the way that he should mainly be honoured, he had hardly any glory. For being stripped of his virtue and power, he was hidden in the company of saints like another member of the community. There was no-one who truly considered this sacrifice to be unique, which he offered to you in the cross and through which he reconciled us to you. There was no-one who relied on its justice alone.

Regarding the confidence in salvation which is ordered and established in your word, it had almost disappeared. But on the other hand, this was received as if it were a sure thing that if someone filled with your kindliness and the justice of your Son felt a certain and sure hope of salvation, for him that was assigned to a stupid arrogance, and (as they said) a rash presumption. There were several bad opinions which subverted from the bottom to the top the first institutions of the doctrine which you have delivered to us by your word. The healthy intelligence of baptism and of your holy communion was corrupted by several lies. And moreover, as everyone shows their faith through good works (not without seriously offending your mercy) and that they take trouble to earn your grace by them, to obtain your justice, purge their sins and please you (all of which things wipe out and nullify the virtue of the cross of Christ), nevertheless they do not know what were good works. For, if they had not been established by your law for justice, they would have made several useless blunders for themselves in order to make you propitious and favourable, with which they were complying as much as they were almost scorning the rule for true justice that you ordered for us by your law. And human traditions had grown so powerful that if they had not taken away the faith that one has in your commandments, at least they had greatly reduced their authority.

But Oh Sir, you have enlightened me by the clarity of your Spirit, in order to think about this. You have placed your word before me, like a torch, in order to lead me to know how wicked and pernicious these things are. Finally you have touched my heart in order that in a fair manner and rightly I should hold them in abomination. As for returning to you the reason for the doctrine, you see what it brings to my conscience, in other words, that I have never thought of going beyond the limits that I knew had been drawn up for those who serve you. Therefore I have not doubted at all that I learned from your mouth, I have wanted to spread it faithfully to the Church. And if it is really certain that I have mainly tended to, and have worked hard towards this, to know that the glory of your kindness and justice seems very clear, the clouds which covered it were chased away and collapsed, and that the virtues and benefits of your Christ glisten in full, all concealment having been removed. For I really thought that it was not too reasonable that those things for which we were born to think and re-think about, should stay in the shadows. And if I did not think that one should show scantily or lightly those things to the size of which any prayer is much too inferior, and if I was not afraid to keeping men for a long time in those which their salvation lay. For it is impossible that this word of God would have contradicted what is called this being of eternal life, to know the true God, and the one that you have sent, Jesus Christ. [Jn 17,3]. As regards what they have objected to me that I have separated myself from the Church, in that I do not feel I am to blame at all. If by chance someone who must be known as a traitor, who sees the soldiers scattered and carried away, wandering here and there and deserting their ranks, lifts the captain's flag and calls them back and puts them into order again. For all your people, Lord, had gone so far astray, that not only were they unable to hear what they were ordered to do, but also it seemed that they may have forgotten both their captain, and the battle, and the oath that they had sworn. And I, in order to bring them back from such a mistake, have not raised a foreign flag, but your noble standard which we need to follow, if we want to be enrolled in the number of your people. In this place, those who had to keep the said soldiers in order, and who had drawn them away by mistake, have put their hands on me and because I persisted, they have resisted me with great violence. And if I had seriously begun to rebel, the battle would have become inflamed until the union was broken.

But on whichever side lies the fault and the blame, it is now up to you, Sir, to say so and to pronounce. For my part, I have always shown in words and in deeds how much I wished for union and harmony. However, I understood this union of the Church to take its beginning from you and ends in you. For however many times you have ordered us into this peace and union, you have stated all the time that you were the sole link to preserve it and maintain it. As for me, if I had wished to be at peace with those who were boasting that they were the leaders in the Church and pillars of the faith, I would have had to buy that by denying your truth. But it seemed to me that I had to submit to all the dangers of the world rather than condescend to such an abominable position. For even your Christ told us that if heaven became mixed with the earth, your word however would remain eternally [Mt 24,35]. Now I did not think that in order to go into battle with such people, I would however be in disunity with your Church. For you have warned us, both by your Son, and by his apostles, that none would be lifted up with those with whom one could not agree. It was not from strangers, of whom he had foretold that they would be ravishing wolves and false prophets, but from those people themselves who would come forward as pastors, that I was ordered to be careful of them [Mt 7,15]. Therefore when he ordered that I should be careful of them, should I have lent them a hand? And your apostles proclaimed to us that there were no more mortal enemies in your Church than those who were in the middle of the body, covered up with the name of

151

pastors (Ac 20,20]. And why should I have feared to separate myself from those that your apostles told me must be known to be your enemies? Day by day I looked at examples of your prophets, whom I saw having so many disputes with the sacrificers and false prophets of their time, who certainly (as it appears) were the first in the Church for the people of Israel. But however, one does not hold your prophets as schismatic, although in order to reinstate the almost ruined service of God, they had not given in at all to the others who were greatly distasteful to them. They therefore stayed within the true union of the Church, although great curses were called down upon them by the sinful sacrificers and were said to be unworthy of being included in the number, not of saints, but also of men.

I therefore, confirmed by their example, persisted so much in this theme, that neither their threats, nor their denunciations, through which they denounced me as schismatic, did not amaze me in any way, so that always constantly and steadily I have not offered resistance to those who, under the shadow of pastors, tyrannically oppressed your poor Church. For I felt within myself a strong desire that I had for its union, provided that truth was the link for such harmony. Of the emotions that followed from that, as they were not stirred up by me, they must not be laid to my charge in this way. You know very well, Lord, and the thing itself is a witness to it towards men, how I have sought nothing else, except that through your word all controversy should subside so that, through a conjunction of spirit, both parties should aim for the widening and establishment of your kingdom. You know too that I have not refused, even at danger to my head (if it were found that I was moved in vain), that peace should be brought back to the Church. But what were our enemies doing? Did they not run suddenly and furiously to fire, gallows and swords? Did they not think that their only solution was weapons and cruelty? Did they not stir up people of all states to this same anger? Did they not reject all conditions of peace? From which it has come about that the thing, which without that could amiably have been calmed down, was lit up and led to such a war. And although in such a great disturbance of things there may have been several opinions, now I am however free from any fear, since we are before your judgment seat, where fairness joined with truth can only judge according to innocence.

There, Sadolet, is the defence of our cause, not that with which to accuse us, you have wished to invent, but that which all people know to be true for the present time, and which in that date will appear clearly to all people. And as for those, who being taught by our preaching shall come with us for this same business, they will have to speak for themselves. For each of them will have the following defence quite ready.

As for myself, Sir, I have always publicly confessed the Christian faith, as I had learnt it from my youth. From which I have not at all from the beginning had any other knowledge than that which at that time was communally observed. Your word which should light your universal people like a lamp was taken away from us, or at least hidden. And in order that nobody should wish for clearer knowledge of this, this persuasion came into the understanding of someone that it was so much better that the investigation of that divine and secret philosophy should be handed to a few people, from which responses and oracles were not required, and that people did not have to have higher intelligence, but only submit themselves to the obedience of the Church. And such were the teachings that had been given to me at the beginning that they did not send me adequately in the direct service of your deity, and did not at all give me enough entry to a sure hope of salvation, and did not send me at all to the work of a Christian life. I had truly learnt to worship you alone for my God, but as much as I did not know the true reason for worshipping you, I stumbled as I went in there. I truly believed, as I had been taught, that by the death of your Son I was redeemed from the obligation of eternal death, but I imagined that this redemption was such that its virtue did not affect me alone. I waited for the day of the resurrection, but I had its recollection in abomination, as though it were an unhappy thing.

And it was not particularly this invented knowledge in my head, but that I had learnt the doctrine that at that time was preached communally by the masters and doctors of the Christian people. These did preach mercy towards men, but only towards those who were thought worthy of it. Finally they placed such great dignity in the justice of works that a person was only received in grace if he had been reconciled with you by his works. However, they did not keep quiet at all among themselves, saying that we were these miserable sinners, who were often falling due to weakness of the flesh. And later, they said that your mercy was for everyone a common haven of salvation, but in order to arrive there they did not give any other means, except to make atonement for our sins. And then, this atonement was a joint thing: first of all, that having confessed all our sins to a priest, we should humbly ask him for pardon and absolution; item that through good works we should wipe out their memory before you; finally, in order to provide what we were lacking, we should add sacrifices and solemn cleansing. And because you were a stern judge, severely avenging sin, they should how you would look upon us in a shocking way. So they ordered that people should first of all apply to the saints: so that by their intercession, you were returned to us and made favourable and accessible. And as I had achieved all these things after a fashion, while I made my confession to a slight extent, I was however a long way from a certain peace of mind. For however and how often I went into myself or lifted my heart to you, such an extreme horror surprised me that it was neither purification, or reparation that could in any way heal me. And the more I considered myself near, the more my conscience was pricked with bitter thorns, so that no other solace or comfort was left to me, but to deceive myself by forgetting myself.

But because nothing better presented itself, I always followed the path that I had started when meanwhile another form of doctrine came up, not in order to turn us away from Christian profession, but to reduce itself into its own source and in order to restore it, as though it were to clear it of any rubbish, in its purity. But I, offended by this novelty, strongly wanted to listen and I confess that at the beginning I valiantly and bravely resisted it. For (as men are naturally obstinate and tenacious in maintaining the institution that they once received) I was annoyed at confessing that all my life I may have been fed in error and ignorance. And in the same way there was one thing, which kept me from believing those people: it was reverence for the Church. But after I had opened my ears sometimes and allowed myself to be taught, I knew well that this fear that the majesty of the Church might be diminished, was vain and superfluous. For they showed that there was indeed a great difference between losing and abandoning the Church and labouring to correct the vices with which the Church is soiled and contaminated.   As for the Church, they spoke about it honourably and truly showed that their main intention was for its union.   And in order that they should not seem to want to fabricate any falsity under the name of the Church, they showed that it was not at all strange that antichrists should take the place of pastors within it [cf 1 Jn 2,18]. On which they gave us several examples through which it seemed clearly that they were not aiming for any other end, but the edification of the Church, and in that they had a similar cause with several servants of Jesus Christ, that we others hold in the number of saints.   As regards the fact that they so freely and openly spoke against the Pope of Rome, held and known to be the vicar of Christ, Saint Peter's successor and as head of the Church, they gave this reason for it: that is to say that such names were only vain scares, through which it was not expedient to dazzle the eyes of the faithful so that they would not dare to look at and discern the matter as the truth.   And that this was raised to such a height and magnificence, when the world was oppressed as though with a deep sleep of ignorance and dizziness. And surely, neither through the word of God, nor through a lawful vocation of the Church, he had not been instituted the prince and head of it, but by his own authority and his own will he had been elected.   Moreover, that the tyranny through which he oppressed the people was not in any way to be tolerated, if we wanted Christ's kingdom to remain safe and sound among us.

However they were not lacking in very strong reasons through which they confirmed everything.   In the first place, they clearly refuted everything that one wished to allege at that time in order to establish the Pope's principality.   And after at that time having taken away all his base, they also demolished, through the word of God, his great eminence.   The matter came to the point, that it was all common and completely clear, both to scholars and to the unlearned, that the true order of the Church was at the time completely lost, the leaders (under which the ecclesiastical order was included) badly adulterated, Christian freedom overturned and Christ's kingdom completely prostrated when this principality was raised. Moreover these new preachers had something with which to prick my conscience so that, predictably, I should not turn a blind eye to their institutions as if they did not belong to me at all, saying that it was really necessary for one to find an excuse for a voluntary mistake towards you – considering that in the same way the one who by ignorance is taken away from the straight path, and is not left unpunished for his mistake, which they proved by your Son's witness which says: If a blind man leads another blind man, both of them fall into the ditch [Mt 15, 14]. And when my mind was equipped to be truly attentive, I began to know, as though someone had brought me into light, in which tangle of mistakes I had fallen and been soiled and with how much mud and stains I was shamed. But therefore I (according to my duty) being vehemently filled with dismay and bewildered for the wretchedness into which I had fallen, and even more for the knowledge of the eternal death which was coming near to me, I thought nothing was more needed by me, having condemned my past life in tears and groans, than to give myself up and withdraw into yours. Therefore now, Lord, what remains for me, a poor and miserable one, but to offer to you for all pleas my humble entreaty: that you do not wish to hold me accountable for this so horrible desertion and estrangement from your word through which by your wonderful kindness you once drew me back?

Now comparing (if it seems right to you) Sadolet, this action to that which you have ascribed to your plain man. It will be wonderful if you doubt which of the two you will prefer to the other. For, without any mistake, the salvation of that one is in great danger whose defence is not turned around or upheld on another hinge, but to say that he will have constantly kept the religion which would have been handed down to him by his ancestors and predecessors. For this reason the Jews, Turks and Saracens escaped God's judgment. Therefore this vain evasion before the court which will be set up not to approve the authority of men, but to maintain the truth of one sole God, the universal flesh of falsity and of a condemned lie. For if I wanted to use drivel like you, what image could I paint, if I do not say of a Pope or a cardinal, or even of some other venerable prelate of your group, (all of whom you almost know well in what colour they could be painted, even by a man who was not too clever) but by which doctor, even the most delightful of all of yours? Surely, I would not now need, in order to condemn him, to bring doubtful surmises or to bring accusations of false crimes, for enough of them would be found true and sufficiently proven, with which he would be too heavily charged. But in order that I do not seem to follow what I pick up in you, I shall keep away from such action. I shall ask them all the more only to return sometimes to themselves and to think and think again in themselves how faithfully they calm down the Christian people, to whom one can feed no bread other than the word of their God. And they do not take pleasure too much in that, with the great recognition and consent of the people, they now play their personalities, for again they have not come to a conclusion. In which, surely, they will not have a ladder to command in order to safely sell their prize horses and abuse faithful consciences by their deceits and inventions, but will remain alive, or they will certainly fall, by God's will only, whose judgment will depend not on the voice and favour of the people, but by his only unchanging fairness. And he will not only enquire into external acts, but will also judge the sincerity or inner malice of the heart. And I do not wish to judge everyone universally. However, who is there among them, when it is a question of fighting against us, who has no remorse of conscience, that in doing so, he is working more for men than for God?

Now, as it may be that through all your Epistle you treat us inhumanely, however in the last clause you openly pour out all the poison of your spitefulness towards us. And although such insults do not affect us at all, and you have partially replied above, tell me, I ask you, why did you remember to reproach us again for greed? Do you think that our people were so dazed, that from the very beginning they did not know very well the path that they were taking to shrink completely from profit and gain of the flesh? Or, in recovering and putting blame on your greed, did they not see that, through that, they were of necessity constrained to live chastely and reasonably, if they did not want to be mocked by small children? When they showed that through a better means one would only be able to correct this by stripping the pastors of this abundance and superfluity of wealth, so that being freed from them, they would take much better care of the Church, did they not close for themselves the road to lead to wealth and abundance of possessions? For what wealth were there at the time, to which they could aspire? What? Was it not the easiest and shortest path to reach to wealth and honours to accept unrestrainedly from the beginning the terms and conditions offered by you? Your Pope, with what sum had he at that time bought the silence of the pastors, and for how much would he buy it back again today? Why, if they had the slightest wish in the world to become wealthy, would they prefer to remain poor perpetually (all hope of increasing their wealth having been taken away), than to become rich in an instant, without any great difficulty? I still do not see why you attacked us like this, considering that those who first of all tried this business could not hope for anything else, but to be shamefully despised and rejected by everybody. And those who came later, knowing and wishing, were exposed to the contumelies and countless criticisms of anyone. But where are these deceits and inner evils? Certainly there is no trace of that in us. Therefore, rather let us talk about these things in your holy college, where every day they are thrashed out.

From such slanders, because I am trying to come to an end, I am happy to turn away. In relation to which, wishing to undertake and do everything on our behalf, we have not found a single person in the whole Church that we might consider worthy of faith, we have now shown that these are only slanders. For while we establish the word of God above all human judgment and we have finally granted some authority to be left to the councils and holy fathers, provided that they comply with its rule, if however we only consider these councils and fathers worthy of the honour and place that they must reasonably hold under Christ. But the most enormous of all the crimes that you charge us with, is that we have made great efforts to disperse and break into pieces the bride of Jesus-Christ. If that were true, we would rightly be considered by you and by the whole world as lost people. However I shall not in any way admit this crime to be in us, if by chance you do not hold the bride of Christ to be torn apart by those who wish to make her into a chaste virgin to Christ, who are called by holy jealousy to keep her whole, which, corrupted by several attempts at match-making, revoke the marital faith, and who in the end are not afraid of corrupting her chastity [cf)Os 2,16 ss]. And have we done something else? Was the chastity of the Church not corrupted and, what is more, violated by foreign doctrines and alien institutions by people of your group? Had she not been violently prostituted by you through countless superstitions? Was she not defiled by this form of adultery, that is, worshipping images? Yes, because we have not allowed that the very holy and sacred resting-place and nuptial chamber of Christ should be thus mocked by you, we are accused of having dismembered his wife. But I, I say that this slashing of which you falsely accuse us is more than obvious among you, and not in the Church only, but in Jesus Christ himself, whom one sees by you to be wretchedly cut up. Therefore as the Church will be joined to its Husband, can it have it healthy and whole? But where is Christ's health when the glory of his justice, holiness and wisdom is transferred elsewhere? Especially, before the war was set alight by us, everything was very peaceful and tranquil. Certainly the laziness of pastors and the astonishment and stupidity of the people meant that among them there was hardly any difference of opinion on the subject of religion. But in colleges, with what stubbornness did the scholars argue? Because you have not a great opportunity to say that your reign was so peaceful, considering that there was no rest, except that Christ was kept quiet and almost forgotten. I did confess that after the Gospel appeared again, several great disputes became overheated, whereas there had been none beforehand. However it would be wrong if these things were attributed to our people, who, through all the abatement of their activity, looked for nothing but

161

to re-establish true religion, the Churches which were scattered and divided by discords and disagreements, were gathered into a good whole union. And so that I do not describe old matters: is it a thing that still they have refused but lately, provided that peace was restored in the Church? But they try everything in vain when you others make every effort to the contrary. For, as much as they ask for a peace with which the kingdom of Christ may flourish and that you others think, everything that is won for Christ is lost for you. And you do have inventions through which you destroy in one day everything that they have built in several months for the glory of Christ. I shall not wear myself out with so many words for I can dispatch the matter in one word. Our people have offered to give reasons for their doctrine and will not refuse to yield, if they are defeated by reason. Who is anxious now that the Church is not enjoying great peace and the light of truth? It goes on now and calls us rebellious, we who do not leave the Church at rest at all. Now, so that you may not forget anything which might serve to aggravate our cause, because in these past years several sects have grown up, by your grace you throw back all the spite upon us, but you should look at how fairly, and in what colour. For, if on that account we are worthy of hate, the name Christian would have in old times been hated rightly by infidels and unbelievers. Either therefore stop tormenting and pursuing us in this place, or confess that the Christian religion, which is the cause of creating so many tumults and revolts in the world, must be removed from the memory of men. Because this must not in any way harm our cause, because by any means Satan works hard to prevent the work of Christ. It was much more suitable and necessary for the thing to look at who is used to attack all these sects which have grown up. Now is it sure that while you others were lazily sleeping, we alone have borne this heavy burden.   May the Lord, Sadolet, work for you and your comrades to hear sometimes that there is no other link in the ecclesiastical union, but that Christ our Lord (who has reconciled us to God his Father) draws us back from this waste of energy in the company of his body, in order that in such a way by his word only and by his Spirit, we may be united in one heart and in one mind.

From Strasbourg, the first day of September 1539.

LITTLE/TREATISE ON/HOLY COMMUNION OF
Our Lord Jesus Christ.
In which is shown the true institution,
Its profit and usefulness:
Together with the reason why several/ of the Moderns
Seem to have written diversely about it.
By Monsieur Jean Calvin.
PRINTED IN Geneva,
By Michel du Bois.
M.D.XLI.

J. Calvin Little Treatise – Introduction

The *Little Treatise on Holy Communion* appeared in Geneva towards the end of 1541 from the printer Michel du Bois, shortly after Calvin's return. The reformer had had to leave the town in September 1538 and had spent nearly three years at the head of the French church in Strasbourg. It was very likely that he wrote the *Little Treatise*, which could explain the short time that passed between his arrival in Geneva and the appearance of the work.[62] Written in French, the treatise will be translated into Latin by Pastor Nicolas Des Gallars, which will ensure a wide circulation for it.

The aim that Calvin is following in this text is double: to try to reconcile the opposing parties within the Reformation, and to give believers a teaching which helps them to understand Holy Communion. Among the great evils of our era, one must count the fact that our Churches are so separated from one another that there is hardly a human society existing between us. This holy communion of Christ's members, which everyone confesses orally, but which few sincerely seek, is not seen to triumph. And thus, with the members torn apart, it is the body which bleeds. As for myself, if my presence were considered useful, I would not fear to cross ten oceans, if it were needed, to deal with such a question.[63] This statement, which is found in a letter of April 1552 which Calvin wrote to Bishop

---

[62] Which makes it understood that Theodore de BEZE in his *Vita Calvini*, calv. Opp.XXI, Col. 62, quoted by Jean CADIER, in his introduction to the *Little Treatise on Holy Communion*, Collection "Les Bergers et les Mages", Paris, 1959, p.9. the publisher of the *Opera Selecta* advances the date of 1537 in referring to a letter from Calvin to Veit Dietrich of Nuremberg, of 17 March 1546, quoted in Note 1 of our Preface.

[63] *Calv. Opp.*XIV, co. 314.

Cranmer, reflects his great care for the unity of the Church. Now the doctrine of Holy Communion constituted "one of the sore points of the emerging Reformation".[64] The four theologians that Calvin names in his text are those same people who in 1529 gathered for a colloquium in Marbourg, but who could not reach an understanding, the "Moderns" mentioned in the title: Luther and Melanchthon on the one hand, Zwingli and Oecolampade on the other. Calvin was very worried about these differences of opinion, and he sought to position his doctrine clearly in relation to the positions that were current.

In Roman doctrine, if one takes *transubstantiation*, in other words the change which takes place in the very substance of the elements of the communion: bread and wine become the substance of the body and blood of Christ, under an unchanged appearance. Out of this one worships the consecrated elements in this tradition, to which all the reformers will object.

He also distances himself from the celebration of the Mass composed as a *repetition of the sacrifice* of Christ, through which credits will be obtained. Finally, he blames the fact that *only, the priests* are empowered to celebrate the sacrament and to pronounce the words that make it valid.

Luther and Melanchthon – as moreover the whole Reformation – state that the *sacrifice of Christ*, is unique and sufficient. In Holy Communion, says Luther, there is no transubstantiation, but *consubstantiation*, which means that the glorified Christ is present "in, with and under" (*in, cum, sub)* the elements: it is an objective fact on which the communicant's attitude has no influence. However, to

---

[64] J. CADIER, p.9

receive communion in a state of unworthiness leads to condemnation [cf I Co 11,29].

The Swiss theologians, Zwingly and Oecolampade, approach the question under a different angle. The place the emphasis on Christ's order: "Do this in memory of me" [Lc 22,19 and I Co 11,25]; Holy Communion is therefore a *memorial*, the sacrament is a sign, a symbol of a spiritual blessing. The emphasis is placed on the operation of the Holy Spirit. The sacraments, according to them, are not essential to salvation. The spiritualist trend is very sensitive in this type of position.

Calvin, as to himself, adopted a type of half-way position. The contacts that he had with Bucer have no doubt confirmed it, but the question of knowing on which exact points and to what extent would demand an enquiry which goes beyond the limits of a simple introduction.

Calvin states firmly that salvation, expected in faith, is inseparable from the Word of God. The sacrament does not affect anything by itself, independently of the Word; it is not on its own an adequate formula. It is thus that the Word, for Calvin, must be preached at each celebration of Holy Communion. He even states that the sacrament is another way of preaching the Word, given by God. The elements – bread and wine in Holy Communion, water in baptism – are *signs* given to make a spiritual reality present; there is no need to look for a bodily and local presence of Christ. The spiritual meaning is "united" to the visible elements. "This is my body" are true words *spiritually*. Thus, Holy Communion is the spiritual food, therefore enough, for the soul, the spiritual substance of the body of Christ, a spiritual gift given to the believer. The unbeliever, by his lack of faith, empties the sacrament of its meaning. In fact, God's gift can only be grasped by faith.   Otherwise, one is there in the presence of a great mystery that one feels more than one can understand.[65]   Calvin "does not put himself on the metaphysical field of the nature of bread in Holy Communion, of the substance which considers the element sacramental *in itself*" and pronounces then that there is transformation of this element, a modification of its being. He puts himself on the religious field of Christ's relationship with us, of the "communion" that he grants us with him, from the gift that he gives us of his living and invigorating power. This is a dynamic way of asking the question.[66] In this text, Calvin was hoping to give justice to the Lutherans as well as to the Zwinglians, while showing some weaknesses in their respective positions.   He thought that he could encourage a reconciliation. Luther had just died when, unaware of this news, Calvin wrote to Veit Dietrich, of Nuremberg, that he did not think he had written anything that could not be negotiated with Luther[67]. The latter, according to Christophe Pezel[68] had had in his hands the Latin translation of Nicolas Des Gallars and would have expressed regret that neither Zwingli, nor Oecolapade would have expressed themselves in the way as Calvin; "we would have been able to understand each other", he would have said. But it was too late, and the lack of understanding between Lutherans and the reformed people was going to fester with time. One had to wait until 1973 and the end of the Concord of Leuenberg[69] for an end to be put to this

---

[65] F. HIGMAN, (*Three French Treatises, 20)* replies on this matter to Calvin, *Institution* IV, XVII, 32.

[66] J. CADIER, p. 9

[67] Letter quoted in note 1.

[68] *Ausfuhrliche, wahrhafte und bestandige Erzahlung durch Christoph. Pezelium...,* 1590, quoted in O.S. I, P. 501.

[69] See below, note 16 of the text.

serious disunity and for the mutual exclusions to be lifted. With the Zurich theologians, Calvin himself could draw up the agreement known by the name of *Consensus Tigurinus*, thanks to which the break was avoided.

Calvin's pedagogic ambition comes out clearly in the first lines of the *Little Treatise*, and Calvin recalls it later in his letter to Veit Dietrich; to teach non-theologian believes in a simple manner. In fact it is essential for members of the Church to understand what they confess and know what they are doing when they take part in Holy Communion; they must not any more allow themselves to be led astray by wrong opinions, nor to be troubled by the various doctrines which are going around. In the *Little Treatise*, the clarity of the argument, the examples and countless images, the stylistic means used as well as the constant use of Scripture respond to this concern and make this text a precious instrument to act as instruction for Christians; in the pedagogic perspective of the Reformation, it is listed after translations of the Bible and compositions of the Confession of faith and the Catechism.

Today's reader, once more, will remember that this work saw the light of day in a time where theological controversies were unfolding in a tone which was always alert, sometimes lively and even bitter. However, it will not take less trouble in making an effort to go into this language whose flavour we have tried to keep. He will find a text which has lost nothing of its depth.

Claire Chimelli

J. Calvin Little Treatise – Text

THE PRINTER TO THE READERS STANZA

Young and old, if you want to learn
Fully where our salvation lies
I ask you sweetly to listen
Not troubling you with a loose mistake;
It's in Jesus who wanted to arrange this,
Having dined with his friends,
Showing them that the indwelling spirit
Wants, and cannot know God's deeds;
So we must, with all desire removed,
Give ourselves to him in order to see this[70]

Because the holy sacrament of Communion of our Lord
Jesus was for a long time tangled up in several great
mistakes and, in these latest years, was still once again
wrapped in various opinions and contentious disputes,
it is no wonder if a great many feeble minds cannot
simply resolve what they must retain of it, but they
remain in doubt and perplexity while, with all disputes
put aside, they wait for God's servants to come to some
agreement. However, because it is a very dangerous
thing to have no certainty in this mystery, whose
understanding is so necessary for our salvation, I
thought it would be useful work to try briefly,
nevertheless clearly to infer the greater part of what we
must know about it. And also considering that some
good people, considering the need for this, have asked
me to do so, and I could not refuse without going
against my duty.

---

[70] The acrostic should be noted: the name of JEAN CALVIN
appears when one takes the first letter of each line (French text).

But in order to come quickly out of any difficulty, it is expedient to note the order that I have decided to follow. Therefore first of all, we shall expose for what purpose and for what reason the Lord has established this holy sacrament. Secondly, what fruit and usefulness we receive from it; where it will similarly be described how the body of Jesus Christ is given to us there. Then afterwards, what is the lawful use of it. Fourthly, we shall recite with what mistakes and superstitions it has been contaminated; where it will be shown what difference the servants of God must have with the Papists. For the last point, we shall state what the source of the dispute was, which as so bitterly been fought, even among those of our time who have brought the Gospel back into light and have applied themselves righteously to build the Church in a holy doctrine.

As for the first article: since it pleased our kind God to receive us by baptism into his Church, which is his house, which he wants to maintain and govern, and that he received us not only to have us as his servants, but as his own children, it remains that, in order to carry out the duties of a good father, he feeds us and provides everything which we require for life. For bodily food, because it is common to everyone and bad people partake of it as well as good people, is not peculiar to his family. It is certainly true that we have already had a witness of his fatherly kindness, in that he upholds us in our bodies, considering that we take part in all the gifts that he gives us with his blessing. But in the same way that the life in which he has restored us is spiritual, but also the meat, in order to keep us and confirm us in that life, must be spiritual. For we must understand that not only has he called us to own at once his heavenly heritage, but that through hope he has already to some extent brought us into this possession:; not only has he

171

promised us life, but already he has transferred us into it, drawing us away from death. It is when, adopting us for his children, he restored us by sowing immortality which is his Word printed in our hearts by his Holy Spirit [I P 1,23].

Therefore in order to sustain us in this life, there is no question of feeding our stomachs with corruptible and worn out meat, but to feed our souls with better and more precious pasture. Now the whole of Scripture tells us that the spiritual food with which our souls are kept alive is the same Word through which our Lord has restored us [Jn 6,31 ss; Mt 4,4 *et al*]; but it adds as regards reason, insofar as it is in Jesus Christ himself, our only life, is given and administered to us. For we must not think that there is life anywhere else than in God. But in the same way that God has established the fullness of life in Jesus in order to give it by his own means, he also established his Word as an instrument through which Jesus Christ, with all his graces, should be distributed. However it always remains true that our souls have no other pasture than Jesus Christ. However the holy Father, being concerned to feed us, gives us nothing else, but rather recommends us to take all our happiness there, as in a fully sufficient refreshment, from which we cannot depart and beyond which there is nothing else to be found.

We have already seen how Jesus Christ is the only food with which our souls are fed, but because it is given to us by the word of the Lord – which is intended for that – as an instrument, it is also called bread and water. Now, what is said about the word applies equally to the sacrament of Communion, by means of which the Lord leads us to communicating with Jesus Christ. For as much as we are so stupid that we cannot receive him in true homage of the heart when he is presented to us by simple doctrine and preaching, the

172

father of mercy, not scorning to condescend into this place to our infirmity, has wanted to add with his Word a visible sign through which he might represent the substance of his promises, in order to confirm and strengthen them in us while freeing us from all doubt and uncertainty.

Therefore then it is a mystery so high and incomprehensible to say that we have communication with the body and blood of Jesus Christ and that, on our part, we are so primitive and unrefined that we cannot understand the slightest things about God, it was his calling to give us to understand, according to our capacity to be able to bear it. For this reason, the Lord established his Communion from your Gospel, trying to make us participants in his body and in his blood, and to give us certainty and assurance that in that there lies our true spiritual food so that having such a pledge, we should conceive a straightforward certainty of salvation. Secondly in order to bring us to recognise his great kindness to us in order to praise and magnify it more fully. Thirdly in order to exhort us to all holiness and innocence, in as much as we are members of Jesus Christ, and singularly in union and brotherly love, as it is especially recommended to us. When we have taken note of these three reasons that the Lord looked at in establishing his Communion, we will already have an entry to a proper understanding and know what we gain from it, and what is our duty to use it directly.

It is therefore time to come to the second point, that is to show how the Lord's Supper is of benefit to us, on condition that we should make good use of his benefit. Now we shall know its usefulness in reckoning our need, for which it comes to our aid. We need to be in enormous difficulties and torment of mind while we look at who we are and examine what is within us. For there is none of us who can find a single grain of justice in himself, but on the other hand, we are all full of sin and iniquity, so much so that we do not need anyone else to accuse us for our conscience or another judge to condemn us. It follows therefore that the wrath of God is created for us and that there is no-one who can escape eternal death. If we are asleep and stupid, this horrible thought must be to us like a perpetual torture to annoy and torment us. For God's judgment cannot come into our memory, as we do not see our condemnation which is to come. We are therefore at the abyss of death, except that our good God pulls us back from it. Moreover, what hope of resurrection can we have when we consider our flesh which is only decay and vermin? So, as much according to the soul as to the body, it cannot happen that we cannot have great sadness and agony of thinking of such wretchedness.

Now the heavenly Father, in order to meet that, gives us Communion as a mirror in which we look at our Lord Jesus crucified in order to do away with mistakes and offences, and he having risen, in order to free us from corruption and death, restoring us into heavenly immortality. Therefore there is a singular consolation that we receive from Communion, in that it guides us and leads us to the cross of Jesus Christ and to his resurrection in order to guarantee to us that, whatever iniquity there may be in us, the Lord does not cease to acknowledge and accept us as righteous; whatever death matter may be in us, he does not cease to revive us; whatever unhappiness we may have, he does not cease to fill us with all happiness. Or in order to declare more easily what this is, as it may be that by ourselves, we become weak in every good thing and we do not have a single drop of the things that must help us to salvation, it gives witness to us that having been made participants in the death and passion of Jesus

174

Christ, we have everything which is useful and wholesome. However, we can say that the Lord gives us all the treasures of his spiritual graces, in as much as he makes us friends of all the possessions and wealth of our Lord. He reminds us therefore that Communion is given to us like a mirror in which we could look at Jesus Christ, crucified in order to save us from damnation, and resurrected in order to obtain justice and eternal life for us. It is certainly true that this same grace is offered to us by the Gospel; however, because in Communion we have a wider certainty and full possession, we rightly acknowledge such a result comes to us from it.

But because the possessions of Jesus Christ do not belong to us in any way other than that he is ours, he must first of all be given to us in the Communion, so that the things that we have said may be truly accomplished in us. For this reason, I habitually say that the matter and substance of the sacraments, is the Lord Jesus, the effectiveness is the graces and blessings that we have through this means. Now the effect of Communion is to confirm to us the reconciliation that we have with God by his death and passion, the washing of our souls that we have in the outpouring of his blood, the justice that we have in obeying him: in short, the hope of salvation that we have in everything that he did for us. Therefore the subject must be united with him or, otherwise, there would be nothing fixed or certain.

From this we must conclude that two things are presented to us in Communion, that is that Jesus Christ as the source and matter of all good, then later, the fruit and effectiveness of his death and passion, which includes also the words which are said to us therein, for in ordering us to beat his body and drink his blood, he adds that his body was delivered for us and his blood was spread for the remission of our sins [Mt 26, 28 *par*]. In which he indicates first of all that we must not simply communicate with his body and his blood without another consideration, but in order to receive the fruit which comes to us from his death and passion; on the other hand, that we can only reach the enjoyment of such a fruit by taking part in his body and his blood, from which it was produced for us.

We begin now to go into this question which was discussed so much in earlier times and in the present time, how these words where the bread is called the body of Jesus Christ and the wine his blood, which could be dismissed without any great trouble if we hold onto the principle that I have but lately held: that all the usefulness that we must week in Communion is destroyed, except that Jesus Christ should be given to us therein as the substance and foundation of everything. Having resolved this, we will doubtless confess that to deny that the true communication of Jesus Christ is presented in Communion, is to make this holy sacrament frivolous and useless, which is an abominable blasphemy and not worthy of being heard. Moreover, if the reason for communicating with Jesus Christ is that we should have a share and portion in all the graces that he obtained for us by his death, it is not only a question that we should be participants in his Spirit, but we must also take part in his humanity, in which he gave complete obedience to God his Father in order to meet our debts, although we say strictly speaking that one cannot be done without the other. For when he gives himself to us, it is in order for us to possess him completely.

For this reason, as it is said, that his Spirit is our life, also from his own mouth he states that his flesh is truly food, his blood truly drink [Jn 6,55]. If these words are not said for nothing, it is right that, in order to have our life in Christ, our souls should be filled with his body and his blood as their own food. There that is especially testified in Communion, when it is said of the bread that we should take it and eat it and that it is his body, that we should drink from the chalice and that it is his blood. Especially, the body and blood are spoken of so that we should learn to seek therein the substance of our spiritual life.

Now, if one needs to know nevertheless if the bread is the body of Christ and the wine his blood, we shall reply that the bread and wine are visible signs, which represent for us the body and blood, but that this name and title of body and blood is given to them because there are like instruments through which the Lord Jesus gives them to us. The reason for this form and manner of speaking is very suitable. For, as it may be that what may be to us an incomprehensible thing not only to the eye, but to our natural sense that the communication that we have with the body of Jesus Christ, is visibly shown to us there, as we have an example which is very suitable in a similar thing. Our Lord, wishing to make his Spirit appear at the baptism of Christ, showed it in the figure of a dove [Mt 3,16 *par*]. Saint John the Baptist, recounting this story, said that he saw the holy Spirit coming down [Jn 1,32]. If we enquire a little more closely, we shall find that he only saw the dove, considering that the Holy Spirit, in his essence, is invisible. However, knowing that this vision was not a vain figure, but a certain sign of the presence of the Holy Spirit, he has no doubt in saying that he saw it, because it showed itself to him according to its capacity. So it is in the communication that we have with the body and blood of the Lord Jesus. It is a spiritual mystery, which cannot be seen by the eye nor understood in human understanding. Therefore it is represented to us by visible signs, as our weakness

177

requires, nevertheless such that it is not a bare image, but united with its truth and substance. Therefore it is right that the bread is called the body, since it not only represents it to us, but also it presents it to us. However we shall indeed grant that the name of the body of Jesus Christ is transferred to the bread, inasmuch as it is sacrament and image. But we shall likewise add that the sacraments of the Lord must not and cannot in any way be separated from their truth and substance. To distinguish them so that one does not confuse them, is not only right and reasonable, but completely necessary. And to divide them in order to establish one without the other, is not in order.

However, when we see the visible sign, we must look at what it represents and from whom it is given to us. The bread is given to us in order to show us the body of Jesus Christ, with the order to eat it; and it is given by God who is certain and unchangeable truth. If God cannot deceive or lie, it follows that he achieves everything that he means. Therefore we must truly receive in Communion the body and blood of Jesus Christ, since the Lord represents to us in this the communion of one and the other. For otherwise, what would it mean that we should eat the bread and drink the wine in a sign that his flesh is food to his and his blood is drink, since he only gave us bread and wine, leaving the spiritual truth behind? Therefore we must confess that if the representation that God makes to us in Communion is true, the inner substance of the sacrament is united with the visible signs; and as the bread is distributed to us in our hands, the body of Christ is also given to us so that we may be made participants. When there would be nothing else, if we really have a matter with which to satisfy ourselves, when we understand that Jesus Christ in communion gives us the true substance of his body and his blood so that we should possess it in full and, in possessing it, should be in company with all his benefits. For since we have it, all of God's wealth, which is contained in him, is exposed to us so that it should be ours. Thus, in order to briefly define this usefulness of communion, we can say that Jesus Christ is offered to us therein so that we should possess him and also the fullness of the blessings that we can desire, and that in that, we have good help in confirming our consciences to the faith that we must have in him.

The second gain that it brings us is that it reprimands us and encourages us to better recognise the benefits that we have received and receive every day from the Lord Jesus, so that we should such a confession of praise as is due to him. For we ourselves are so negligent that it is wonderful to meditate on the goodness of our God, unless he awakens our laziness and drives us to do our duty. Now we do not have a needle to point us more in life than when he makes us, in a manner of speaking, sees with our eyes, touch with our hands and obviously feel such a priceless benefit, that is to say to feed us with his own substance. It is what he means by ordering us to announce his death until he comes [I Co. 11,27 ss]. Therefore if it is something so necessary for salvation not to ignore the blessings that God has given us, but to reduce them diligently into our memory and to magnify them towards others so that we should mutually enlighten ourselves, in that we see another singular usefulness of communion, that it takes ingratitude away from us and does not allow us to forget the benefit that the Lord Jesus gave us in dying for us, but leads us to give thanks and, almost by public confession, to protest how much we are obliged to him.

The third usefulness lies in that we have therein a vehement admonishment to live in a holy manner and above all to keep charity and brotherly affection between us. For since therein we are made members of Jesus Christ, being incorporated in him and united with him as to our leader, it is also a very good reason that, first of all, we should be made true to his purity and innocence, as all the members of the same body should be, although in order to directly hear of this usefulness, it must not be considered that our Lord should only warn us, encourage and inflame our hearts by the outward sign. For the main thing is that he works in us internally through his Holy Spirit, in order to have his decree made effective that he intended for that as an instrument through which he wished to carry out his work in us. Because, in as much as the virtue of the Holy Spirit is united with the sacraments when one duly receives them, we have to hope for a good means and help in order to make us grow and gain in holiness of life, and singularly in charity.

Let us come to the third main point that we have put forward at the beginning of this treatise, that is for lawful use which is to reverently observe the Lord's institution, for whoever approaches this holy sacrament with scorn or listlessness, not carrying a great deal about following where the Lord calls, he perversely takes advantage of it and, in taking advantage, contaminates it. Now to pollute and contaminate what God has sanctified so much, is an intolerable sacrilege. Therefore it is not without reason that Saint Paul denounces such a serious condemnation on all those who will take it unworthily. For if there is anything in heaven or earth of greater price and dignity than the body and blood of the Lord, it is not a small mistake to take it thoughtlessly and without being well prepared. However he asks us to experience this in order to use it appropriately (I Co 11,27*ss*]. When we understand what this examination should be, we shall know what the usage is that we seek

Here now we must keep watch carefully. For, as we cannot put too much application into examining ourselves, as the Lord commands, also on the other hand the philosophical doctors have put poor consciences into a much too dangerous perplexity, or rather a horrible torture, requiring I know not what examination of which it was not possible to come to an end[71]. In order to take us away from all these troubles, we must reduce everything, as I have already said, to the Lord's command as to the rule, which will not let us fail when we follow it. In following it, we have to experience whether we have true repentance in ourselves and true faith in our Lord Jesus Christ, which are two things that are so united that one cannot exist without the other. For if we think that our life is placed in Christ, we must acknowledge that we are dead in ourselves [cf Rm 6,3ss]. If we seek our virtue in him, we must understand that we become feeble in ourselves. If we think that our happiness is in his grace, we must understand what our wretchedness is without it. If we have our rest in him [cf Mt 11,28], we ourselves must understand that in ourselves we only feel torment and anxiety.

Now such an attachment cannot be, that it does not first of all create a dissatisfaction with our whole life, then later a concern and fear, in the end a desire and love of justice. For he who knows the baseness of his soul and the unhappiness of his state and condition, though he is estranged from God, is so ashamed of it that he is obliged to dislike himself, to condemn himself, to groan and sigh very sadly. Moreover, God's

---

[71] Calvin grasps here the Roman theologians and to the practice of a magnified examination of conscience.

judgment shows itself as unchaste, which presses the sinful conscience with amazing anguish, so much that it sees that there is no means of escape and has only to reply for his defence. When with such acknowledgment of our wretchedness we can taste God's goodness, then we wish to arrange our life according to his will and renounce all our previous life in order to be made into new creatures [cf. 2 Co 5,17].

Therefore if we duly wish to communicate with the holy Lord's Supper, we must in strong trust in our hearts hold the Lord Jesus for our only justice, life and salvation, receiving and accepting the promises that are given to us by him as certain and guaranteed, on the other hand renouncing all contrary trust, in order that in us and from all creatures, we should rest completely in him and be happy with his grace alone. Now, because that cannot be, unless we do not know the need that we have that he should come to our aid, it is our occupation that we should also be touched deeply within our hearts with a true feeling of our wretchedness, which makes us hungry and thirsty for him. And in fact, what mockery it would be to come looking for food without an appetite? Now, in order to have a good appetite, it is not enough that the stomach should be empty, but it needs to be well inclined and capable of receiving its food. From this therefore it follows that our souls must be beset by famine and have a desire and burning zeal to be fed to really find their food in the Communion of the Lord.

Moreover, it remains to be noted that we can desire Jesus Christ without aspiring to God's justice, which lies in the sacrifice of ourselves and obedience to his will, for there is no order that we should claim to be from the body of Christ, abandoning us to all licence and leading a dissolute life. Since in Christ there is only chastity, benignity, sobriety, truth, humility and all such virtues, if we want to be his members, it is necessary for all lewdness, superiority, intemperance, lying, pride and similar vices to be far away from us. For we cannot mix these things with him without doing great dishonour and shame to him. He must always make us remember that there is no more conformity between him and sin than between light and shade. That is how we shall come to him in true repentance if we are aiming to make our life comply with the example of Jesus Christ.

However, although that may be general in all parts of our life, if it particularly has a place in charity, as it is above all recommended in this sacrament, for which reason it is called the link to that.[72] For as bread is sanctified there for the common use of all of us is made of several grains which are so mixed together that one could not distinguish one from the other, so we must be united between us with insoluble friendship. And what is more, we all receive the same body of Christ there, so that we may be made members of it. Therefore if we have disagreements and discords together, it is not up to us that Jesus Christ should not be torn to pieces, and we will be guilty of a similar sacrilege as if we had done so. Therefore it is not necessary for us to presume not to approach it at all if we carry some hatred or bitterness to a living man, and mainly to any Christian who may be in the unity of the Church. We must also, in order to carry out the instruction of the lord, bring another attachment: it is to confess with our mouth and witness how much we are indebted to our Saviour [cf Rom 10,9] and give him thanks, not only so that his name may be glorified in us, but also in order to

---

[72] Quotation from Saint Augustine, *In Joannis Evangelium Tract.* (Commentary on the Gospel of John) 26, 13 (MIGNE PL 35,1613).

enlighten others and teach them by our example for what they have to do.

But in order that a man will not be found on the earth who has gained so much in faith and in holiness of life that he may not still have a great deal of weakness as much in one way as another, there would be a danger that several good consciences were not troubled by what was said, if one did not come forward in moderating the lessons that we have taught, as much in faith as in repentance. However, it is a dangerous way of teaching that some people have, to require a perfect heartfelt trust and perfect penitence and to exclude all those who do not have this. As it may be, who will be the one who cannot boast not to be tainted with some defiance? Not to be subject to some vice or weakness? Certainly, the children of God have such faith that they always have the need to pray that the Lord should come to their incredulity [cf Mc 9,24]. For it is a sickness which is so well rooted in our nature that we are never completely cured of it, that we may not be delivered from this prison of our body.

Moreover, they travel to such an extent in purity of life that they have a need to pray every day as much for remission of sins as to ask for grace to gain more from it. Although some may be more imperfect, others less so, however there is no-one who does not fail in many ways. Thus Communion not only would be of no use to anyone, but also pernicious if we had to bring to it integrity of faith or of life which there would be nothing to find fault with. What is contrary to the intention of our Lord, for he has given nothing more beneficial to his Church. However, when we shall feel an imperfect faith in us and we will not have such a pure conscience that it does not accuse us of a great many vices, that does not prevent us from presenting ourselves at the holy table of the Lord, on condition

184

that in the middle of this weakness we should feel in our hearts that, without hypocrisy and pretence, we are expecting the salvation of Jesus Christ and wish to live according to the rule of the Gospel. I say particularly: that there is no hypocrisy, for there are a great many people who deceive themselves with vain flatteries, making themselves trust that it is enough to condemn their vices, although they are still being committed, or to release themselves for a while so that they can come back immediately afterwards. Now true penitence is fixed and steady; however, it works in us not for a day or a week, but endlessly and ceaselessly to struggle against the evil that is within us.

Therefore when we feel a strong distress and hatred of all vices coming from the fear of God and a wish to live well in order to please our Lord, we are capable of taking part in Communion, notwithstanding the residue of weakness that we carry in our flesh. Even, if we were not weak, subject to distrust and with an imperfect life, the sacrament would be of no use to us and it would have been superfluous to establish it. Since it is a remedy that God has given us to meet our weakness, strengthen our faith, increase our charity, improve us in all holiness of life, so much more must we use it as we feel that our sickness urges us on. It is so important that it such a thing must not prevent us from it. For if we allege, in order to exempt us from coming to Communion, that we are still weak in faith or in integrity of life, if is as if a man excused himself from taking medicine, because he is ill. Therefore that is how weakness of faith that we feel in our hearts and the imperfections which are in our lives must encourage us to come to Communion as a singular remedy for correcting them. Only, that we should not come there devoid of faith and repentance, the first of which is hidden within the heart; however, our conscience must give witness of it in front of God. The second is manifest in works, however it must not appear at all in our life. As for the time to partake of it, it cannot be limited for everyone for sure. For there are some times of special hindrances which excuse a man if he abstains. And moreover, we have no express commandment to oblige all Christians to use it every day that it is presented to them. However, if we look carefully at the end to which the Lord leads us, we shall know that it must be partaken of more often than it is used by a great many people.[73] For in so far as feebleness besets us, we have a duty to exert ourselves so much more often in what can and must act to confirm us in faith and advance in purity of life. However this custom must be, in all well ordered Churches, to celebrate Communion often as much as the people are able to sustain it. And each person in his particular place must prepare himself to receive it as often as it is administered in the congregation, unless there is a great hindrance which forces him to keep away. Although we do not have an express commandment which defines for us the time and day, it must be enough for us to know that our Lord's intention is such that we should partake of it often, otherwise we do not know really well how useful it is to us.

The excuses that some people make, on the other hand, are too frivolous. Some of them say that they do not think they are worthy and, under the shade of that, they keep away from it for the whole year. Others are not content with looking at their worthy, but claim that they could not communicate with others whom they see

---

[73] In 1537, Calvin had offered to celebrate Communion every week. In 1541, on his return from Strasbourg, he recommended it should be done once a month, but the Council upheld the rhythm of four celebrations per year.

186

coming without proper preparation. There are also others who think that it is a superfluous thing to partake of it often, because if we have once received Jesus Christ, there is not now a duty to return so soon after receiving it. I ask the first of these, who are covered in their unworthiness, how their conscience can bear to stay for more than a year in such a poor state that they cannot directly call upon God. For they will confess to me that it is rashness to call upon God as our Father if we are not members of Jesus Christ, which cannot be less than that the substance and truth of Communion are not accomplished in us. Now if we have the truth, we are for a stronger reason capable of receiving the sign. Therefore we see that the man who wishes to exempt himself from receiving Communion as he is unworthy excludes himself from praying to God. As for the rest, I do not intend to force consciences which are tormented by some scruples so that they may presume without knowing how, but rather I counsel them to wait until the Lord has delivered them. Similarly, if there is a lawful reason which prevents them, I do not deny that it may not be right to differ. I only want to show that no-one should agree to that, to keep away from Communion due to being unworthy, considering that, in so doing, he deprives himself of the communion of the Church in which all our benefits lie. Moreover, he should make an effort to fight against all the hindrances that the devil will put before him, in order not to be excluded from such a great benefit and as a result, from the all graces which follows from privation.

The second group of people have some colour, because they take this argument, in other words, that it is not lawful to eat bread in common with those who call themselves brothers and lead a dissolute and wicked life [Co 5,11]; for a stronger reason, we must keep ourselves from communicating with them in the bread of the Lord, which is blessed for us to represent and dispense the body of Christ. But the reply is not too difficult: that it is not the duty of a particular person to judge and discern in order to admit or send away as he seems fit, considering that this prerogative belongs to the whole Church generally[74], or even to the pastor with the Old Christians that he must have in order to help him in governing the Church. For Saint Paul does not order us to examine others, but for everyone to examine himself [I Co 11,28]. It is true that our duty is to counsel those that we see living in a reckless manner, and if they do not wish to listen to us, to warn the pastor so that he can deal with them by ecclesiastical authority. But it is not the means of withdrawing from the company of wicked people by leaving the communion of the Church. Moreover, most often it will happen that the crimes are not so notorious that one could be brought to excommunication. For although the pastor may judge some man unworthy, however he does not have the power to proclaim him as such and to forbid Communion to him, unless he may be convicted by an ecclesiastical judgment. In such a case, we have only the measure of praying to God that he may deliver his Church more and more from all scandals, waiting for the last day in which the straw will be completely separated from the good grain [cf Mt 3,12].

The third group of people have no appearance of verisimilitude. For the spiritual bread is not given to us in order that we should eat it straight away, but rather so that in having had some taste of its sweetness, we should long for it more and should partake of it when it

---

[74] On this subject see *Institution* IV, XII, 2 and 5. The ecclesiastical discipline proposed by Calvin foresaw excommunication as the ultimate sanction of ecclesiastical authority.

is offered to us. It is what we have explained above, that while we converse in this mortal life, Jesus Christ is never communicated to us in such a way that our souls may be satisfied at all, but he wants us to be fed continually.

In order to come to the fourth main point, the Devil, knowing that our Lord had left nothing more useful to his Church than this holy sacrament, according to his usual manner made a great effort from the beginning to contaminate it with mistakes and superstitions in order to corrupt and destroy the fruit, and has not stopped carrying out this work until he has almost completely overturned the Lord's decree and to change it into a lie and vanity. My intention is not to mark in what period each such abuse began to happen and in what period it was increased. It will be sufficient for me to note by articles which mistakes the Devil has introduced, of which we must beware if we wish to have the Lord's Supper in its fullness.

For the first part, as it may be that the Lord has given us his Communion in order that it should be distributed among us in order to witness to us that in communicating with his body, we are taking part in the sacrifice that he gave on the cross to God his Father for the expiation and satisfaction of our sins, men, in their own heads, have on the other invented that it is a sacrifice through which we obtain remission of our sins before God. That is a sacrifice which cannot in any way stand. For if we do not recognise the death of our Lord Jesus and hold it as a unique sacrifice through which he has reconciled us to the Father, blocking out all the mistakes for which we were accountable to the Father, we are destroying its virtue. If we do not confess that Jesus Christ is the only Sacrificer – that we commonly call a priest – through the intercession of which we are reduced in the grace of the father, we strip him of his honour and greatly insult him [cf Hb 4,14 *ss*; Rm 8,34]. Therefore then that this opinion that one has had of Communion, that it was a sacrifice to obtain remission of sins, does not derogate to that, it must be condemned as diabolical. Now if it does derogate to it, it is too notorious a thing. For how would one reconcile these things together that Jesus Christ in dying should have offered a sacrifice to his Father through which he as once forever obtained remission and grace for all our mistakes [cf Hb 10,9 *ss*], and that one must daily make a sacrifice in order to obtain what one must only look for in that death?

In the beginning this mistake was not so extreme, but little by little it gathered strength, until it has come to this. It seems that the old Fathers called Communion sacrifice. But they give as the reason that the death of Jesus Christ is represented in it. So their story comes back to this, that this name is given to it only because it is a remembrance of this single sacrifice before which we must stop completely, although I cannot faithfully excuse the custom of the old Church. It is that one represented, by gestures and way of acting, a type of sacrifice which was almost like a similar ceremony that took place in the Old Testament, except that instead of a wild beast, bread was used as the host. Because that goes too near to Judaism and does not respond to the Lord's institution, I do not approve of it. For in the Old Testament, at the time of images[75], the Lord had ordered such ceremonies while waiting for this sacrifice to be made in the flesh of his beloved Son, which was the fulfilment of it. Since he was perfect, there is nothing left except for us to receive the communication,

---

[75] The Old Testament is considered here as the prefiguration of the New Alliance, and his people and events as images of Christ and episodes of his earthly life. On this matter the development of the Bible of Olivetan, can be read in the present volume.

because it is superfluous to have another image. And thus stands the order that Jesus Christ left us: not that we should offer or sacrifice, but that we should take and eat what was offered and sacrificed.

However, although there may be some weakness in such an observation if there were not an impiety as it has come down to us. For we have completely transferred to the Mass what was proper for the death of Christ, that is to satisfy God for our debts and, by these means, to reconcile ourselves with him. Moreover, the role of Jesus Christ has been assigned to those that are called priests, that is to sacrifice to God and, in sacrificing, to intercede for us to obtain grace and pardon for our mistakes. I do not wish to hide the solutions which the enemies of truth put forward: that is that the Mass is not a new sacrifice, but only an application of the one sacrifice of which we have spoken. Although they put a little colour into their abomination by speaking in this way, however it is only simple hair-splitting. For it is not only said that Christ's sacrifice is unique, but that it must never be repeated in as much as its effectiveness remains forever [Hb 10,18]. It is not said that Christ offered himself once to the Father in order that others later might make the same offering in order for us to apply the virtue of his intercession, but that he entered the heavenly sanctuary and there, he appears in order to make the Father favourable to us by his intercession [Hb 9,24].

As for applying for ourselves the merit of his death so that we should feel the benefit of it, that is done not in the way that has been considered in the papal Church, but when we receive the message of the Gospel, as it is witnessed to us by the preaching of ministers, whom God has established as his ambassadors, and sealed by the sacraments. The opinion of all the people was approved by all their

191

doctors and prelates that in hearing or having the mass said, through this devotion one would deserve grace and justice with God. We say that in order to feel any benefit from Communion, we do not need to bring anything of ourselves in order to deserve what we are seeking, but that we only have to receive in faith the grace which is presented to us therein, which does not dwell in the sacrament, but sends us back to the cross of Jesus Christ, as it proceeds from it. Therefore there is nothing more contrary to the true understanding of Communion than to make a sacrifice of it, which takes us away from recognising the death of Christ as a single sacrifice, the virtue of which lasts forever.

Having understood that, it will appear that all Masses in which there is no communion such as the Lord has established are only an abomination. For the Lord has not ordained that a single priest, after making his sacrifice, should play his part separately, but he wished the sacrament to be distributed to the gathering, in the example of the first Communion that he took with his apostles. But after this cursed opinion, this opinion itself like from a chasm there came a custom that the people, contenting themselves with being present there in order to take part in the merit of what is done there, abstain from communion because the priest asserts himself in offering his host for everyone, and particularly for his assistants. I am refraining from talking about the abuses which are so heavy that they are not worthy of mention, as to assign his mass to each saint and transfer what is said in the Communion of the Lord to saint William and Saint Gautier. Likewise to have fun in the ordinary way in order to sell and buy, and such other offences that the word sacrifice has created.

The second mistake that the Devil has sown in order to corrupt this holy mystery has been in creating and inventing a practice that after the words pronounced with the intention of consecrating, the bread is transubstantiated into the body of Christ and the wine into his blood. This lie, first of all, has no foundation in Scripture and is not witnessed at all by the old Church and, what is more, can in no way go along with or exist with the Word of God. Is it not a forced explanation when Jesus Christ, showing the bread, calls it his body, to say that the substance of the bread is annihilated and in its place there comes the body of Christ? But it is not right now to put the matter back into question, considering that the truth is obvious enough to disprove this absurdity. I am leaving endless testimonies, as much in Scripture as in the old fathers, where the sacrament is called bread. I only say that the nature of the sacrament needs this, that the material bread remains for a visible sign of the body. For it is a general rule for all sacraments that the signs that we see there must have some similarity with the spiritual thing that appears there[76] Therefore as in baptism we have the certainty of the inner washing of our souls when the water for it is given to us as a witness, which cleans our bodily dirt, it is also necessary that in Communion there should be material bread in order to give witness to us that the body of Christ is our food. For otherwise, what meaning would the whiteness have for us? Therefore we see clearly how all the representation, which the Lord wanted to give us to yield to our weakness, would perish, unless the bread remained. For the words that the Lord uses imply as much, as he said: in the same way as man is sustained and kept alive according to the body in eating bread, so my flesh is the spiritual food with which souls are brought alive.

---

[76] Calvin has exposed in detail his idea of the sacrament in *The Institution* IV, XIV.

193

Moreover, what would the other similarity given by Saint Paul become? It is as if several grains of wheat are mixed together in order to make a loaf, so we need to be united together, since we all share in one bread [I Co 10,17][77]. If there was only whiteness without substance, would it not be a mockery to speak like this? However, no doubt we conclude that this transubstantiation is an invention forged by the Devil in order to corrupt the truth of Communion.

From this fantasy several other stupid ideas came out later. And may it please God that there may be only stupid ideas and not gross abominations. For I have thought of any local presence and I thought that Jesus Christ, in his divine humanity, was attached to this whiteness without considering all the absurdities which follow from it. Although the old doctors in the Sorbonne may argue more subtly how the body and blood are united with the signs, however one cannot deny that this opinion was not received by the great and the small in the papal Church and that it is not today cruelly upheld by fire and sword, that Jesus-Christ is contained under these signs and that there, one must seek him. Now, in order to uphold that, one must confess either that the body of Christ is endless, or that he can be in various places. And in saying that, we come in the end to the point that it is no different at all from a ghost. Therefore to wish to establish such a presence through which the body of Christ would be enclosed within the sign or united with it locally, is not only a dream, but a damnable mistake, opposing the

---

[77] It is in the *Didache* (or Doctrine of the Lord by the Twelve Apostles) 9,4 which uses this image on the basis of I Co 10, in the Eucharistic prayer: "As this bread broken first of all scattered on the hills was gathered in order to make only one, so that your Church may be the same..." (trad. Fr. De France QUERE, *Les Peres apostoliques,* Seuil, coll. Points/Sagesses, 1980).

glory of Christ and destroying what we must grasp of his human nature. For Scripture teaches us everywhere that as the Lord Jesus has taken on our humanity on earth, he has also exalted it to heaven, taking it away from a mortal condition, but not by changing its nature [*cf* Ph 2,6 *ss*].

Thus we have two things to consider when we speak about this humanity: it is that we do not take away the truth of its nature and that we do not derogate to its glorious position. In order to observe that properly, we always have to lift our thoughts on high in order to look for our redeemer. For if we do not want to bring him down under the corruptible elements of this world, over and above destroying what Scripture shows us of his human nature, we are annihilating the glory of his Ascension. Because several others have fully dealt with this matter, I am going to go beyond it. I only wanted to note in passing that to include Jesus Christ by fantasy under the bread and the wine, or unite him in such a way with them, that our understanding enjoys itself there without looking up to heaven, is a diabolical dream. And also we shall deal with this again in another place.

Now this perverse opinion, after being received once, as given rise to a great many superstitions, and first of all this fleshly adoration, which is only pure idolatry. For to prostrate oneself in front of the bread of Communion and worship Jesus Christ in it as if he were inside it, is to make it into an idol instead of a sacrament. We are not ordered to worship, but to take and eat. Therefore it was no need to try that in such a reckless manner. Moreover, it has always been noticed in the old Church that before celebrating Communion, the people were solemnly exhorted to lift up their hearts on high in order to show that one did not need to stop in front of the visible sign in order to truly worship Jesus

Christ.[78]   But one has only to argue at length on this point when the presence and unity of truth with the sign, of which we have spoken and shall speak later, will be well understood.   The other superstitious practices come from a similar source, such as carrying the sacrament in pomp through the streets once a year[79] and to make a tabernacle for it on another day and, throughout the year, to keep it in a cupboard in order to entertain the people, as if it were God. Because all of that was not only invented without the Word of God, but is also directly contrary to the institution of Communion, it must be rejected by all Christians.

We have shown where this calamity in the papal Church comes from, that the people abstain from communicating with Communion throughout the year, that is because it is held as a sacrifice, which is offered by one person in the name of everyone. But again, when it is a question of partaking of it once a year, it is shabbily destroyed and as if torn into pieces, for instead of distributing the sacrament of the blood to the people, as the Lord's commandment orders it, they are made to believe that they must be content with the other half. Thus the poor faithful people are wickedly defrauded of the grace that the Lord had given them. For it is not a small blessing to communicate with the Lord's blood for our food, it is too great a cruelty to take it away from those to whom it belongs.

In that, we can see with what audacity and impudence the Pope has tyrannised the Church after it once occupied the domination.   Our Lord, having ordered his disciples to eat the bread which was sanctified in his body, when it comes to the chalice he does not say simply: drink, but he adds especially that

---

[78] This is the *Sursum corda (Lift up your hearts)* of the old liturgy.

[79] Calvin refers here to the processions of Corpus Christi which take place on the Thursday after Trinity Sunday.

all should drink it [Mt 26,26 *par*]. Would we want anything clearer than that? He says that we should eat the bread without using the word universal. He said that we should all drink from the chalice. Where does this difference come from, unless he wanted to confront the Devil's evil? And nevertheless the pride of the Pope is that he dares to say: all of you, do not drink of it. And in order to show that he is cleverer than God, he alleges that it is right for the priest should have some privilege beyond the people in order to honour the priestly dignity. As if our Lord were not aware of how one must be discerned by the other.

Moreover, he objects to the dangers which could occur if the chalice were commonly given to everyone, it is that sometimes a drop could be spilled. As if our Lord had not foreseen that. Is it not to be argued with God quite openly that he confused the order that he had to observe and put his people in danger without any purpose? In order to show that there is no great problem in this alteration, he shows that under one type, everything is included, all the more as the body cannot be divided from the blood, as if the Lord had distinguished one from the other, in vain. For if one can leave one of the parts behind as superfluous, that would have been crazy to recommend them distinctly.

Some of his henchmen, seeing that it was effrontery to uphold this abomination, wanted to cover it otherwise: it is that Jesus Christ, in instituting the sacrifice, only spoke to his apostles whom he had set up in a priestly order. But what would they answer to what Saint Paul says, that each person should eat of this bread and drink of this chalice [I Co 11,23]? And in fact, who revealed to them that our Lord gave Communion to his apostles as to priests? For the words sing the opposite when he orders them to act according to his example. Therefore he gives them the rule, which

197

he wants to be held forever in his Church, as it was held in olden times, until Antichrist, having gained tyranny, has openly raised his horns against God and his truth in order to destroy it completely. Therefore we see that it is an intolerable perversity to thus divide and tear the sacrament apart, separating the parts that God has united.

In order to come to an end, we will understand under an article what could otherwise be distinguished. It is that the Devil has introduced the manner of celebrating Communion without any doctrine and, instead of the doctrine, has substituted a great many ceremonies which are partially foolish and useless, also partially dangerous and from which a great deal of evil has come, such that the mass, which is held for Communion in the papal Church, in order to define it properly, is only a pure monkey trick and transport of the mind. I call it a monkey trick because in that there is an attempt to fake the Lord's Communion for no reason, like a monkey, thoughtlessly and without discretion, following what he sees he can do.

So it may be, the main thing that our Lord has recommended to us is to celebrate this mystery with true intelligence. It therefore follows that the substance lies in doctrine. If that is taken away, it is no more than cold ineffective ceremony. That is not only shown by Scripture, but also witnessed by the Pope's canons in an alleged sentence of Saint Augustine where he asks what the water of baptism can be without the word, except a corruptible element, the word, he says afterwards at once, not insofar as it is pronounced, but understood[80]. In that he means that the sacraments take their virtue from the word when it is preached

---

[80] Saint Augustine, *In Joannis Evangelium* Tract, 70 (MIGNE *PL* 35, 1840).

intelligently; without that, that they are not worthy of being called sacraments. Now it is so necessary to have intelligible doctrine in the mass, that on the other hand one would think that the whole mystery was spoilt, except that everything should be done and said secretly, so that nothing is heard. However their consecration is only a type of sorcery, considering that in the style of socerers, by murmuring and making a great many signs, they think that they can force Jesus Christ to come down into their hands. Therefore we see how the mass, being so ordered that it is an obvious desecration of the Communion of Christ, rather an observation of it and that the true and that it lacks the main substance of the Communion, which is that the mystery should be well explained to the people and the promises clearly spoken, not that a priest should aside murmur everything low, without sense or reason.

I also call it a transport because the hotchpotch and grimaces that are present there a more suitable to a farce than to such a mystery as the sacred Communion of the Lord. It is really true that the sacrifices in the Old Testament were done with several decorations and ceremonies. But because there was a good meaning and that everything was suitable for teaching and leading the people in piety, it could be said that they were like those that are practised now, which are useful for nothing but to entertain the people without being useful at all. Because the Mass-goers[81] allege this example of the old Testament in order to defend their ceremonies, we must note what a difference there is between what they do and what God had ordered the people of Israel to do. When that was the only thing, what one saw then was based on the Lord's commandment and, on the other hand, all their

---

[81] Those who partake of the Mass.

frivolities have no foundation other than men, still there would be great dissimilarity.

But we have a great deal more with which to reprimand them, for it is not without reason that our Lord had ordered such a form for a time, so that it should come to an end and should be repealed sometimes. For because he had not yet given his doctrine in a very clear manner, he wanted the people to be led in more symbols in order to compensate for what was lacking in another place[82]. Since we have seen the body, we must chase the shadows away, for if we want to restore the ceremonies which are abolished, that is to rebuild the veil of the Temple that Jesus Christ tore down by his death and darken the clarity of his Gospel all the more. Thus we see that such a multitude of ceremonies in the mass is a form of Judaism which is completely contrary to Christianity. I do not wish to reprimand the ceremonies, which serve honesty and public order and increase reverence for the sacrament, through which they should be made sober and suitable. But such an endless abyss without end and measurement is in no way tolerable, considering even that it has given rise to a thousand superstitions and has put the people almost into stupidity, without bringing any incitement to virtue.

From that one may also see the difference which those to whom God has given knowledge of his truth, with the papists. First of all, they will not doubt that it may not be an abominable sacrifice to state that the mass is a sacrifice through which the remission of sins may be obtained for us, or even that the priest may be like a mediator in order to apply the merit of the death and passion of Christ to those who will buy his mass or

---

[82] Calvin developed this idea of the usefulness of the ceremonies of the Old Alliance in *Institution* Ii, VII, 1 and XI, 4 in particular.

who will attend it or who are devoted to it, but on the contrary, they will have concluded that the death and passion of the Lord is the only sacrifice through which he was satisfied in the anger of God, and perpetual justice is obtained for us; similarly, that the Lord Jesus has gone into the heavenly sanctuary in order to appear there on our behalf and to intercede with the virtue of his sacrifice [Hb 9,24 *ss*]. Apart from that, they will indeed concede that the fruit of that death is communicated in Communion, not by the merit of the work, but on account of the promises that are given to us therein, through which we should receive them in faith.

Secondly, they should not at all accept that the bread should be transubstantiated into the body of Jesus Christ, nor the wine into his blood, but must persist on this question that the visible signs retain their true substance in order to represent to us the spiritual truth we have mentioned. Thirdly, it may already be that they must hold as true that the Lord gives us in Communion what he shows us there and thus we truly receive the body and blood of Jesus Christ. Nevertheless, they will not seek it as though it were inside the bread or locally attached to the visible sign, it is so necessary for them to worship the sacrament, but they will rather lift up their understanding and their hearts upwards in order to receive Jesus Christ than to worship him. Out of this it will occur that they will scorn and condemn as idolatry all those superstitious both to carry the sacrament in pomp and procession, and to build tabernacles to have him worshipped, for our Lord's promises do not extend beyond the use that he has left us.

Later, they will maintain that to deprive the people of one of the parts of the sacrament, in other words the chalice, is to violate and corrupt the Lord's decree, and

201

that in order to observe it properly, both should be distributed completely. Finally, they will state that it is not only a useless superabundance, but also dangerous and unsuitable for Christianity, to use so many ceremonies taken from the Jews, beyond the simplicity that the apostles have left us, and that it is even more perversity to celebrate the Mass through affectations and any overwhelming raptures, unless the doctrine is recited there, but rather it is buried inside it, as if Communion was a type of magic art.

In order to come to an end, it is time to come to the last main point: it is the dispute which has been fought in our time on this matter. Now because it was unhappy, as doubtless the Devil stirred it up in order to prevent, indeed even to break the circulation of the Gospel, I would like the memory of this to be completely abolished, while it is necessary for me to refrain to make a long speech about it. Nevertheless, because I see a great many good consciences upset because they do not know which way to turn, I shall briefly say what counsel seems to be required in order to show them how they must resolve this.

First of all, I would ask all faithful people in God's name not to be too offended that such a great dispute was stirred up between those who must be like captains in order to put truth back into light. For it is not a new thing that the Lord should leave his servants in some ignorance and allow them to fight with one another, not in order to leave them there forever, but only for a period in order to be humble. And in fact, if everything came to perfection until now without any hardship, men could become misunderstood, or God's grace might have been less well-known than it appeared. Thus the Lord wanted to take away every type of glory from men in order to be the only glorified one. Moreover, if we consider in what an abyss of shadows the world was found when those who stirred up this controversy began to reduce us to truth, we are not at all amazed that they did not know everything in the beginning. Rather it is a miracle that our Lord, in such a short space of time, enlightened them so much that they were thus able to come out of this mire of mistakes and withdraw the others, into which we had been plunged for so long. But there is nothing better than to describe how the thing went because from that it will appear that we did not have such a great opportunity to be offended in this place, as we think communally to such an extent.

When Luther began to teach, he dealt in such a way with the matter of Communion that, on the bodily presence of Christ, he seemed to think that he should leave it as the world viewed it for the moment. For in condemning transubstantiation, he said that the bread was the body of Christ especially as he was united with it. Further, he added similarities, which were rather hard and severe. But he did so as through compulsion, because he could not explain his thinking otherwise. For it is difficult to make such a high thing understood, unless one refers to some impropriety.

On the other hard Zwingli and Oecolampade[83] who, considering the abuse and deceit that the Devil had used in establishing such a bodily presence of Christ that had been taught and upheld for more than six hundred years, thought that it was not permissible to hide it, even since that included an abominable idolatry in that Jesus Christ was worshipped within it as though he were enclosed under the bread. Now because it was too difficult to take way this opinion deep-rooted for such a long time in the hearts of men, they applied all their understanding to shout against it, pointing out that

---

[83] Oecolampade (from his German name Johannes Hausschein, 1482-1531), reformer of Basle, was very close to Zwingli (1484-1531), the reformer of Zurich.

it was a heavy mistake not to acknowledge what is so well testified in Scripture, on the Ascension of Jesus Christ, and that he was received in his humanity in heaven, where he shall remain until he comes down to judge the world. While they were dawdling on this point, they forgot to show which presence of Jesus Christ one must believe to be in Communion and what communication from his body and his blood is received there, such that Luther thought that they should not wish to leave anything but the naked signs, without their spiritual substance. So he began to resist them head-on until he denounced them as heretics. From the time that the dispute first started, it always became inflamed with time and thus was tossed about too bitterly over the space of fifteen years or about that, without some of them had wanted to listen to the others with a peaceful heart. For although they had once conferred together,[84] nevertheless there was such estrangement that they came back without any agreement. Even, instead of coming near some good allowances, they always withdrew more and more, not looking at anything other than to defend their judgment and refute everything that was contrary.

Therefore we have the matter in which Luther failed on his part and in which Oecolampade and Zwingli failed on theirs. It was on order from Luther to warn that he did not intend to establish such a local presence as the papists dreamed of; *item*, to protest that he did not want to have the sacrament worshipped instead of God; thirdly, to abstain from these similarities which were so rough and difficult to imagine, or to make use of them moderately, interpreting them so that they could not create any scandal. Once the debate had been stirred up, it knew no bounds, both in declaring his

---

[84] They had met at Marbourg in October 1529.

opinion and in blaming the others with too strict a bitterness of tongue. For instead of exposing himself in such a way that one could accept his judgment, according to his usual vehemence, in order to impugn the objectors, he used hyperbolic forms of speech, which were very hard to bring to those who otherwise were not very well-disposed to believe what he said.

The others offended too, en that they were so eager to cry out against the superstitious and fantastic opinion of the papists, on the local presence of the body of Jesus Christ within the sacrament and the perverse adoration which followed from it, that they tried harder to ruin the evil than to build up the goodness. For although they had not denied the truth, however they had not taught it as clearly as they should have. I understand that by taking too much trouble to uphold that the bread and the wine re named the body and blood of Christ because they are signs of him, they did not take trouble to add that they are such signs that truth is united with them, and thus to protest that they did not claim at all to cloud the true communion that the Lord gives us in his body and his blood through this sacrament.

One party and the other has erred in not having the patience to listen to each other in order to follow the truth unaffectedly where it would be found. Nevertheless, surely we must not stop thinking what our duty is; it is not to forget the graces that the Lord has given them and the blessings that he has given us through their hands and through their own means. For if we are not ungrateful and repudiating of what we owe to them, we can truly forgive that and more, without passing censure on them or slandering them. In short, since we see them to have been and still be, partly, of a holy life and excellent intelligence, and full of outstanding zeal to build the Church, we must always consider them to speak with modesty and reverence, and even, since in the end it pleased our good God, after having thus humiliated them, to put an end to this unhappy quarrel or at least to calm it down, while waiting for it to be finally decided. I say that because there is still no formula which has been published where the agreement was drawn up, as ought to be done. But that will be when it pleases God to gather in one place who wish to draw it up.[85] However, it must suffice for us that there is brotherhood and communion between the Churches and that we all agree as far as necessary to meet together, according to God's commandment.

Therefore we all confess with one mouth that in receiving the sacrament in faith, according to the Lord's command, we are truly all made participants in the true substance of the body and blood of Jesus Christ. However that is done, some can deduce it better and more clearly expose it than the others. On the one hand we must, in order to keep out all earthly fantasies, lift up our hearts to heaven, not thinking that the Lord Jesus came down here to be included in some corruptible elements. On the other hand, in order not to lessen the efficacity of this holy mystery, we must think that that is done through the secret and miraculous virtue of God and that the Spirit of God is the connection with this participation, for which reason it is called spiritual.

---

[85] In 1549, Calvin and Bullinger, Zwingli's successor in Zurich, drew up the "Zurich Agreement". (Consensus Tigurinus) But the doctrinal differences with the Lutherans did not stop them poisoning themselves. The official reconciliation between Reformed people and Lutherans took place in our century, with the Concord of Leuenberg in March 1973, an agreement script which cancels the excommunications that were pronounced. The French text will be found in *Lutheran Positions* 21/3, July 1973.

VERY USEFUL NOTICE
Of the great benefit which would come to Christianity,
If it made an inventory of all the holy bodies, and relics,
Which are in Italy, in France, Germany, Spain and other Kingdoms and countries.
By Monsieur Jean Calvin
PRINTED IN GENEVA,
By Jean Girard.
1543.

J. Calvin Treatise on Relics – Introduction

Historic circumstances

The year 1541 marks the publication of several treatises written by Calvin against the Roman Catholic Church. Beyond the *Treatise on relics,* the text of which we reproduce here, the Reformer in the same year brings out the *Defence of the doctrine of the Serbian judge* aimed against the famous Catholic disputant Albert Pigge (ca.1490-1542)[86], the *Entreaty and admonishment on the fact of Christianity and the Church reformation sent to the Emperor*[87] and the *Little Treatise showing what a faithful man should do among the papists*[88]. The first two treatises appeared first of all in Latin, while the *Little Treatise*, like the *Treatise on Relics,* were written and published straight away in French. The question of the language of writing is closely linked with its aim and for the public which

---

[86]*Calv. Opp.VI, 225-404.*
[87] Ibid.453-543
[88] Ibid.637-588.

were described by Calvin in each of his works. The *Reply to Pigge* (who himself was dead at the time of the publication) is placed within the family of scholarly polemic literature. It is the work of a theologian addressed to another theologian. As for the *Entreaty to the Emperor*, it represents an official step that Calvin took to Charles the Fifth, in order to ask him to continue *the effort* in the way of reforming the Church.

The public covered by the *Little Treatise* and by the *Treatise on Relics* is broader. It is a question, in the case of the first, of exhorting the faithful not to give in to "papist idolatry", even when they are in a place where worship has not been reformed. The aim of the second text, as we shall see, is to put the faithful on their guard against the worship of relics. In spite of the diversity of aims, the theology of the four treatises stays the same and is a witness to Calvin's basic preoccupation at that time. The main thing is to purify the Church from any human work which only clouds the glory of God. In the *Reply to Pigge*, the Reformer underlines, by quoting Jn 15,5, that man cannot be saved unless he puts his whole confidence in God. In the *Entreaty*, he emphasises the true worship of God as being exempt from "human superstitions". In the *Little Treatise*, he emphasises that yielding to "idolatry" even if "the heart stays pure", is to turn away from God and place one's confidence in men. It is appropriate to note that during the years 1541-43, Calvin was above all preoccupied by pastoral and ecclesiastical questions. He wanted to build the reformed Church of Geneva on the model which had already been designed in 1537 before his expulsion. It is this same preoccupation which is manifest in his literary activity during these years.

Usually considered as a monument of the French language[89], this treatise is counted also among the most openly satirical works of Calvin. Not being addressed to the theological public, his argumentation is well defined and easy to discern. According to Calvin, the worship of relics is bad in itself as it turns the faithful away from the true adoration of God. Instead of seeking Christ "in his word, in his sacraments and in his grace, one takes pleasure in his robes, his shirts and his flags". It is the same for the apostles and the other saints. These should not be worshipped either in themselves, nor through the objects which would have belonged to them. We must meditate on their piety, in order to be able to follow their example. In a different way from some other reformers, in particular Philippe Melanchthon, Calvin does not consider relics and images as *adiaphora* or things which are unimportant for salvation. According to him it is impossible to acknowledge the existence of relics without that leading to venerating them and from that to idolatry. He rejects the whole main argument put forward by the Roman Church, according to which saints' relics must be honoured not on account of themselves, but on account of God. This doctrine which goes back to Jerome, to Basil of Caesarea and to Augustine, receives its definitive formulation in the *Theological Summary* of Thomas Aquinas. It was confirmed by the Council of Trent in 1563 against the Reformers.

Having thus resumed his theology on relics, which he elaborates elsewhere in *The Christian Institution* 1,11, Calvin passes to what in fact will constitute the

---

[89] On Calvin's French style v. F.M. HIGMAN, *The style of John Calvin in his French Polemical Treatises*, Oxford 1967.

main point of his work, that is the worship of false relics. By beginning with the relics of Jesus Christ himself, Calvin deals in a "descending" order with those of the Virgin Mary, Saint Michael, John the Baptist, the apostles and several other saints. The argument is the same each time and consists in fact of three questions. First of all, Calvin asks, is it possible that a single and same relic, for example the body of an apostle, should be kept in several places? The reply dictated by common sense is "no". How, then, can one believe the different churches which claim to have the true relic of such or such same saint? The third question also appeals to the common sense of his faithful people: is it possible that such and such an object mentioned in the Gospel may be kept and used as a relic? The example par excellence is that of the robe of Christ. The pagan soldiers did not dare to divide it for their own use, but the Christians do not hesitate to expose some pieces of it in several churches. By referring to the biblical account, Calvin exposes very well the difference between Scripture (which is the same as truth) and human fabrication.

Nobody up to now has discovered the sources that Calvin would have used in order to compile his inventory of the "doubled" relics. M. Higman, in the introduction to his critical edition of the *Treatise*[90], rightly states that the information given by Calvin can be largely proved to accurate. It is also striking to ascertain that Jean Cochlee 91479-1552), Roman Catholic disputant who in 1549[91] published a reply to

---

[90] *Three French Treatises*, p.16.

[91] *De sacris reliquiis Christi et sanctorum eius, Brevis contra Ioannis Calvini calumnias et blasphemias responsio, per Ioannem Cochlaeum* _(Moguntiae, F. Behem) 1549. Cochlee did not know French. His reply was aimed against the Latin version of the *Treatise* entitled *Ioannis Calvini Admonito qua ostenditur quam e*

the *Treatise* does not find any mistake in it. Cochlee's move consists rather in finding a scriptural and patristic basis for the worship of relics.

In fact, the title that Calvin himself gives to his *Treatise*: *Useful warning for the great profit which would come to Christianity if it made an inventory of all the holy bodies and relics which are so much in France, Germany, Spain and other kingdoms and countries* shows itself to be revealing as to the probable sources that he would have used. Which, the Reformer claims, is a general inventory of all relics. Now at the time there existed inventories of relics about a single place or a single church. We think in particular of the *Reliquie rhomane urbis atque indulgentie* which consists of an inventory of the relics preserved in the main churches in Rome beginning with the church of Saint John Lateran, often mentioned by Calvin. The *Reliquie* was printed towards 1500[92]. There were other inventories either printed or in manuscript to which Calvin could have had access. By comparing them, he could very easily count the number of "doubled" relics, from which his wish to see a general inventory which would clearly illustrate the falsity of such worship.

As for the sources which were explicitly named by Calvin within the *Treatise,* we have already noted the use that he made of the evangelical account. His other sources have nothing amazing. Among patristic writings, he uses the writings of Ambrose, Eusebe-Rufin's *Ecclesiastical History* and the *Tripartite History* of Cassiodorus. His attitude towards ancient

---

re Christianae reipublicae foret sanctorum corpora et reliquias velut in inventarium redigi..E. Gallico Per Nicolaum Gallasium in sermonem Latinum conuersa (Geneva, Jean Girard, 1548 – v. *Calv. Opp.* VI, XXVII).

[92] See Ludwig HAIN, *Repertorium bibliographicum*, Leipzig 1890, nr. * 13855.

writers is, as might be expected, completely positive. Ambrose's authority about the piety of Helen who looked for the cross of Christ is not questioned. As regards the fate of the cross itself which was found by Helen, Calvin raises the contradictions in various ancient writings without however criticizing them. Rather he uses them to show that "what is held today of the true cross is a vain and frivolous opinion". He uses a similar process in speaking of the body of John the Baptist. Several churches boast of possessing the head and several other parts! Now according to the old stories, whose writings are however different from one another, it is clear that the whole body, with the exception of the head, was burnt "except for some small parts which the Jerusalem hermits took secretly". There is only one passage in which Calvin allows himself an open criticism of Eusebius's *Ecclesiastical History*. This case is particularly interesting. In speaking of king Abgar and the countenance portrait from life that Christ had sent him, Calvin wrote: "Eusebius truly writes in the *Ecclesiastical history* that he sent King Abagarus his life portrait, but that must also be true of one of the comments of the chronicles of Melusina". In fact Eusebius, in his *Ecclesiastical history* (1,13), speaks well of the miraculous healing of King Abgar. However, he does not mention Christ's portrait.

This legend is attributed to Eusebius by several mediaeval chroniclers including Haymo de Halberstadt. Calvin almost certainly knew the original story of Eusebius, in the same way as Haymo's work, and he must therefore know that Eusebius does not speak about Christ's portrait. Since a lengthy discussion on authenticity does not even interest non-specialist readers of the *Treatise*, Calvin contents himself with saying that the story of the portrait is false, without any other detail.

One should remember that the story of Christ's portrait constituted one of the main arguments for divine origin of the worship of images which the Roman Catholic disputants used, such as Jean Eck (1486-1543). However Eck attributed the story of the portrait to Eusebius himself.

The greatest number of saints that Calvin mentions in the last part of the *Treatise* appear in the *Legenda aurea (Golden legend)* of the Dominican Jacques de Voragine (ca. 1230 – ca. 1298). This collection of the life of saints had a great fortune throughout the Middle Ages until the 16th century. There was a French translation of it from the 14th century. However the *Legend* could only provide Calvin with the *names* of the saints, since Jacques de Voragine does not speak about relics and even less about doubled relics. Moreover, the names of the saints were in every way publicly well-known. It is therefore difficult to consider the *Legend* as one of the sources of the *Treatise* in the strict sense of the word.

Calvin was not the first one to criticize the worship of relics and one is often struck by the relationship between his *Treatise* and the *De pignoribus sanctorum* composed around 1119 by Guibert de Nogent, abbot of Nogent-sous-Coucy[93]. A. Lefranc, who was the first person to deal with this question, draws our attention to the fact that Guibert de Nogent and Calvin laugh their heads off at John the Baptist in almost identical terms[94].

---

[93] The treatise itself is reproduced in MIGNE PL 156. V. also Abel LEFRANC, The Treatise on relics by Guibert de Nogent and the beginnings of historical Criticism in the Middle Ages in: historic studies of the Middle Ages, dedicated to Gabriel Monod, Paris 1896. 285-306.

[94] Ibid. 305-306, Lefranc refers also to other similar passages.

However, it is ruled out that Calvin may have had access to Guibert's treatise, since there was only one manuscript copy before its publication in 1691. It is suitable to note also that in spite of certain parallels, Calvin's theology does not correspond to that of Guibert de Nogent. The latter does not attack the worship of relics in itself. He even emphasises that in the case of doubled relics, those who worship relics of one saint while thinking that it is another one, are not sinning[95].

In fact, a survey of Calvin's more direct "predecessors" proves to be a revelation. The theology of the 14th and 15th centuries comprises two contradictory trends. On the one hand Gregory of Rimini (d. 1358), a general of the Augustinian Order whose theology is often considered as having influenced Luther, placed a heavy accent on grace as a necessary element of any good human work. On the other hand, Jean de Palz (d. 1511), also an Augustinian, insisted on penitence and good works who act to reassure the sinner and to diminish his fear of eternal damnation.

These two contradictory trends are found in the sermons of the late Middle Ages and in particular in the 15th century, where popular religion is directed more and more towards "the theology of works", which has particularly had the result of an increase in indulgences and pilgrimages, as well as the growing popularity of the worship of saints and relics. Gabriel Biel (d. 1495) one of Luther's masters, emphasises in his sermons the importance of relics on the one hand, and the real dangers of venerating false relics on the other hand. The preacher and "reformist" of Strasbourg, Johann Geiler von Kaisersberg (1445-1510), goes further than

---

[95] *De pignoribus sanctorum* 1,4, MIGNE PL 156,628.

Biel in exhorting his faithful people to abandon their excessive devotion to relics and pilgrimages, without however touching the central question of the theology of relics. *The Imitation of Christ* (ca.1418), a devotion manual which was a huge success in the 15th and 16th centuries, even more openly denies the human initiative in the work of salvation and condemns pilgrimages and relics in a manner which is almost categorical than Calvin does one hundred and twenty-five years later. The author of the *Imitation*(1.1.23) states: "There are a great many people who visit various places to see the relics of saints and admire their deeds. They look at the magnificent buildings where the relics are found and they embrace the bones of saints covered in silk and gold. And thou, Lord, thou art thy very self in my heart."

The main elements of Calvin's thought on relics are found therefore in the religious literature of the late Middle Ages. The preachers of the 15th century are aware of the fact that some relics are not authentic and that there is no relationship between the worship of "saints' bones" and veneration due to God himself. The arguments presented by Calvin in the Treatise on Relics are certainly more developed. However, it would be wrong to separate them completely from the "reformist" tradition of the end of the Middle Ages.

There were seven editions in French of the Treatise between 1543-1599. Here is the transcription of the title page of the first edition:

VERY USEFUL WARNING of the great benefit which would come back to Christianity, if it makes an inventory of all the holy bodies, and relics, which are as much in Italy, as in France, Germany, Spain and other Kingdoms and countries./ by Monsieur Jean Calvin. PRINTED IN GENEVA, by Jean Girard. 1543.

8 0. A-G 8. Pages numbered 1-10. Last page blank: copies available in the National Library and University of Strasbourg, in the National Library of Vienna and in the Zurich Library. The copy in the Zurich Library contains instead of pages 49-64, the folio D 8 of another treatise by Calvin dating from the same year: *Little Treatise showing what a faithful man among the papists should do.* This substitution, which must go back to the 16th century, suggests that there was at that time a tendency to group these two treatises together and to consider them as a whole.

The other editions which contain relatively little in variations date from 1544, 1545 and 1551 (Geneva, Jean Girard), from 1557? (Geneva, Francois Jaquy, Antoine Davodeau and Jaques Bourgeois), from 1563 (Geneva, for Jean Crespin. By Marmet Requen) and from 1599 (Geneva, Pierre de la Roviere)[96]. The text published in the Opera Calvini[97] is that of the first edition.

We would draw attention also to two other modern editions: 1. that of Albert Autin, which also reproduces the text of the first edition with modern spelling[98] and which contains several mistakes and omissions; 2. The

---

[96] Here is the list of libraries which hold copies of these editions: 1544: Geneva BPU, Bibl. Of   Gotha.1545: Geneva BPU, Cambridge St John's College,1551: Wolfenbuttel, Herzog-August-Bibl.1557? Geneva, Museum of History of the Reformation, 1563 and 1599: Geneva BPU.

[97] Jean Calvin, Treatise on relics followed by the Excuse to the Nicodemites. Introduction and notes by Albert Autin, Paris 1921. v. ibid.p. 71 for the list of other editions of the Treatise dating from 1822, 1842, 1863 and 1909.

[98] Jean Calvin, Treatise on relics followed by the Excuse to the Nicodemites. Introduction and notes by Albert Autin, Paris 1921. V. ibid. p. 71 for the list of the other editions of the Treatise dating from 1822, 1842, 1863 and 1909.

critical edition of Francis Higman[99] based on the 1543 text and taking into account variations of the editions of 1544, 1545, 1557 and 1563. It is this last edition that we use here to a great extent as a basis, while modernising the spelling and in retrieving the text of the copy of the BNUS Strasbourg in the places where that of the Zurich ZB, used by Higman, is found to be defective.

Irena Backus

---

[99] Three French Treatises, 47-97.

J. Calvin Treatise on Relics – Text

Saint Augustine, in the book that he entitled *On the labour of Monks*[100] complaining of some bearers of scraps which, already in his time, operated a bad and dishonest market carrying here and there martyrs' relics, adds: even if they are martyrs' relics. By which words he means that at that time abuse and deceit were committed, by making the plain people believe that bones gathered here and there were the bones of saints. Since the origin of this abuse is so old, it must not be doubted that it was well multiplied meanwhile for such a long time, even considering that the word has been wonderfully corrupted since that time and has always declined by getting worse, until it has come to the extremity where we see it now.

Now the first sin, as the root of evil was that instead of seeking Jesus Christ in his word, in his sacraments and in his spiritual graces, the world, according to its habit, took pleasure in his robes, shirts and flags; and in so doing it has left the principal to follow the accessory. It did the same thing to apostles, martyrs and other saints. For, instead of meditating on their lives in order to follow their example, it undertook all its studies to contemplate and hold as treasure their bones, shirts, belts, hats and similar rubbish.

I know very well that there is some kind and colour of good devotion and zeal, when one alleges that one is keeping the relics of Jesus Christ for the honour that one brings to him and in order to have a better memory of him, and similarly of the saints. But what Saint Paul said had to be considered: that all service of God invented in man's head, whatever appearance of

---

[100] *De opera monachorum 28*, PL 40, 575.

218

wisdom it may have, is only vanity and foolishness, if it does not have a better and more sure foundation than our show [cf Ga 1,8-12]. Moreover, the benefit which cannot come with the danger had to be counter-balanced. And in so doing, it was found that it was something which was not very useful, or in every way superfluous and frivolous, to have reliquaries in this way; on the contrary, that it is very difficult, or completely impossible, to avoid declining little by little from that into idolatry. For one cannot hold back from looking at them and handling them without honouring them; and in honouring them there is no step which may incontinently honour them may be attributed, which was due to Jesus Christ. Thus, in order to say briefly what this is about, the wish to have relics is almost never without superstition and, what is worse, it is the mother of idolatry, to which is ordinarily united.

Everyone acknowledges that what moved our Lord to hide the body of Moses [cf. Dt 34,6] was for fear that the people of Israel would abuse it by worshipping it. Now it should be put forward that what was done in one saint was done to all the others, considering that it is the same reason. But while we may leave the saints there, we must note what Saint Paul said about Jesus Christ himself. For he protests not to know him any more according to the flesh after his resurrection [cf 2 Co 5,16], warning by these words that everything which is of the flesh in Jesus Christ must be forgotten and put behind in order to use and place all our affection into looking for him and owning him in the Spirit. Therefore now, to claim that it is a good thing to have some memorial, both of him as of the saints, in order to encourage us to devotion, what is that but a false cover in order to load up our stupid greed which is not based on any reason? And even when it would seem right that this reason was sufficient, since it openly rejects what the Holy Spirit pronounced by the mouth of Paul, what more do we want?

Although there is no need to have a long argument on this point, that is, whether it is good or bad to have relics in order to keep them only as precious things, without worshipping them. For, as we have said, experience shows that one is hardly ever without the other. It is true that Saint Ambrose, speaking of Helen[101], mother of Constantine the Emperor, who with great trouble and great expense looked for the cross of Our Lord, said that she only worshipped the Saviour who had been hung and not the tree. But it is a very rare thing to have a heart which relates to any relic, that one is not contaminated and polluted from time to time by some superstition. I admit that one does not come straight away to manifest idolatry, but little by little one comes from one abuse to another, until one falls completely. There are so many people who call themselves Christian who have come to that, that they are fully worshipping idols in that place, as pagans always did. For people prostrate themselves and kneel before relics, as before God. Torches and candles are lit as a sign of homage. People put their trust in them. If idolatry is nothing other than transferring the honour of God elsewhere, shall we deny that that is idolatry? And it is no excuse that that was an immoderate zeal by some rough and stupid people or by simple women. For it was a general immoderation, approved by those who had the government and conduct of the Church. And people have even spoken to the bones of the dead and all other relics on the great altar, instead of the highest and most eminent in order to have them worshipped more authentically. Therefore that is how

---

[101] Addition in the margin (ed. 1543) "in the prayer on the death of Theodosius" V. AMBROSE, *Oratio de obitu Theodossii*, 46, MIGNE PL 16, 1464.,

the stupid curiosity that people had in the beginning in treasuring relics came into this completely open abomination, which not only turned away completely from God in order to enjoy corruptible and vain things, but, by a deplorable sacrilege, they worshipped dead and unfeeling creatures, instead of the one living God.

Now, as an evil is never alone but attracts another one, this unhappy state of affairs came about since the people received as relics, both of Jesus Christ and of his saints, I do not know what rubbish where there is no reason or purpose, and the world was so blinded that, whatever title was given to each piece of jumble that was offered to them, they received it without any judgment or enquiry. Thus, with any donkey's or dog's bone that the first derider wanted to put forward as a martyr's bone, they had no problem in accepting it devotedly. It was the same for all the others, as will be discussed later. For my part, I have no doubt that it was a fair punishment by God. For since the world became fond of relics in order to abuse them in perverse superstition, that was why God allowed one lie after another came about. In this way he became used to avenge dishonour which is given to his name when his glory is carried elsewhere [cf Rm 1, 21-23; 2 Thu 2, 11-12]. However, as there are so many false relics and lies everywhere, that did not come from another reason, except that God allowed the world to be doubly deceived and disappointed, since it liked deceit and lying. It was the duty of Christians to leave the bodies of saints in their tombs in order to obey this universal sentence that each man is dust and shall return to dust [Gn 3,19], not to lift them up in pomp and sumptuousness in order to make a resurrection in time. It was not understood, but in a contrary way, against God's command, to unearth the bodies of faithful people in order to magnify them in glory, instead of

221

their being in their bed of rest while awaiting the last day. People craved to have them and they put their trust in them. They were worshipped; all the signs of reverence were made to them. And what came out of it? The Devil, seeing such stupidity, did not stay content for having deceived the world in one way, but he put forward this other deception of giving the name of saints' relics to things that were completely profane. And, without making further enquiries, they accepted everything that was offered to them without knowing the difference between white or black.

Now, for the present, my intention is not to deal with what an abomination it is to abuse relics, both of our Lord and of the saints, so that up to now and as is done in most of Christianity, as a whole book would be required to reason out this matter. But because it is a notorious thing that most of the relics that are shown everywhere are false and have been put forward by deriders who have impudently abused the poor world, I have taken it upon myself to say something about this in order to give everyone an opportunity to think about it and to be careful of it. For, sometimes we approve of something thoughtlessly, as our minds are so preoccupied, so that we do not take time to study what is to be given good and straight judgment. And thus we go wrong through lack of thought. But when we are warned, we begin to think and are all amazed at how we were so weak and so idle to believe in what was not at all likely. Thus it came about in what is heard said – there is the body of such and such saint, there are his slippers, there are his shoes – allows people to be persuaded that this is true. But when I have shown obviously the fraud which was committed there, anyone would have a little prudence and reason when they open their eyes and apply themselves to consider what they had never thought about

Although I cannot do in this little book what I wanted so much to do. For there would be a need to have registers of all parts in order to know which relics are said to be in each place in order to make a comparison of them. And then one would know that each apostle would have more than four bodies, and each saint at least two or three. There would be as many of all the rest. In brief, when one would have gathered such a heavy pile, nobody would be amazed to see such stupid and heavy derision, which nevertheless was able to blind the whole world. I thought that, since there is no cathedral church which is not so small that it does not have something like an assembly of the crowd of two or three thousand dioceses, of twenty or thirty thousand abbeys, more than forty thousand convents, and so many parish churches and chapels? But still the main thing would be to visit them and not just to name them. For one does not know them all to name them. In this town they had, one said, in past times, an arm of Saint Anthony: when it was enshrined, people used to kiss it and worship it, when it was brought out, it was found to be the limb of a deer. There was one at the great altar of the brain of Saint Peter. When it was enshrined, there was no doubt, for it would have been blasphemy not to trust in it at sight. But when the nest was peeled off and it was looked at more closely, it was found that it was a sponge stone. I could recite many similar examples, but these will be sufficient to enable one to understand how rubbish was discovered, if one once made a good universal visitation of all the relics in Europe. Even prudently, in order to know how to discern what was there. For some people, when they look at a reliquary, close their eyes out of superstition so that, in seeing, they will not see a drop [cf Mt 13,13]: that is to say that they do not dare to cast an eye wisely in order to consider what that is. Thus some people who boast about having seen the body of Saint Claude or another saint, in its full size, have never had this bravery to lift their eyes to see what it was. But someone who has the freedom to see the secret and the effrontery to use it would know well how to say otherwise. Such is the head of the Madgalene that is shown near Marseilles, with the piece of pulp or wax attached over the eye. It is made into a treasure, as if it was a god come down from heaven. But if one studied it, it would clearly be found to be a cheat.

Therefore it would be something to be desired to have certainty about all the rubbish that is held here and there as relics, or even at least to have a register and enumeration in order to show how many false ones there are. But since it is not possible to do this, I would like to have only the inventory of ten or twelve towns, such as Paris, Toulouse, Reims and Poitiers. When I had that, I would still see wonderful rabbit-warrens, or at least it would be a rather muddled shop. And it is a wish that I have been used to having often, to be able to gather such a list. However, because that would be far too difficult for me, I thought in the end that it would be better to give this little warning that follows, in order to wake up those who are asleep and to make them think what the total could be, when in such a small part there is so much to find fault with. I understand that when so many lies have been found in what I will call relics, which is not nearly the thousandth part of which is shown, what could one guess for the others? Moreover, if it appears that those that have been held to be the most authentic were fraudulently fabricated, what could one think of the more doubtful ones?

And may it please God that the Christian princes should think a little about that. For they would have a duty not to allow their poor subjects to be seduced in this way, not only by false doctrine, but visibly by making them believe that deer bladders are lanterns, as the proverb says. For they will have to give an account to God about their pretence, if they keep quiet as they see it, and it will be a mistake which is sold at a high price to have allowed God to be mocked where they could have put things right. However that may be, I hope that this little treatise will be useful to everyone, giving every person an opportunity to think in his own place about what the name carries. It is that if one had a register of the relics in the world, one would clearly see how much one had been blinded by the following, and what shadows and stupidity there would have been all over the world.

The relics of Christ

Let us begin therefore with Jesus Christ, on which, because one could not say that he had a natural body (for from the miraculous body they find the means to forge it, even in such number and all and as many times as they liked) that instead a thousand other pieces of rubbish were gathered to fill this gap. Although it was not allowed that the body of Jesus Christ should escape without some piece of it being retained. For, apart from the teeth and hair, the abbey of Charroux in the diocese of Poitiers boasts of having the foreskin, that is to say the skin which was cut off him at the time of circumcision. I ask you, from where did this skin come to them? Saint Luke the Evangelist writes clearly that our Lord Jesus was circumcised [cf Lk 2,2], but that the skin was cut off in order to preserve it as a relic, he does not mention at all. And over the space of five hundred years it was never mentioned in the Christian Church. Therefore where was it hidden in order to find it again so suddenly? Moreover, how was it stolen for Charroux? But, in order to prove it, they say that several drops of blood fell from it. That is what they say, which would be proof. That is why one can see very well that it is only a fraud. However, while we grant to them that the skin which was cut off Jesus Christ was kept and that it could be here or there, what will we say about the foreskin which is displayed in Rome, at Saint John Lateran? It is certain that they was always only one of them. It cannot therefore be in Rome and in Charroux together. Thus that is a completely manifest falsehood.

Then there is the blood next, over which there have been great battles. For several people wanted to say that no blood of Jesus Christ was found, except in a miraculous form. Nevertheless, it is shown as natural in more than a hundred places. In one place, several drops, as at La Rochelle in Poitou, which Nicodemus [cf. Jn 19,39] gathered in his glove. In other places, full phials, as at Mantua and elsewhere. In others, in full goblets, as in Rome, in Saint Eustace. But people were not content to have plain blood, but it had to be mixed with water, as it came out of his side when it was pierced on the cross. This product is found in Saint John Lateran in Rome. I leave judgment to everyone as to how certain one can be. And even if it is not an obvious lie to say that the blood of Jesus Christ was found seven or eight hundred years after his death in order to be spread by everyone, considering that in the old Church it was never mentioned.

Then there is that which dealt with the body of our Lord, or everything that they could gather up to make relics in his memory instead of his body. First of all, the manger in which he was placed at his birth [cf Lk 2,7], is displayed in Rome in the church Our Lady the Great. Also there, in the church of Saint Paul, the cloth in which he was wrapped, although there is a scrap of it in San Salvador in Spain. His cradle is also in Rome, with the shirt [cf Jn 19,23-24] that the Virgin Mary his mother made for him. *Item*, in the church of Saint James in Rome, the altar on which he was placed in the temple at his presentation is displayed [cf Lk 2,27]. As if there were altars at the time, as one had under the papacy what one wanted. Thus they are lying about that without blushing. That is what they have for the time of his infancy. It is not right here to argue too much as to where they found all this stuff, so long after the death of Jesus Christ. For, there is no judgment so small that it does not see some folly. In all the history of evangelism, there is not a word of all these things. In the time of the apostles it was never mentioned. About fifty years after the death of Jesus Christ, Jerusalem was sacked and destroyed[102]. So many old doctors wrote about it since then, describing things which happened in their time, even the cross and the nails that Helen found[103]. Of all this little rubbish, they do not say a word. What is more, in the time of Saint Gregory, there is no question that there was none of that in Rome, as can be seen from his writings. After the death Rome was several times taken, pillaged and almost completely destroyed. When all of that is considered, what could else could one say, except that all of that was contrived in order to abuse the plain people? And in fact, the sneaks, both priests and monks, do confess that this is the case, by calling them *pious frauds*, that is to say honest deceits in order to move the people to devotion.

Then later the relics belong to the time between the childhood of Jesus Christ until his death. Between them is the pillar that he leaned against while arguing in the temple, with eleven other similar ones from

---

[102] The destruction of Jerusalem by the Romans, in the year 70.
[103] V. n. 2 above.

227

Solomon's temple. I ask: what was revealed to them from Jesus Christ leaning against a pillar, for the Gospel does not say anything about it while telling the story of this argument [cf Lk 2,46]? It is not likely that he was given a place as to a preacher, considering that he was not held in esteem or authority, so it appears. Moreover, I would ask, while he was leaning on a pillar, how do they know that it was this one? Thirdly, where did they acquire these twelve pillars that they say came from Solomon's temple?

Then later there are the pitchers containing the water that Jesus Christ changed into wine at the wedding at Cana in Galilee [cf Jn 2,1 *ss*], which they call water-jars. I would like to know who was looking after them for so long in order to distribute them. For we must always note this: that they were found only eight hundred or a thousand years after the miracle was done. I do not know all the places where they are shown. I know that there are some in Pisa, Ravenna, Cluny, Angers and at San Salvador in Spain. But, without writing a longer description of them, it is easy, on sight alone, to accuse them of lying. For some do not hold more than five quarts of wine, at the very highest, others even less, and others hold about a hogshead[104]. One may allow these records, if one can, and then I shall allow them their water-jars without making a controversy out of them. But they were not only happy with the vessel, if they had not known about the liquid at the time.   For in Orleans they say they have the wine, which they call the architriclin. For because Saint John, describing the miracle, talks about the architriclin [Jn 2, 8-9], that is to say, master of

[104] According to Jn 2, 6, each water-jar holds 2-3 *metretes* = about 81-107 litres. Five quarts = about 5 litres. A water-jar varied in Calvin's time according to the area. E.g. about 270 litres in Paris, about 730 litres in Montpellier!

ceremonies, it seems to them that it was the proper name of the bridegroom, and they amuse the people with this stupid trick. Once a year, they allow the end of a small spoon to be licked by those who wish to bring their offering, telling them that they are drinking the wine that our Lord created at the party. And the amount of it never goes down, by means of properly filling up the jug. I do not know what size the shoes that are said to be in Rome in the place called *Sancta Sanctorum*, and whether he wore them when he was a child, or when he was a already a man. And when everything is said, one of them is worth the other. For what I have already said shows adequately what impudence it is to produce Jesus Christ's shoes now, which even the apostles did not have in their time.

Let us come to what relates to the last supper that Jesus Christ had with his apostles [cf Mt 26,17 *ss*]. Its table is in Rome, in Saint-John Lateran. There is bread from it in San Salvador, in Spain. The knife with which the pascal lamb was cut is in Treves. Note that Jesus Christ was in a borrowed house when he held his supper. As he left there, he left the table; we do not read at all that it was ever recovered by the apostles. Jerusalem, some time later, was destroyed, as we have said. How likely is it that this table was found seven or eight centuries later? Moreover, the shape of tables at that time was completely different from what it is now. People were lying down as they ate, not seated, which is expressly stated in the Gospel [cf Mt 26,20]. The lie is too obvious. And do we need something else? The cup from which he gave the sacrament of his blood to be drunk, to his apostles [Mt. 26,28] is shown at Notre Dame de l'Ile, near Lyon and in Albigeois, an Augustine convent. What should one believe? It is even worse in the case of the plate on which the pascal lamb was placed, for it is in Rome, in Genes, and in

229

Arles. It should be said that the practice of that time was different from our own. For instead of changing the food as now, one would change the plate for one type of food. Even if one wanted to add faith to these holy relics. Would one want to see a more obvious falsehood? This is also the case with the cloth with which Jesus Christ dried the feed of his apostles, after having washed them [cf Jn 13,5]. There is one of them in Rome, in St John Lateran, another at Aix in Germany, in Saint Cornelius, with the sign of Judas's foot. What will we make of this? Let people fight one another, until one of the parties has proved its case. However, let us consider that it is only deceit to wish to make people believe that the sheet that Jesus left in the boarding-house where he held his supper, five or six centuries after the destruction of Jerusalem, was stolen in Italy or in Germany.

I had forgotten about the bread with which five thousand men were fed in the desert [cf Mt 14,13 *ss*], a piece of which is shown in Rome, in the church of Notre-Dame the New and a small piece in San Salvador, in Rome. It is said in Scripture that there was a small portion of manna reserved for the memory that God had miraculously fed the people of Israel in the desert [cf Ex 14,20]. But of the surplus that was left of the five loaves, Scripture does not say that there was anything left at such an end [cf Mt 14,20], and there is no ancient story that mentions it, nor any doctor of the Church. It is therefore easy to judge that what is shown now has been made since then. One may make the same judgment of the rod which is in San Salvador, in Spain. For they say that it is the one that Christ was holding in bloom when he went into Jerusalem on Easter day [cf Mk 11, 1-10]. Now the Gospel does not say that he was holding it. Therefore it is a false thing. Finally, one must put into this category another relic which appears to be the same. It is about the ground where Jesus Christ had his feet stood when he resurrected Lazarus [cf Jn 11, 38-44]. I would ask you, who marked his place so well, that after the destruction of Jerusalem[105], everything changed in the land of Judea, one could have gone to the place where Jesus Christ had once walked?

It is time to come to the main relics of our Lord. There are those which relate to his death and passion. And first of all we must speak about the cross on which he was hung. I know that it is held to be true that it was found by Helene, mother of Constantine, the Roman Emperor. I know too that some ancient doctors have written about the seal of approval, in order to certify that the cross found by her was no doubt that on which Jesus Christ had been hung[106]. Of all that, I am relating to what accounts there are. There are so many accounts that it was her stupid curiosity, or a crazy and thoughtless devotion. But still, let us take the case that it was a praiseworthy action of hers to take the trouble to find the true cross, and that our Lord declared at the time by a miracle that it was the true one that she had found. Only let us consider the case in our time. It is maintained that this cross that Helen found is still in Jerusalem. And nobody doubts that, although ecclesiastical history particularly contradicts it. For there it is written that Helen took a piece of it to send to the emperor her son, which he put on a porphyry pillar in Constantinople, in the middle of the market; on the other hand it is said that she placed it in a silver case

---

[105] V. n. 3 above

[106] There are several accounts of this, in particular: AMBROSE, *Oratio de obitu Theodosii*, 46, MIGNE *PL* 16, 1464; SOCRATES, *Hist eccl.* 1, 17 *in Hist trip*,2, 18, CSEL 31,114.

231

and handed it for safe keeping to the Bishop of Jerusalem[107].

Thus, either we shall argue the history of lying, or what is held today of the true cross is a vain and frivolous opinion. Now let us be aware on the other hand of how many pieces of it there are in the whole world. If I wanted to write only what I could say about it, there would be a role to fill a complete book. There is no town so small where there is not some of it, not only in the cathedral church, but in some parishes. Similarly, there is no really wicked abbey where no part of it is shown. And in some places, there are some great fragments of it, as at the Sainte-Chapelle in Paris, and in Poitiers, and in Rome where there is a fairly large crucifix which is made of it, as it said. In short, if one wanted to gather everything which is found of it, it would be the size of a fairly large boat. The Gospel testifies that the cross could be carried by a man [cf. Jn 19,17]. Therefore what audacity was it to fill the world with pieces of wood in such an amount that three hundred men could not carry it? And from this fact, they have made up this excuse that, whatever one makes of it, it is never diminished. But it is a falsehood so crazy and heavy that even superstitious people know that. Therefore I would allow people to wonder what certainty one could have about all the true crosses that are worshipped here and there. I would allow people to say where some pieces came from and by what means. As some people say that what they have of it was carried by angels, others say that it fell from heaven. The people of Poitiers say that what they have of it was brought by a servant of Helen, who had found it; and as she ran away, it was lost near Poitou. They add to the legend that she was lame. These are the

---

[107] THEODORET, *Hist. eccl. In Hist. trip.* 2, 18, CSEL 31, 114.

wonderful foundations that they have for persuading people to idolize. For they were not content to charm and abuse plain people, by showing ordinary wood instead of the wood from the cross; but they decided that it had to be worshipped, which is a diabolical doctrine. And Saint Ambrose specifically condemns it as a pagan superstition[108].

After the cross, there follows the name that Pilate had put on, where he had written: Jesus of Nazareth, king of the Jews [Jn 19,19]. But one would need to know both the place and the time, and how it was found. Someone will tell me that Socrates, a Church historian, records it[109]. I will acknowledge it. But he does not say what became of it. Thus, this testimony is not worth very much. Moreover, it was writing done in haste and on the spot, after Jesus Christ was crucified. However, to show a plaque which was curiously made, to be held for show, would not serve any purpose. Thus, when there would be only one of these, one could say it was a falsehood and a fake. But when the town of Toulouse boasts of having it and the Roman people contradict that, showing it in the church of Holy Cross, they disown one another. Therefore they may fight as much as they want. In the end both parties will be found guilty of lying, when somebody wants to study what is left of it.

There is an even great battle about the nails [cf Jn 20,25]. I shall give a list of those that have come to my attention. On that, there would be no small child who does not consider that the Devil laughs too much at the

---

[108] *De obitu Theodosii*, 46, MIGNE *PL* 16, 1464.

[109] *Hist. eccl.* 1,17, MIGNE *PG* 67,119. Quoted here according to *Hist. trip.* 2, 18, CSEL 31, 114.

11First edition 1543 adds in the margin "In the second book of the three-part History". In fact, *Hist. trip.* 2, 18, CSEL 31,115. (Cf. THEODORET, *Hist. eccl.* 1, 17, MIGNE *PG* 82, 959).

world, taking away his sense and reason, so that he cannot notice anything in this place. If the old writers are telling the truth, and in particular Theodoret, the historian of the ancient church, Helen had one enclosed in her son's helmet; of the other two, she put them in her horse's bit.[110] Although Saint Ambrose does not say this at all, for he says that one was placed in Constantine's crown; about the other one, his horse's bit was made of it; the third one, that Helen kept it[111]. We see that already over more than twelve hundred years it was in dispute as to what had become of the nails. Therefore how sure can we be at the moment? Now, in Milan, they boast about having the one that was placed in Constantine's horse's bit. The town of Carpentras contests this, saying that they have it. Now Saint Ambrose does not say that the nail was attached to the bit, but that the bit was made out of it[112]. This can in no way agree with what the people of Milan and the people of Carpentras say. Later, there is a piece of it in Rome, in Saint Helen's, a similar one in Holy Cross church, another in Siena, in Germany, two, one in Cologne, in Trois-Maries, another in Treves. In France, there is one in the Sainte Chapelle in Paris, the other in the Carmelite convent, another in Saint-Denis in France, one in Bourges, one in Tenaille, one in Draguignan. That makes a total of fourteen. Each place alleges good approval in its place, it seems. There are so many of them that each one has as good a right as the others. However, there is no better method than to

---

[110] First edition 1543 adds in the margin: "In the second book of the three-part History". In fact, *Hist. trip.* 2,18, CSEL 31,115. (Cf THEODORET, *Hist. eccl.* 1, 17, MIGNE *PG* 82, 959)

[111] *De obitu Theodosii*, 47, MIGNE *PL* 16, 1464-1465.

[112] *Ibid.*

make them all go through a *fidelium*[113]. It should be considered that everything that was said about them was only a lie, since otherwise one cannot come to a conclusion.

After this, the blade of the sword [cf Jn 19,34] which could only be one; but it must be said that it went through the furnace of some alchemist. For it was multiplied by four, without those who may be here and there, which I have not heard of. There is one in Rome, the other in the Saint-Chapelle in Paris, the third in the abbey of La Tenaille, in Saintonge, the fourth at the Sauve, near Bordeaux. Which will one choose now as the true one? However, the shortest answer, is to leave all four of them for what they are. But still, when there would only be one of them, I would really want to know where it came from. For none of the old Stories, nor any of the other written ones, make any mention of it at all. Therefore they must have been newly forged.

As regards the crown of thorns [cf Jn 19,2] it must be said that there pieces were re-planted in order to bloom again. Otherwise I do not know how it could be increased in this way. For one *item*, there is a third part of it in the Sainte-Chapelle in Paris, in Rome, in the Holy Cross church, there are three thorns from it in the church of Saint-Eustace, in Rome itself, some quantity, in Siena, I do not know how many thorns, in Vicence, one, in Bourges, five, in Besancon, in the church of Saint John, in Mont-Royal, three, in San-Salvador, in Spain, I do not know how many, in Saint

---

[113] *Fidelium*. The word which ends the *requiem* mass. Some priests in the Middle Ages who were not very conscientious sang a single mass for several dead people, instead of singing an individual mass every time. This practice gave rise to the maxim used here by Calvin which means "gathering several things together into one category". V. HUGUET, *Dict*. S.v. *fidelium*.

James church in Galicia[114], two, in Albi, three, in Toulouse, in Macon, in Charroux in Poitou, in Clery, in Saint-Flour, in Saint-Maximin in Provence, in the De la Salle abbey, in the parish church of Saint Martin in Noyon, in each of all these places, there is one of them. When one would have carried out a diligent enquiry, one could name more than four times as much. What trust therefore can one have of some, or the others? With this, it should be noted that in the whole old Church, one never heard what this crown had become. That is why it is easy to conclude that the first plan began to grow a long time after the passion of our Lord Jesus Christ.

Then later there is the purple robe, which Pilate put on our Lord for scorn [cf Jn 19,2] especially as he was called a king. Now, this was a precious robe which was not to be thrown away carelessly. And it should not be presumed that Pilate or his people would allow it to be lost, after once having laughed at our Lord. I would really like to know who was the businessman who bought it from Pilate in order to keep it in a reliquary. And in order to colour their lie, they show several drops of blood on it, as if the wicked people wished to spoil a royal robe, as they put it in jest on the shoulders of Jesus Christ. I do not know if there is another one also, somewhere else. But of the robe which was woven from top to bottom without a seam, over which lots were cast [cf Jn 19, 23,24], because it more suitable to move plain people to devotion, several of them have been found. For at Argenteuil, near Paris, there is one, and another one in Treves. And if the records of San Salvador in Spain are true, the Christians, through their thoughtless zeal, have done worse than the unbelieving soldiers. For the latter did not dare to tear it in pieces,

---

[114] Saint James of Compostela

but, in order to spare it, cast lots over it [cf Jn 19,24] and the Christians cut it up in order to worship it. But yet, what will they say to the Turk who laughs at their madness, saying that it is in his hands? Although it is not now right to make them plead against the Turk, it is sufficient that among themselves they settle their question. Meanwhile we will be excused from believing either one or the other, for fear of favouring one of the parties more than the other, without knowing why. That would be against all reason. What is more, if they want to add credence to their story, they would need, in the first place, to agree with the writers of the Gospels. Now is it true that this robe, over which lots were cast, was a sagum or a smock, that the Greeks call *choeton*, and the Romans *tunica* [Jn 19,23].

When one sees that the robe in Argenteuil, or the one in Treves, are in such a shape, one will find that they are like a folded chasuble. Thus, while they cross the eyes of people, one would know that they are false by touching them with the hands. In order to finish this article, I would gladly ask one small question. When the soldiers divided Christ's garments between them, as Scripture bears witness [cf Jn 19,23], it is certain that it was to use them for their gain. What I want to know, is, who was the Christian who bought them from the soldiers, both the smock and the other garments which are displayed in other places, such as in Rome in the church of Saint Eustace, and elsewhere? How is it that the Evangelists forgot that? For it is an absurd thing to say that the soldiers together plundered the garments, without adding that they were purchased from their hands, in order to make them into relics. Moreover, how is that that all those who wrote in old times were so disagreeable as not to say a word? I shall give them space to answer me on these questions, when men will have any more sense or understanding in order to

237

judge. The best thing is that with the robe they also wanted to have dices, with which the lot was cast by the soldiers [cf Jn 19,24]. One is in Treves, and two others in San Salvador in Spain. Now in that, they naively showed their stupidity. For the Evangelists say that the soldiers threw lots, which come out then from a hat or from a bowl, as when one wants to play the king of Twelfth Night, or when one is drawing a raffle.[115] To sum up, one knows that it is casting lots. That is done communally in shares. These beasts imagined that casting lots was a game of dice[116], which was not then in use, at least as we know it in our time. For instead of six and an ace, and other points, they had certain marks, which they called by their names, such as Venus or Dog. So that now people go to kiss the relics, for the credit of such heavy liars.

It is time to deal with the shroud [cf Jn 20,7], with which they have again showed better both their impudence and their stupidity. For, apart from the shroud of Saint Veronica, which is shown in Rome in Saint Peter's, and the handkerchief that the Virgin Mary, as they say, placed on the private parts of our Lord, which is shown in Saint John Lateran, which is really again for the Augustines of Carcassonne; *item*, the shroud which was placed on his head in the tomb, which is shown there also; there are half a dozen towns, at least, which boast about having the shroud from the tomb in a whole state: such as Nice, the one which as taken there from Chambery, *item* Aix in Germany; *item*

---

[115] *Playing blank.* Ed. 1543: blank. A lottery of Italian origin. The participants bought tokens on which there appeared a figure and a maxim. The draw was done by a blind man. V.M. PSICHARI, *Gargantua's games in the Review of Rabelaisian studies 6* [1908], 336-337.

[116] *Game of dice. Venus and Dog* in fact meant combinations of dices, and not what appeared on a dice.

the Trect; *item* Besancon; *item* Cadouin in Limousin; *item* a town in Lorraine, situated at d'Aussois harbour; not to mention the pieces which are scattered from one side and another, such as at San Salvador in Spain, and with the Augustines in Albi. Again I am leaving out another whole shroud which is in Rome, in a women's convent, because the Pope forbade it from being shown solemnly. I ask you, has the world not been infuriated, to trot a hundred or one hundred and twenty leagues far, with great expense and great trouble, in order to see a sheet of which nothing can be guaranteed, but rather was obliged to doubt it? For whoever thinks that the shroud is in a certain place, makes all the others forgers who boast about having it. As, for example, the person who believes that the sheet at Chambery is the true shroud, also condemns those at Besancon, Aix, Cadouin, Trect and Rome as liars, who wickedly make the people idolatrize by persuading them and making them believe that an unhallowed sheet is the shroud in which our Redeemer was wrapped.

Let us come now to the Gospel. For it would be a small thing if they contradicted one another; but the Holy-Spirit, contradicting them all, makes them all confused together, some of them and also the others. For the first part, it is a wonder that the Evangelists do not mention this Veronica, who wiped the face of Jesus Christ with a handkerchief, considering that they speak about all the women, who were with him at the cross[117]. It was truly a notable thing and worthy of being placed on the record that the face of Jesus Christ should have been miraculously printed in a shroud. On the other hand, it seems right that it is not credible to say that some women had accompanied Jesus Christ on the

---

[117] Cf, Matth. 27, 55-56; Mark 15, 40-41; Luke 23,49. Nothing suggests that the Evangelists talk about *all* the women.

cross, without any miracle happening to them. Therefore how is it that the Evangelists describe minor things of slight importance, keeping quiet about the main things? Surely, if such a miracle had taken place, as one is led to believe, we would have to accuse the Holy Spirit of forgetfulness or indiscretion, that he would not have prudently chosen what was the proper thing to describe. That is for Veronica, so that one should know what an obvious lie that is, which they want to be believed.

As for the winding-sheet in which the body was wrapped [cf Jn 20,7], I am making a similar request to them. The Evangelists diligently describe the miracles that were performed upon the death of Jesus Christ and leave out nothing which belongs to history. How is it that something escaped them so that they did not say a word about such an excellent miracle? It is that the effigy of the body of our Lord Jesus had remained on the shroud in which he was buried. That was also well worth describing as well as several other things [cf Jn 20,6-7]. If there is any miraculous portraiture, he does not talk about it at all. It should not be presumed that he would have suppressed such a work of God, if there had been something like that. There is still another doubt to bring up; it is that the Evangelists do not say at all that any of the disciples, or the faithful women, carried the shrouds, with which we are concerned, out of the tomb. But rather they let it be known that they have left them there, although that is not expressly stated[118]. Now the tomb was guarded by soldiers who then would have had the shroud in their power. Should it be presumed that they handed it over to some man of faith so that relics could be made out of it, considering that the Pharisees had corrupted them in order to

___

[118] In fact, only Jn 20,6.

perjure themselves, saying that the disciples had stolen the body [cf Mt 28,13]? I am keeping away from charging them with lying by actually seeing the portraits which are shown of it. And I cannot be astounded enough, at first of all how they were so dull as not to be more crafty in order to deceive; and even more, how the world was so foolish as to allow itself to have its eyes dazzled, in order not to see such an obvious thing. What is more, they have shown very well that they had the painters under their thumb. For when one shroud was burnt, a new one was always found the next day. They really said that this was the same one as was there before, which was miraculously saved from the fire. But the painting was so fresh that the lie did not work at all, if one had eyes to see it. There is, to end the matter, a peremptory reason through which they were all convinced by their immodesty. Everywhere that they say they have the holy shroud, they show a large shroud which covered the whole body with the head, and there one sees the effigy of a body in one block. Now, the Evangelist Saint John says that Jesus Christ was buried with the method of the Jews [cf Jn 19,40]. Now, this method, not only can be understood by the custom that the Jews still keep today, but also through their books which show the old practice. This is to wrap the body separately up to the shoulders, then to wrap the head within a headdress, tying it at four corners. What the Evangelist also states, when he says that Saint Peter saw the cloths from one side, where the body had been wrapped, and from another side the shroud, which had been placed on the head [cf Jn 20,6-7]. For such is the meaning of this word *winding-sheet*, to take it as a handkerchief or headdress, and not as a great shroud which is used to wrap up the body. In order to come briefly to an end, Saint John the Evangelist must be a

241

liar, or really all those who boast about having the holy shroud are convinced by forgeries, and one sees clearly that they have deceived the poor people by an effrontery which is too extreme.

That would never be done, if I wanted to follow in detail all the mockeries that they practise. In Rome, in Saint John Lateran they show the rod that was put into the hand of Jesus Christ instead of a sceptre, when he was scourged as a mockery in Pilate's house [cf Mt 27, 29-30]. There too, in Holy Cross church, is the sponge with which the gall and myrrh were put into his mouth [cf Mt 27,34]. I ask you, where were these found? It was the unbelievers who had them in their hands. Did they hand them over to the apostles to make relics out of them? Did they bury them themselves in order to keep them for a future time? What sacrilege is it to thus abuse the name of Jesus Christ thus to cover up myths which were so coldly created? So it is with the denarii that Judas received for having betrayed our Lord. It is said in the Gospel that he gave them to the Pharisees' synagogue and that a field was bought with them for burying foreigners [cf Mt 27, 3-7]. Who took back these denarii from the merchant's hands? If one says it was the disciples, that is far too ridiculous. One should look for a better colour. If one says that this was done a long time afterwards, it is even less credible, considering that the money could have been passed through a great many hands. Therefore it must be shown, either that the merchant who sold his goods to the Pharisees in order to make a cemetery had done so in order to purchase the denarii, in order to make relics out of them, or in fact he sold them back to the faithful flock. Now, about that, there was never any news of that in the old Church. It is a similar cheat as regards the steps of Pilate's judgment-hall [cf Jn 19,9] which are at Saint John Lateran in Rome, with holes, where they say that drops of blood fell from the body of our Lord. *Item*, even there, in the church of Saint Praxedes, the column to which he was attached when he was flogged, and in Holy Cross church, three others, around which he was paraded, going to his death. Of all these columns, I do not know where they were dreamt up. There are so many of them that they are imagined in their own fantasy. For in the whole story of the Gospel[119] we read nothing about them. It is truly stated that Jesus Christ was flogged [cf Mt 27,26]; but that he was attached to a pillar, that is their criticism. Therefore one can see that they have done nothing else, but to gather something like a sea of lies. In which they gave themselves such licence, that they were not ashamed to simulate a relic from the tail of an ass on which our Lord was carried [cf Jn 12,14]. For they show it in Genoa. But we must not be amazed by their effrontery any more, than the foolishness and stupidity of the world which has received such a mockery with great devotion.

Here someone could object that it is improbable that all the reliquaries that we have named above so authentically that one could not allege when they came from, and from whose hands they were received. To that I could reply in a word, that in such obvious lies, it is not possible to claim any truth. For all something to which they arm themselves with the name of Constantine, or King Louis, or some pope, all of that does nothing to prove that Jesus Christ was crucified with fourteen nails, or that a whole hedge was used to make his crown of thorns, or that a sword created three others, or that his cassock would be multiplied by three and have changed into a chasuble, or that out of a

---

[119] *Of the Gospel... Virgin, I understand nothing.* This part of the text is missing in the copy in Zurich Library.

single winding-sheet there would come a clutch, like chickens from a hen, and that Jesus Christ was buried in a way other than what the Gospel describes. If I displayed a lump of lead and said: this gold nugget was given to me by such and such a prince, people would think I was a crazy old man, and according to me the lead would not change its colour or its nature in order to be changed into gold. Thus, when one says to us: that is what Godefroy de Bouillon[120] sent from there, after conquering the land of Judaea, and that reason shows us that it is only a lie, must we allow words to be abused, in order not to look at what we see with our eyes? But yet, so that it may be known how sure he is to trust everything they say in order to approve of their relics, it should be known that the main relics, and the more authentic ones which are in Rome, were brought there, as they say, by Titus and Vespasian[121]. Now, it is such a tall story, as if one said that the Turk went to Jerusalem to acquire the true cross in order to put it in Constantinople. Vespasian, before he was emperor, conquered and destroyed a part of Judaea; later, having become emperor, his son Titus, whom he had left as his lieutenant, took the city of Jerusalem. Now they were pagans, who were so unconcerned with Jesus Christ that he might never have existed. Thus one may consider whether they did not dare to lie so openly, by alleging Godefroy de Bouillon or Saint Louis, as they alleged Vespasian. Moreover, one wonders what judgment the king called Saint Louis, or similar people, really had. There was truly a devotion and zeal with which to increase Christianity. But if one had shown

---

[120] (1061-1100) General of the 1st Crusade and first Christian King of Jerusalem.
[121] Vespasian led the war against the Jews, 67-69. Titus who succeeded him, is responsible for the destruction of Jerusalem in the year 70.

them goats' dung and said to them: here are the prayers of Our Lady, they would have worshipped them without contradiction and would have brought them in their ships from over there, in order to plump them down honourably somewhere. And in fact, they consumed their bodies and their wealth, and a good part of the substance of their country, in order to bring back a pile of small trinkets with which they had been pestered, thinking that they were the most precious jewels in the world. In order to let you know even more fully what is to be found of this, it should be noted that all over Greece, Asia Minor and Mauritania, which we call today in common talk the Indies, one is shown with great assurance all this old lumber that the poor idol-worshippers think they have around us. How can one judge between one and another of them? We shall say that these relics were brought from those countries. The Christians who live there still say that they have them and laugh at our stupid boasting. How can one decide this case without an inquisition, which cannot be done and will never be done? Because the only remedy is to leave the thing as it is, without worrying about one side or the other.

The last relics which belong to Jesus Christ are those that have been held since his resurrection, like a piece of roast fish, that Saint Peter presented to him, when he appeared to him on the edge of the sea [Lk 24,42; Jn 21,13]. One must say that it has been well spiced, that a wonderful spicy sauce has been made out of it, so that it could be kept for such a long time. But, without laughing, should it be presumed that the apostles had made a relic out of the fish that they had prepared for their dinner? Anyone can see that that is an open mockery of God, I leave it like a beast who is not worthy of being shown beforehand.

There is also the miraculous blood which came out of several victims, such as in Paris, in Saint John of Greve, in Saint John of Angely, in Dijon, and elsewhere in a great many places. And in order to make the pile even higher, they have added the holy knife with which the Paris victim was stabbed by a Jew, which the poor foolish Parisians hold in greater reverence than the victim himself. With which our master of Quercu[122] was not happy at all. And he reproached them for being worse than Jews, in that they worshipped the knife which had been the instrument for violating the precious body of Jesus Christ. What I am alleging, because as much can be said about the sword, the nails and the thorns, is that all those who worship them, according to the judgment of the master of Quercu, are more wicked than the Jews who crucified our Lord.

In the same way, we are shown the shape of his feet where he walked when he appeared to some people after his ascension. As there is one of these shapes in Rome, in Saint Lawrence church, at the place where he met Saint Peter when he foretold to him that he would suffer in Rome. There is another one in Poitiers, in Sainte-Ragonde. Another one in Soissons. Another one in Arles. I am not disputing at all whether Jesus Christ could print the shape of his feet on one stone. But I am disputing only the fact and say, since there is no legitimate proof, that one must consider that to be a myth. But the rarest of this kind of thing is the shape of his buttock which is in Reims, in Champagne, on a stone behind the great altar. And they say that this was made in the time that our Lord had become a mason in

---

[122] Guillaume Duchesne, one of the most conservative doctors of theology at the Sorbonne and priest of Saint John en Greve, Paris. See A.RENAUDET, *Pre-reform and humanism in Paris*, Paris 1953, p.537.

order to build the porch of their church. This blasphemy is so execrable that I am ashamed to mention it any more.

Let us therefore go beyond this, and let us see what is said about his images; not those which are made commonly by painters, or stone-cutters, or carpenters, for their number is infinite, but about those which have some special dignity for being held in some singularity as relics. Now, there are two types of them: some were made miraculously, such as the one which is shown in Rome, in Saint Mary's church, which is called *in Porticu*; *item*, another one in Saint John Lateran; *item*, the one in Luques, which is said to have been made by the angels and which is called *Vultus sanctus*. These are such frivolous myths that it seems to me to be labour lost, and even if I held myself up to ridicule and were inept, I would be happy to disprove them. That is why it is enough to have noted them in passing. For it is well known that angels are not professional painters, and that our Lord wants to be known otherwise by us and to confine himself to our memory, than by earthly images. Eusebius describes well in the Ecclesiastical History that he sent King Abagarus his live portrait[123], but that must be as true as one of the comments in the Chronique de Melusine[124]. However, as it was, how is that they obtained it from King Abagarus? For in Rome they boast about having it. Now Eusebius does not say that she stayed alive until his time, but he speaks through hearsay as of a distant matter. It is right to presume that, six or seven years later, she was resuscitated and came from Persia

---

[123] In fact, Haymo DE HALBERSTADT, *Historiae Sacrae Epitome* 2, 5, *MIGNE PL* 118,825 where the story of the portrait is attributed to Eusebius.

[124] *Chronicles of Melusine*. A very popular prose novel by Jean d'Arras dating from 1392-93.

to Rome. They have also made images of the cross, as of the body. For in Bresse they boast about having the cross which appeared to Constantine[125] with which I have nothing to discuss upon meeting them; but I send them back to the people of Courtonne who strongly maintain that it is theirs. Therefore they are claiming together. Then, let the party who has won his case come, and we will answer him. Although one may say that the answer may be easy, in order to convince them of their stupidity. For what some writers have said, that a cross appeared to Constantine, is not to be understood as a material cross, but a figure which was shown to me in heaven in a vision. Therefore while this may be true, one can see that they have erred seriously through lack of intelligence. And thus they have built their abuse without any foundation.

As for the second type of images, that are held as relics due to some miracles that they have performed, in this number there are included the crucifixes in which the beard grows, such as the one in Burgos, in Spain; *item*, the one in San Salvador and the one in Aurenge. If I stop to show what madness, or rather what stupidity it is to believe that, I will be laughed at. For the thing in itself is so absurd that already it is not right that I should go to the trouble of disproving it. However, the whole world is so stupid that most of it holds this as true as the Gospel. Similarly in this category I would put the crucifixes which have spoken, which are numerous. But let us be content with one as an example, that is, the one in Saint-Denis, in France. It spoke, they say, to give witness to the fact that the church was dedicated. But again, I ask them, how is it that the crucifix could be in the church at that time?

---

[125] *The cross which appeared to Constantine.* V. EUSEBIUS, *Vita Constantini* 1, 28, MIGNE *PG* 20, 943-44; *PL* 8, 22.

Considering that, when one wants to dedicate churches, all the images are taken away. How is it therefore that it was hidden in order to avoid being carried away with the others? It should be said that they did not think about deceiving the world completely at their ease, considering that they did not take care to contradict themselves openly, but it was enough for them to lie out loud, not taking care that replicas could be made of these. Finally there are the tears: one in Vendome, one in Treves, one in Saint-Maximin, one in Saint-Pierre-le-Puellier in Orleans, of which I know nothing. Some, as they say, are natural, like that in Saint-Maximin, which, according to their chronicles, fell upon our Lord as he washed the feet of the apostles [cf Jn 13,5]; the others are miraculous. As if it could be believed that wooden crucifixes were so offended that they could weep. But they must be forgiven for this mistake, for they were ashamed that their urchins made as much of them as those of the pagans. Now, the pagans have pretended that their idols wept sometimes. Thus, we can put one with the other.

The relics of the Virgin Mary

As for the Virgin Mary, because they maintain that her body is no longer on earth, they do not have the means of boasting that they have her bones. Otherwise I think that they would have made people believe that it had a body to fill a large charnel-house. For the rest, they avenged themselves on her hair and on her milk, in order to be able to have something from her body. Of her hair, there is some in Rome, in Sainte-Marie-sur-Minerve, in San Salvador in Spain, in Macon, in Cluny, in Noyers, in Saint-Flour, in Saint-Jacquerie, and in several other places. About the milk, it is not right now to number the places where there is some. And also that would never be done. For there is no really small town, nor any wicked convent either of monks, or of young nuns, where there is not shown some of it, in some of them a great deal, in other less. Not that they would be ashamed to boast about having some in jugfuls, but because they thought it right that their lie would be more hidden in what could be held inside a glass or crystal display, so that it would not be examined more closely. There is so much of this that if the holy Virgin had been a cow and she had been a wetnurse all her life, she could hardly have produced such an amount. On the other hand, I would gladly ask how this milk which is shown everywhere today, was collected in order to keep it in our time. For we do not read that anyone was ever curious about this. It is well said that the shepherds worshipped Jesus Christ [cf Lk 2,8-13], that the wise men offered him their gifts [cf Mt 2, 1-13], but it is not said at all that they had taken away some milk as a reward. Saint Luke [2,25-33] describes well what Simeon foretold to the Virgin, but he does not say that he asked her for some of her milk. When one does not look into this point, one must not now argue more for showing how much this madness is against all reason and without any cover. It is a miracle, since they could have nothing else from the body, that they did not decide to cut her nails and similar things. But it must be said that everything is not remembered by them.

The remainder of the relics of Our Lady that they hold is her luggage. First of all, there is one of her night-gowns in Chartres, out of which a rather famous idol is made, and another in Aix in Germany. There I leave a comment as to how they were able to obtain them. For it is a true matter that the apostles and true Christians of their time were not so playful as to take pleasure in such underhand practices. But one has only to look at the shape, and I leave the game, one can see their impudence with one's eyes. In Aix in Germany, when the shirt that we said was there, it is shown at the end of a rod like a long alb of a priest. When the Virgin Mary had been a giant, she would have worn such a long night-gown with some difficulty.

And in order to give her more lustre, from time to time one is shown Saint Joseph's socks which would be for a small child or a dwarf. The proverb says that a liar has to have a long memory, for fear of giving oneself away due to forgetting. They have kept this rule badly, when they have not thought of making a better proportion between the socks and the wife's night-gown. One should go now to kiss relics very devotedly, which have no other appearance of truth. Of his head-dress, I only know two: one in Treves, in Saint-Maximin abbey, in Lisio in Italy, another. But I would like to know what cloth they are made of, and if they were worn in such a way in that time in the land of Judaea. I would also like a comparison to be made between one and the other to see how they resemble each other. In Boulogne, they have a frontal of it. Someone will ask me if I think that this frontal was a contrived thing. I shall answer that I think of it in the same way as of his belt which is in Prat, and of the one which is in Notre Dame de Montserrat. *Item* of his slipper which is in Saint-Jacquerie, and one of his shoes which is in Saint Flour. When there would be nothing else, any man of medium prudence knows very well that it was not the way of the faithful flock to gather socks and shoes in this way in order to make them into relics, and that there was no mention of them for over five hundred years after the death of the Virgin Mary. Therefore what more must be argued about this, as if the matter was doubtful? They have even wanted to

251

make people believe as regards the Virgin that she was very meticulous in decking herself out and doing her hair. For they show two of her combs, one, in Rome in Saint Martin's church, and the other one, in Saint John the Great in Besancon, not to mention those which could be shown elsewhere. If that is not to laugh at the holy Virgin, I do not understand at all[126] what mockery is. They have not forgotten her wedding ring at all. They have it in Perouse. Because now the custom is for the husband to give a ring to his wife when they get married, they imagined that it was done that way at that time, and without making a longer inquisition into it, they have appointed a ring for this use, beautiful and rich, not considering in any way the poverty in which the holy Virgin lived. Of her clothes, they have some in Rome, in Saint John Lateran; *item* in Saint Barbe church; *item* in Saint Mary-on-Minerve; *item* in Saint-Blaise church, and in San Salvador in Spain; at least they say they have some pieces of them. I have also heard people speak of other places, but I do not remember them. In order to show the falsehood in this place, one would only need to look at the material. For it seemed right to them that it was as easy to attribute clothing to the Virgin Mary at their station, like dressing images as they dress themselves.

It remains to speak about images; not the common ones, but those which by recommendation are above the others, for some peculiarity. Now they want to believe that Saint Luke painted four of them in Rome, at the place where the Sainte-Marie church is, that they call *Inviolata*[127]. One is shown there in an oratory, which he made, they say, for her devotion, with the ring with which Saint Joseph had married her. Another of

<hr>

[126] Here the text takes up the 1543 edition in the copy in the Zurich Library.

[127] Distortion of the phrase: *in via lata.*

252

them is even shown in Rome in Sainte-Marie la Neuve, which they say was made in this way by Saint Luke in Troade, and which later was brought to them by an angel. *Item*, there is another in Sainte-Marie Ara Coeli, in such a form that she was beside the cross [cf Mt 27,56]. But in Saint-Augustin they boast about having the main one. For this is the one, if they are to be believed, that Saint Luke always carried with him, until it was buried in his tomb. I ask you, what blasphemy to make a perfect idolater out of the holy Evangelist? And even what colour have they in order to persuade us that Saint Luke was a painter? In fact, Saint Paul calls him a doctor [Col 4,14]. But the profession of a painter, I do not know where they dreamt that up. And when it is thus mixed up, it can be presumed that he would have liked to paint the Virgin Mary like a Jupiter or a Venus, or some other idol. It was not the custom of Christians to have images, and it was not long afterwards, until the church was corrupted by superstitions. On the other hand, all the corners of the world are full of images of the Virgin Mary that are said to be made by him, as in Cambrai, and here and there. But in what form? There is as much honesty as if someone wished to paint a loose woman.

That is how God has blinded them, that they have had consideration no more than that of wild beasts. Although I am not too amazed at what they have imputed to Saint Luke for having made images of the Virgin, considering that they have in fact imposed the same thing on the prophet Jeremiah, le Puy in Auvergne testifies. It would be time, I think, that the poor world should open its eyes in order to see what is so widespread. I shall refrain from mentioning Saint Joseph whose slippers are held by some people, such as in Saint-Simon Abbey in Treves, others have his socks, as we have already said, and others his bones. The example that I have alleged is enough to reveal what foolishness is there.

The relics of Saint Michael

I shall place Saint Michael here so that he may keep the Virgin Mary company. One would think that I am enjoying myself in listing the relics of an angel. For even those who play jokes are mocked. But however the sneaks have not refrained from knowingly abusing the poor people. For in Carcassonne, they boast about having relics of him, and similarly in Saint-Julien in Tours. At the Great Saint Michel which is so well frequented by pilgrims, one is shown his double-edged sword which is like a dagger used by a small child, and his shield of the same kind which is like the boss on a horse's bit. There is no man or woman so simple as to be unable to judge what a mockery that is. But because such lies are covered under the shadow of devotion, it seems right that it was not a bad thing at all to laugh at God and his angels. They will reply that Scripture bears witness to the fact that Saint Michael fought against the Devil [Jude 9]. But if the Devil had to be beaten by a sword, that would have to be stronger and with a sharper point and sharper than this one. Are they so stupid as to imagine that it was an earthly war that both the angels and the faithful flock had against the devils, which was fought by a material sword? But it is what I said in the beginning, that the world really deserved to be charmed into such stupidity, to the extent that it was so perverse as to wish to have idols and gross figures to worship, instead of serving the living God.

254

So as to keep things in order, we must now deal with Saint John the Baptist, who, according to the Gospel history, that is the truth of God, after being beheaded, was buried by his disciples [cf Mt 14, 12]. Theodore[128], old chronicler of the Church, states that his tomb in Sebast, a town in Syria, was opened by the pagans some time afterwards and that his bones were burnt by them, and the ashes were spread in the air. Although Eusebius[129] adds that some men of Jerusalem came there and took a little of the ashes in a casket which was brought to Antioch, and buried there by Athanasius in a town wall. On the matter of his head, Sozomenus [130] another chronicler, said that it was brought by the Emperor Theodosius to the town of Constantinople. That is why, according to the Ancient Histories, the whole body was burnt, except the head and all the bones and ashes were lost, except some small parts which the hermits of Jerusalem stole. Let us see now what is found of them. The people of Amiens boast of having the face and, in the mask that they show, there is the mark of a knife on the eye, that they say that Herodias gave him. But the people of Saint Jean d'Angely contradict this and show the same part. As for the rest of the head, the top from the forehead to the back was in Rhodes and is now in Malta, as I think. At least the commanders[131] led people to believe that the Turk had given it to them. The back [of the head] is in Saint-Jean in Nemours; the brain is in Nogent-le-

---

[128] THEODORET, *Hist. eccl.* 3, 3, MIGNE *PG* 82, 1092 *in Hist. trip.* 6, 15, CSEL 31,328.

[129] In fact, RUFIN, *Hist. eccl.* 2, 28, MIGNE *PL* 31.536.

[130] SOZOMENUS, *Hist. eccl.* 7, 21, MIGNE *PG* 67, 1481-5 *in Hist. trip.* 9, 43, CZEL 31, 568.

[131] Those who presided over the order of the Knights of Malta.

Rotrou.   Notwithstanding that, the people of Saint-Jean-de-Maurienne hold onto stating that they have a part of the head. His jaw is not denied to be in Besancon, at Saint-Jean le Grand. There is another part of it in Saint John Lateran, in Paris[132] and in Saint-Flour in Auvergne, a part of the ear. At San Salvador in Spain, the forehead and the hair. There is also some part of it in Noyon, which is shown very authentically. In the same way there is a part in Lucques, I do not know where it is from.   Was all that done? If one goes to Saint John the Baptist in Rome and to the monastery of Saint Sylvester, one will hear people say: here is the head of Saint John the Baptist. Poets pretend that in the old times there was a king in Spain called Gerion[133] who had three heads. If our forgers of relics could say the same about Saint John the Baptist, that would be very useful in order to help them to lie. But since this myth was not based on fact, how will they excuse themselves?   I really do not wish to press them so closely as to ask them how the head was thus torn to shreds in order to be broken up in so many and various places, not how it is that they had it in Constantinople. I only say that Saint John must have been a monster, or that they are shameless abusers to show so many pieces of his head.

What is worse, the people of Siena boast about having his arm. Which is contrary, as we have said, to all the ancient histories. Nevertheless, this abuse is not only tolerated, but also approved. As nothing is found wrong in the kingdom of Antichrist, through which he holds the people in superstition. Now they have made up another myth: it is that, when the body was burnt, that the finger with which he pointed out our Lord

---

[132] More likely: Rome!

[133] One of the labours of Hercules.

Jesus Christ stayed whole, remaining unviolated. That not only does not comply with the ancient histories, but it can even easily be disproved by them. For Eusebius and Theodore[134], in particular, say that the body was already reduced to bones when the pagans carried it off. And they did not take care to forget such a miracle, if something had been known about it, for they are only otherwise too curious to talk about it, even as a joke. However, as it was, let us hear a little about where the finger is. In Besancon, in Saint John the Great church, there is one of them, in Toulouse another, in Lyon another, in Bourges another, in Florence another, in Saint John of the Adventures, near Macon, another. I am not saying a word above, but I ask the readers not to harden their hearts upon meeting such a clear and certain warning, and not to close their eyes to such clarity in order to allow themselves to be beguiled as in the shadows. If they were always players of conjuring tricks who dazzle our eyes, it would seem so much that there were six of them, still we would have this idea of fear of being abused. Now there is no subtlety here. It is only a question of whether we want to believe that Saint John's finger is in Florence and that it is elsewhere in five places. The same for Lyon and Bourges and the others, or, to state it briefly: whether we wish to believe that six fingers are only one, and that one only is six. I am not speaking except about what has come to my notice. I have no doubt that, if one enquired more diligently, one would find even half a dozen elsewhere. And about the head, if even more pieces which would amount to the size of a cow's head, even beyond what I have said about it. Or for fear of leaving nothing behind, they have also made a pretence of having the ashes, of when there is one part in Genoa,

---

[134] V. nn. 29-30 above.

the other part in Rome, in Saint John Lateran church. Now we have seen that most of was thrown into the air[135]. However, they do not stop having, as they say, a good part of it, and mainly in Genoa.

Now there remain, after the body, other belongings such as a shoe, which is with the Carthusians in Paris, which was stolen twelve or thirteen years ago. But unrestrainedly, a new one was found. And in fact, unless the trade of shoe-making dies out, they will never lack such relics. In Rome, in Saint John Lateran, the boast about having his hair-shirt, which is not mentioned at all in the Gospel, except that, because he said that he wore a camel-skin [cf Mk 1,6], they wanted to change it into a camel-skin robe. Even there, they say that they have the altar on which he prayed in the desert, as if, at that time, they had made altars for any purpose and in such a place. It is a miracle that they do not make one believe about him that he had said mass. In Avignon there is the sword with which he was beheaded, and in Aix in Germany the shroud, which was spread out under him. I would like to know how the executioner was so gracious as to line the floor of the prison, when he wanted to kill him. Is it not a crazy thing to fabricate that? But again, how one another did they come into their hands? Do you think that it is really true that the one who put him to death, if he were a soldier or an executioner, would give away the shroud and his sword to make a relic of them? Because they wanted to make such a set of all parts, they left out Herodias's knife, with which she struck his eye, all the blood which was spilt, and even his tomb. But also I could be wrong. For I do not know if all these objects are somewhere else.

---

[135] V. nn.29-30 above.

Now the apostles have to have their turn. But because the number of them could lead to confusion, if I put them all together, we shall take Saint Peter and Saint Paul separately, then we shall speak about the others. Their bodies are in Rome, half in St Peter's church, and the other half in Saint Paul's church. And it is said that Saint Sylvester weighed them in order to send them out in this way in equal parts. Both heads are also in Rome, in Saint John Lateran, although in the same church there is a tooth of Saint Peter's separately. After all that, one does not stop having their bones everywhere: as in Poitiers, there is the jaw with the beard, in Treves, several bones from one and the other, at Argenton in Berry, one of Saint Paul's shoulders. And when would that be done? For wherever there is a church which bears their names, there are relics of them. If one asks which ones, one remembers the brain of Saint Peter mentioned above, which was on the grand altar of that town. Just as one finds that it was a sponge stone, in the same way one would find a great many bones of horses or dogs that are attributed to these two apostles.

With the bodies the story continues. At San Salvador, in Spain, they have a slipper; as to the shape and of the material, I cannot answer. But it is right to presume that it is a similar object to those that they have in Poitiers, which are of gold satin brocade. That is how they made him gallant after his death, in order to reward him for the poverty that he suffered during his life. Because the bishops of today are small-minded in this way, when they are settled in their diocese, it seems right to them that it would lower the dignity of the apostles if they did not do so. Now painters can easily fake little figures at their leisure, gilding them and decorating them from head to toe, then afterwards put the name of Saint Peter or Saint Paul. But we know what state they were in while they lived in the word, and that they had no apparel other than that of poor people. Also in Rome there is the Episcopal throne of Saint Peter with his chasuble, as if in that time bishops would have had thrones to sit on. But it was their duty to teach, to control, to exhort in public and especially, to show an example of true humility to their flock, not to make idols, as the people of today do. As for the chasuble, the custom of disguising oneself had not yet come, for one did not play any tricks in the Church, as they do now. Thus in order to prove that Saint Peter had a chasuble, first of all one would have to show that he would have been a juggler, as our priests are today, in wishing to serve God. It is true that they could truly have given him a chasuble, when they assigned an altar to him. But one has as much colour as the other. It is known which masses were sung at that tie. The apostles in their time simply celebrated our Lord's supper, at which it is not necessary to have an altar. About the mass, one did not know yet how stupid it was, and it has not been known for a long time afterwards.

Therefore one can see clearly that, when they invented their relics, they never doubted having objectors, considering that they dared so impudently to lie at the top of their voice. Although they cannot agree among themselves about this altar. For the people of Rome state that they have one, and the people of Pisa show it in the suburb going down to the sea. In order to gain from all this, they have not forgotten the knife which which Malchus had is ear cut off [cf Jn 18,10]. As if it was a jewel worthy of being made into a relic. I had forgotten his cross, which is shown in Saint Stephen of the stones in Paris, of which one may think in the same way as the altar or the chasuble. For it is the same reason.

There is a little more semblance of truth in his staff, as it is right to presume that he could have been armed with such a stick, going to the fields. But they spoil everything in not being able to agree with each other. For the people in Cologne are very proud to have it, and the people in Treves speak in the same way. Thus, while bothering one another, they surely bring about the situation where nobody has any faith in either of them. I am avoiding mentioning Saint Paul's chain, with which he was tied up, which is shown in Rome in his church. *Item*, of the pillar on which Saint Peter was martyred, which is at Saint Anastasia. I only leave the readers to consider, where was this chain taken from to make a relic of it. *Item*, one would need to know if at that time they executed men on pillars.

We shall deal with all the other apostles in common, in order to do so more quickly. And first of all, we shall list where there are whole bodies of them, so that by comparing one with another, we can judge what opinion we can have of their statements. Everyone knows that the town of Toulouse thinks they have six of them, that is Saint James the Major, Saint Andrew, Saint James the Minor, Saint Philip, Saint Simon and Saint Jude. In Padua there is the body of Saint Matthias, in Salerno, the body of Saint Matthew, in Orthon, that of Saint Thomas, in the kingdom of Naples, that of Saint Bartholomew. Let us find out now which of them have two or three bodies. Saint Andrew has a second body in Melphe, Saint Philip and Saint James the Minor, each have another one in Rome, *Ad sanctos Apostolos*, Saint Bartholomew in his church. So there are already six of them which have two bodies each. And again, as a surplus, the skin of Saint Bartholomew is in Pisa. However, Saint Matthias

261

has won over all the others, for he has one body in Rome, at Saint-Mary-the-Major, and the third one in Treves. It is true that the parts of Saint Andrew which are here and there, are half rewarding. For in Rome, in Saint Peter's church, there is a head, in Saint Chrysogone a shoulder, in Saint Eustace a rib, and in Holy Spirit an arm, in Saint Blaise I do not know which part, in Aix en Provence, a foot. Who would join up this group, it would be enough to make two quarters of them, by means of putting them into proportion properly. Now, as Saint Bartholomew has left his skin in Pisa, there is also a hand; in Treves, there is an unknown member, in Frejus, a finger, in Rome, in Saint Barbe, other relics. Thus there are none in the poorest churches. The others have not so many. However each one has some relic. As Saint Philip has a foot in Rome, *Ad sanctos Apostolos*, and in Saint Barbe, I do not know which relics. *Item* more in Treves. In these last two churches, he has similarly for company Saint James, who has similarly a head in Saint Peter's church and an arm in Saint Chrysogone, and another *Ad sanctos Apostolos*. Saint Matthew and Saint Thomas remained the poorest, for the first, with his body, has nothing other than some bones in Treves, an arm in Rome, in Saint Marcel, and in Saint Nicholas, a head. Unless, by chance, something has escaped me, which could easily happen. For in such an abyss who would not be confused?

Because they find in their chronicles that the body of Saint John the Evangelist vanished immediately after it was put in the grave[136], they have not been able to produce his bones. But in order to make up for this deficiency, they flung themselves on his belongings.

---

[136] Jacques DE VORAGINE, *Legenda Aurea* ed. Th. Graesse 1890 (reprint Osnabruck Otto Zeller 1969) chap. 9, p. 62

And first of all, they were told about the chalice from which he drank the poison, being condemned by Domitien[137]. But because two people wanted to have it, we must believe what the alchemists say about their multiplication, or these people, with their chalice, are the laughing-stock of the world. One is in Boulogne and the other one in Rome, in Saint John Lateran. Later they contrived his smock, and a chain to which he was tied, when he was brought as a prisoner from Ephesus[138], with the prayer-stool on which he used to pray, while in the prison. I would like to know if at that time there were carpenters on hire to make prayer-stools for him. *Item*, who familiar were the Christians with his guard, in order to take away the chain and make a relic out of it? These mockeries are too idiotic and made for taking advantage of small children. But the most ferial. jewel is the twelve combs of the apostles, that are shown in Notre Dame of the Island above Lyon. I really think that they were placed there in the beginning in order to make people believe that they were for the twelve peers of France; but since then, the legend has grown, and they have become apostolic.

Relics of other saints

We must from now on hurry up, or otherwise we shall never come out of this forest. We shall therefore briefly list the relics of saints that are held, which were from the time when our Lord Jesus Christ lived; then, as a result, ancient martyrs and other saints. On that the readers will have to judge what respect they will have

---

[137] Cf. *Legenda aurea*, p. 56-57/
[138] *Ibid.*

263

for them. Saint Anne[139], mother of the Virgin Mary, has one of her bodies in Apt en Provence, the other, in Notre Dame of the Island, in Lyon. Apart from that, she has one head in Treves, the other, in Duren-en-Juliers, the other, in Thuringe, in an town named after her. I shall omit the parts which are in more than a hundred places; and between others I remember that I have kissed part of it in the Abbey of Ourscamp near Noyon, for which there is a great festival. Finally, she has one of her arms in Rome, in Saint Paul's church. One may make a foundation from the above, if one can.

Then later there is Lazarus and Magdalene his sister. Regarding him, there are only three bodies, that I know of: one is in Marseilles, the other, in Autun, the third, in Avallon. It is true that the people of Autun had a long legal battle upon meeting the people of Avallon. But after spending a great deal of money on one side and the other, they both won their case; at least, they remained in possession of the name. Because Madeleine was a woman, she had to be inferior to her brother; however, she had only two bodies, of which one is in Vezelay, near Auxerre, and the other, which is more famous, in Saint Maximin in Provence, where her head is separate with her *noli me tangere* [cf Jn 20, 17], which is a small piece of wax, that is thought to be the mark that Jesus made on her in defiance, because he was irritated that she wanted to touch him. I am not talking about her relics which are scattered all over the world, both her bones and her hair. What one would want to know about that, if one was enquiring, first of all, to find out whether Lazarus and his two sisters Martha and Magdalene ever came to France to preach. For in reading the ancient Histories and in judging

---

[41] Cf. Leg. Aur. Chap.131, De natiuitate beatae Mariae virginis, p. 585.

everything reasonably, it is obvious that this is the most foolish myth in the world, and which has as much credibility as if one said that clouds are calves' skins; and nevertheless they are the surest relics that one has. But yet if it was, it was enough to abuse a body in idolatry, without making two or three for a trick.

Indeed they have also canonised the one who pierce the side of our Lord [cf Jn 19,34] on the cross, and called him Saint Longin[140]. After having baptised him, they gave him two bodies, of which one is in Mantua, the other, in Notre Dame of the Island, near Lyon. They did the same thing to the wise men who came to worship our Lord after his nativity [cf. Mt 2,1-13]. First of all they specified him by the number, saying that there were only three of them[141]. Now the Gospel does not say how many they were; and none of the ancient doctors said that they were fourteen, like the one who wrote the imperfect Commentary on Saint Matthew, who is entitled Chrysostom[142]. Afterwards, at the place where the Gospel calls them philosophers [cf Mt 2,2], they have made them into three kings[143] in haste, without countries and without subjects. Finally, they baptised them, giving one the name Balthasar, the other Melchior, and the other, Gaspard[144]. Now, if we grant all their legends to them, except that they died there. Who transported them since then? And who knew them, in order to mark them, in order thus to make relics of their bodies? But I am getting carried away, inasmuch a it is foolishness on my part to disprove such

---

[140] Cf. Leg.aur. chap 47, p. 202s.

[141] Three. This tradition goes back to ORIGINE, *Homilies on Genesis* 14, 3, MIGNE PG 12,238.

[142] Cf MIGNE *PG 56,637.*

[143] *Kings.* In fact, this tradition already goes back to Tertullian. *Contre Marcion 3.13* MIGNE *PL* 2,339.

[144] The attribution of the names dates from the 6th century.

obviously ridiculous things. I am only saying that the people in Cologne and those in Milan fight about who will have them. For they both claim together to have them, which cannot be done[145]. When their case is cleared, then we shall announce that it must be done.

Among the ancient martyrs, Saint Denis [146] [cf Ac 17,34] is one of the most famous, for he is held as one of the disciples of the apostles and first evangelist in France. On account of this dignity, his relics are held in several places. However the body has only remained intact in two of them: in Saint Denis in France and at Ratisbon, in Germany. Because the French claimed to have it, the people of Ratisbon brought the case to Rome, about a hundred [147] years ago, and the body was judged by a final decision, with the French ambassador present, from whom they had a beautiful bull. Who would say, in Saint Denis near Paris that the body is not there at all, he would be stoned. Whoever would want to state that it is in Ratisbon will be held as a heretic, inasmuch as he will be a rebel of the apostolic Holy See. Thus, the most advisable thing will be not to intervene at all in their quarrel. They may turn a blind eye to one another, if they wish; and in so doing, may they gain nothing from it, but to discover that their whole case rests on a lie.

Of Saint Stephen[148] [cf Ac 7]. They have in the same way a part of the body which is whole in Rome in his church, the main one in Arles, and bones in more than a hundred places. But in order to show that they are followers of those who murdered him, they have

---

[145] In fact, the relics were transferred from Milan to Cologne in 1162.

[146] *Denis.* Cf. *leg. Aur.,* chap. 153, p. 680ss.

[147] The incident, in fact, took place in 1052. *Cf* MIGNE *PL* 143, 789-94.

[148] On Saint Stephen generally, v. *leg. Aurea* cap. 8, p. 49ss.

canonised the stones with which he was killed. One would wonder where it was that they could be found and how they obtained them, by which hands and by which means. I would reply briefly that this request is foolish, for it is well known that pebbles can be found everywhere, in such a way that the transport does not cost anything at all. In Florence, in Arles with the Augustinians, at Vigan in Languedoc, they re shown. Someone who would like to those their eyes and their hearing will believe that they are the very stones with which Saint Stephen was killed. Someone who would like to consider this a little, will laugh at it. And in fact, the Carmelites in Poitiers found one of them fourteen years ago, to which they assigned the duty of delivering women who are in labour. The Dominicans[149], from whom a rib of Saint Margaret was stolen[150] for this purpose, quarrelled a great deal about it, shouting against their abuse. But in the end they won by holding their own.

I had almost decided not to speak at all about the Innocents[151] because, when I had gathered an army, they always replied that that does not go against history, in that the number of them is not defined at all. I shall therefore keep away from speaking about the crowd. Only, that one notes that there are some in all regions of the world. Now I would ask how it is that their tombs were found such a long time after, considering that they were not considered as saints when Herod killed them. Afterwards, when were they taken away? They cannot answer me with anything other than that it was five or six hundred years after

---

[149] *Dominicans.* The French Dominicans. Their first convent in this country was established in 1218 in the Rue Saint-Jacques in Paris.

[150] Saint Margaret, cf *Leg. Aur.* Chap. 151, p. 676. Patron of women in labour.

[151] *Innocents,* cf .*Leg. Aur.* Chap. 10, p. 62ss.

their death. I would like to go back to the poorest simple people that could be found, if one must add faith to such absurd things. After that, while someone from among them may have been found, how could it be that several bodies were brought to France, to Germany, to Italy, in order to scatter them in towns that were so far from one another? Therefore I am leaving aside this falsehood to be believed by everyone.

However as Saint Lawrence is among the number of ancient martyrs[152], we shall give him his place here. I do not know whether his body is in more than one place, that is to say in Rome, in the church dedicated to his name; it is true that afterwards there is a vessel of his burnt flesh. *Item*, two full phials, one of his blood and the other with his fat. *Item*, in the church called Palisperne, his arm and some of his bones, remains which are shown only in France, and in Saint Sylvester, other relics. But if one wished to gather all the remains which are shown only in France, there would be enough to make two bodies, in length and in width. Then there is the grill on which he was roasted, although the church that is called Palisperne boasts about having one part. Now, for the grill, I shall leave that aside; but there are other relics which are too ridiculous, therefore it is not permissible for me to keep quiet, like ashes which are shown in Saint Eustace church. *Item*, a cloth with which the angel burnt his body. Since they have taken their time to dream up such musings in order to abuse the world, those who will see this warning will also take time to think about them, in order to prevent being laughed at more in this way. His tunic came out of the same forge, which is shown in Rome itself, in Saint Barbe's church. Because they heard that Saint Lawrence was a deacon,

---

[152] *Innocents,* cf *Leg. Aur.* Chap. 10, p. 62ss.

they thought that he would have the same belongings with which their deacons were equipped, while playing their part in mass. But it was another position in that time, in the Christian Church, which is not at the moment within the papacy; they were the stewards or deputies for distributing alms, and not jugglers for playing games. Thus they did not have to wear tunics, or dalmatics, or other fools' garments in order to distinguish themselves.

We shall add to Saint Lawrence, Saint Gervais and Saint Protais[153], whose tomb was found in Milan in the time of Saint Ambroise, as he himself testifies, in the same way as those of Saint Jerome and Saint Augustine and several others[154]. Thus the city of Milan maintains that it still has the body. Notwithstanding that, they are in Brisach, in Germany and in Besancon, in the parish church of Saint Peter, without the infinite parts which are spread out in various churches, to such an extent that each of them must have had four bodies at least, or that all the bones which are shown under false marks were thrown into the fields.

Because Saint Sebastian[155] was given the duty of curing the plague, that has meant that he was more in demand and that everyone wanted him more strongly. This credit made him multiply into four whole bodies, of which one is in Rome, in Saint Lawrence, the other in Soissons, the third in Piligny near Nantes the fourth near Narbonne, the place of his birth. In addition he has two heads: one in Saint Peter's in Rome, and the other with the Dominicans in Toulouse. It is true that they are hollow, if one refers to the Franciscans of

---

[153] *Gervais and Protais.* V. *Leg.Aur.* Chap.85, p. 354.

[154] In fact: AMBROISE, *Epist.,* MIGNE *PL* 16, 1062-3; AUGUSTINE, *Confessions* 9, 7, MIGNE *PL 32, 770;* GREGORY OF TOURS, *Libri miraculorum 1,47,* MIGNE *PL* 71,748-9.

[155] *Sebastian.* V, *Leg. Aur.* Chap.21,p. 104ss.

Angers, who are said to have his brain. *Item*, moreover, the Dominicans in Angers have an arm of his. There is another one in Saint Sernin in Toulouse, another in Chaise-Dieu in Auvergne, and another in Montbrison in Forez, without the small pieces that are in several churches. But when one has properly weighed it all up, one has to guess where is the body of Saint Sebastian. Even if they were not happy with all of that, if they did not also make relics of the arrows which were fired at him, of which they show one in Lambesc in Provence, one in Poitiers with the Augustinians, and the others here and there. Through that one can see very well that they did not think about taking account of their deceits.

A similar reason caused Saint Anthony[156] to multiply his relics. For, to the extent that he was an irascible and dangerous saint, as they claim, who burns those who annoy him, by this opinion he is feared and dreaded. The fear gave rise to devotion, which whetted the appetite for wishing to have his body, for profit. That is why the city of Arles had a great battle against the Antonians of Vienne; but the outcome was none other than what was usual in such a matter, that is to say that everyone was confused. For, if one wished to dilute the truth, none of the parties had a good case. With these two bodies, there is a knee with the Augustinians in Albi, in Bourg, in Macon, in Dijon, in Chalons, in Ouroux, in Besancon, relics of various members, without the finders being named, which is not a small amount at all. That is what it is to have the fame of being bad. For without that, the good saint would have remained in his grave, or in some corner, without anyone being aware of it.

---

[156] *Saint Anthony.* V. *Leg. Aur.* Chap.21, p. 104ss.

I had forgotten Saint Petronella[157], Saint Peter's daughter, whose whole body is in Rome in her father's church. *Item*, there are some relics separately in Saint Barbe[158]. But however she is not without another one in Le Mans, in the Dominican convent, which is held there in great solemnity, because it heals fevers. In the same way there are several saints called Suzanne, I do not properly know if their intention was to double the body of one of them. But the fact remains that there is one body of Saint Suzanne in Rome, in the church dedicated to her name, and another in Toulouse. Saint Helen was not so lucky. For apart from her body which is in Venice, the only extra part she gained was a head, which is in Saint Gereon of Cologne. Saint Ursula[159] surpassed her in this, her body, first of all, is in Saint John of Angely; then she has a head in Cologne, one part with the Dominicans in Le Mans, another with the Dominicans in Tours, the other in Bergerac. Of her companions, who are called the eleven thousand virgins, they may well be everywhere. And in fact, they are well helped in that by daring to lie more freely. For, over and above a hundred cart-loads of bones which are in Cologne, there is hardly a town in the whole of Europe which does not have some of them, either in one church or in a few.

If I began again to describe common saints, I would be going into a forest from which I could not find the way out. That is why I shall be content to allege some examples in passing, from which one can pass judgment on all the rest of them. In Poitiers, there are two churches who are fighting over the body of Saint Hilaire, that is to say the canons of his church and the

---

[157] *Saint Petronella* V. *Leg Aur.* Chap. 78, p. 343..

[158] *Saint Barbe,* V. *ibid.* chap.202, p.898

[159] *Saint Ursula and the eleven thousand virgins* V. *Leg. Aur.* Chap. 158, p. 701-705.

monks of La Selle. The lawsuit for this is hanging on a hook, until one makes a visitation to it. The faithful flock will allow the body to rest wherever it is, without caring about it. As regards Saint Honorat[160], his body is in Arles and also in fact on the isle of Lerins, near Antibes. Saint Giles[161] has one of his bodies in Toulouse, and the other in a Languedoc town, which bears his name. Saint William is in an abbey in Languedoc called Saint-William-the-Desert, and in a town in Aussoy called Ecrichen, with the head separate, although there is another head in the suburb of Duren, in Juliers, in the Williamite abbey. What shall I say about Saint Saphorin our Symphorien[162], which is in so many places, in body and in bones? It is the same in the case of Saint Loup[163], who is in Auxerre, in Sens, in Lyon, and one is led to believe that he was in Geneva. The same applies to Saint Ferreol, who is in a whole state in Uzes in Langueoc, and in Briouze in Auvergne. At least they make some good transactions together, so that their lies may not be discovered, as the canons in Treves did with those in Liege, on Saint Lambert's head[164]. For they decided with a sum of money, for the interest of offerings, not to show it publicly, for fear that one might be amazed to see it in two towns that were so close together. But it is what I said in the beginning: they never thought of having an examiner who might dare to open his mouth in order to reveal their impudence.

I could be asked how these builders of relics, considering that thus they gathered out of season everything that came into their heads, and as they

---

[160] *Saint Honorat.* V. *Leg. Aur.* Chap. 228, p. 942.

[161] *Saint Giles, ibid.* chap. 130, p. 582

[162] *Saint Symphorien,* ibid. chap. 122, p. 589.

[163] *Saint Loup, ibid.* chap. 128, p. 579.

[164] *Saint Lambert, ibid.* chap. 133, p.596.

puffed, faked everything they liked, have left out important things from the Old Testament? I do not know what to reply to that, except that they have scorned them, because they did not hope to gain a great deal from them, although they must not have forgotten them completely. For, in Rome, they say they have bones of Abraham, Isaac and Jacob, in Saint Mary *supra Minervam*. In Saint John Lateran, they boast about having the Ark of the Covenant, with the rod of Aaron. And nevertheless this rod is in fact also in the Sainte Chapelle in Paris. And the people of San Salvador in Spain have a part of it. Over and above that, the people in Bordeaux maintain that Saint Martial's rod, which is shown there in the church of Saint Severin, is that of Aaron. It appears that they wanted to make a new miracle, by envying God. For as this rod was changed into a snake by his virtue (cf Ex 4, 2-4), now as well they have changed it into three rods. It may well be that they have a great many other items from the Old Testament, but it is sufficient to have mentioned this matter in order to show that they behaved as loyally in this area as in all the others.

I would now ask the readers to remember what I said in the beginning: that is that I have not had commissioners to visit the sacristies in all the countries that I have mentioned above. However, one must not all take what I have said about relics as a register or complete inventory of which of them can be found. In Germany I have only named about half a dozen towns. In Spain I have named only three, as far as I know; in Italy, about fifteen, in France, thirty to forty, and of those I still do not know all of them. Therefore if everyone thinks for himself what an awkward situation it would be, if one placed in order the great number of relics which are to be found throughout Christianity. I am only talking about countries that we know and which we visit. For the main thing is to note that all the relics which are shown here and there of Jesus Christ and the prophets, can be found as well in Greece and in Asia and in other regions where there are Christian churches. Now I am asking, when the Christians of the eastern Church say that everything that we think we have is on their behalf, what decision could one take on that matter? If we contradict them, alleging that such a holy body was brought by merchants, another by monks, another by a bishop, a part of the crown of thorns was sent to a king of France by the emperor of Constantinople, the other, conquered by war, they will toss their heads in laughter. Now in so doing, they will always win. For everything that they have to say on their side is more likely than everything that one could claim on the other side. That is an annoying point to unravel for those who would like to defend the relics.

In order to come to an end, I would ask and exhort all readers in the name of God to wish to listen to the truth while it is shown to them so openly, and to know that this is done by a singular providence of God, that those who so wished to beguile the poor world have been so blinded that they have not thought of covering up their lies in another way. But like Midianites, with their eyes blinded, they have stood up one against the other. As we see that they go to war against one another and mutually contradict all reason to his knowledge, while he is not fully instructed that it is an abominable idolatry to worship any relic, whatever it may be, true or false, nevertheless, seeing such an obvious falsehood, will never have the courage to kiss any one of them; and whatever devotion he may have had before that, he will be completely averse to it.

The main thing that would be good, as I said at the beginning, is to abolish between us Christians this pagan superstition of canonising relics, both of Jesus

Christ and of his saints, in order to make idols of them. This activity is a pollution and filth that should not be tolerated in any way in the Church. We have already shown, by reasons and testimonies in Scripture, that this is true. If anyone is not happy with that, he should look at the customs of the ancient fathers, in order to follow their examples. There have been a great many patriarch saints, a great many prophets, holy kings and other faithful people in the Old Testament. God had ordained more ceremonies in that time than we need to have. Even the tomb had to be made in a grander style than nowadays, in order to show the glorious resurrection in figures, because it was not so clearly revealed in words, as we have it. Do we read that at that time saints were pulled out of their tombs, to be made into dolls? Abraham, the father of all the faithful people, was he ever taken up? Sarah too, a princess of the Church of God, was she taken out of her grave? Were they not left, with all the other saints, at rest? What is more, was the body of Moses not hidden by God's wishes, without anyone ever being able to find it? Did the Devil not fight about it against the angels, as Saint Jude [9] says? Why is it that our Lord was taken away from the sight of men, and that the Devil wanted to take him back? It is, as everyone acknowledges, that God wanted to take the opportunity of idolatry away from his people. The Devil, on the other hand, wanted to establish it. But the people of Israel, someone will say, were addicted to superstition. I ask what is that to us? Is there not, without comparing, more perversity among the Christians in this area they there has ever been among the Jews?

Let us state what was done in the ancient Church. It is true that faithful people have always taken the trouble to take back the bodies of martyrs, so that they should not be eaten by animals and birds, and they have buried them honestly, as we read of both Saint John the Baptist and Saint Stephen [Mt 14,12; Ac 8,2]. But in the end it was putting them in a grave in order to leave them there until the day of resurrection, and not to pace them in the sight of men, to kneel in front of them. This unhappy ceremony of canonising them was only introduced into the Church, until everything was perverted and almost profaned, partly through the stupidity of prelates and pastors, partly through their greed, and partly because they could not turn away from the practice, since it was accepted. And also the people wanted to be deluded, giving themselves rather to childish foolishness than to the true adoration of God. However, what began badly and placed above all reason should have been completely thrown out, which would justly correct the delusion. But if one cannot first of all come to this knowledge, at least one should come to the other activity, that one should open one's eyes to discern what are the relics that one is shown. Now it is not difficult to see who would want to hear that. For among so many very obvious lies as I have revealed, where would one choose a true relic, of which one could be sure? Moreover, it is nothing that I have dealt with, at the price of what remains of it. In the same way, while this book was being printed, I was warned of a third foreskin of our Lord which is shown in Hildesheim, which I had not mentioned. There is an infinite number of similar cases. Finally, visitation would discover one hundred times more than what I have been able to describe. Thus each person in his place is advised not to allow himself to his knowledge to be dragged like a wild beast to wander across fields, without being able to see either a way or a path in order to have a certain address. When the feast of Saint Stephen was coming, there were as many hats and trinkets on the tyrants who were stoning him (for they are so called in common language) as on his own image. The poor women, seeing the tyrants so ordered, took them for the friends of the saint, and each of them had his candle. What was done to the Devil close to Saint Michael. That is the way with relics. Everything around them is so jumbled and confused that one may be in danger of worshipping the bones of some bandit or their, or even of a donkey, or a dog, or a horse. One would not know if one is worshipping a ring belonging to Our Lady, or one of her combs or belts, or that one may be in danger of worshipping the rings of some debauchee. However one may wish to keep out of danger, nobody in future can claim the excuse of ignorance.

Saint Paul in the third chapter of the second letter to the Thessalonians [!]

The one who does not wish to honour the Creator who is eternally blessed, is a just vengeance of God that he serves creatures. And the one who does not wish to obey the truth, is the reason why he may be subject to a lie [cf Th 2,11; Rm 1,25].